Special Praise for *On the O*

"*On the Other Side of Chaos* is an invaluable resource for the families and loved ones of those trapped in addiction. Van Vechten's combination of compassion for the one suffering with a substance use disorder, written from her perspective as a family member of someone who suffered with addiction, along with comprehensive information on this baffling disease and it's treatment provides readers with a critical resource. Her book is likely to become a staple in the treatment of addiction for anyone who wants to learn more about how to cope with this cunning disease. This is recommended reading for our families."

Brad M. Reedy, PhD
Cofounder and Clinical Director of Evoke Therapy Programs
Author of *The Journey of the Heroic Parent*

"*On the Other Side of Chaos* is a comprehensive and useful resource for family members of individuals with substance use disorders. It is a valuable tool for families attempting to understand, navigate, and cope with the complex process of substance use and recovery for themselves and their loved ones. I am going to recommend this book to my clients."

Janice Gabe, LCSW, LCAC
Owner and President of New Perspectives of Indiana, Inc.

"Making our way through the turmoil of a loved one's addiction is daunting for the one with the disease and his or her family. Blame, shame, not understanding the disease, not knowing where to turn, and what help is available only add to the confusion. Now comes Ellen Van Vechten who provides a much-needed resource that guides loved ones suffering from a substance use disorder and their families away from the blame and shame and toward clarity about the true impact of addictive substances, the nature of the disease, and the way through the chaos."

Chuck Hutchcraft, LCSW
Psychotherapist and mindfulness meditation teacher

"*On the Other Side of Chaos* is a timely and relevant text that offers practical, sound, and heartfelt information and support for the family and loved ones of those living with addiction. Armed with evidence-based and practice-informed data, Ellen Van Vechten walks readers through pertinent information on substance use and treatment, as well as providing a call for family and loved ones to engage in their own recovery. Perhaps most importantly, Ellen uses her own experience of living through a loved one's addiction to bring empathy and grace to what is often such a challenging experience."

Brian L. Kelly, PhD, MSW, CADC
Assistant Professor
Director, Advanced Accredited Alcohol and
Other Drug Abuse Counselor Training Program
Loyola University Chicago School of Social Work

"Why does anyone pick up a drink or a drug? After so many personal disappointments and heartaches, why would anyone go back to using again? Is there any hope for these individuals? Can they be cured? Why do loved ones take them back again and again? Can any of us make life-giving changes and gain a sense of peace?

"These are some of the questions presented in this eye-opening book that will be most informational and useful to a wide audience. Substance use can cause deep heartache for the one using it and for anyone related to him or her.

"The author presents us with this difficult subject in a manner that is clearly understood and indicates her deep caring for those affected by this disease. She has brought current research into the subject in an appealing format that can reach many who do not have the opportunity to look into this on their own."

Patricia L. Bogie, MSW, LCSW, CADC, MISAII
Director of Addiction Counseling and Education Services
Catholic Charities of the Archdiocese of Chicago (Retired)

"At a time when the opioid crisis is impacting thousands, families of these individuals are at a loss to understand what is going on with their loved ones caught up in this downward spiral. Ellen's *On the Other Side of Chaos* captures a comprehensive up-to-date view of substance use disorders detailed in plain layman's language, including some of the self-defeating behaviors happening with their addicted family members. Thumbs up."

Rick Love, MHS, CAADC, PCGC
Director of Staff Training and Development
Haymarket Center, Chicago (Retired)

"Myths abound when it comes to the issues of addiction to alcohol and other drugs. Perplexities, shame, frustration, self-blame, fatigue, and hurt are common feelings endured by many when these issues are connected to our close loved ones. In *On the Other Side Chaos,* Van Vechten debunks these myths using neurobiological evidences and unpacks the scientific knowledge related to many different types of addictive substances and how these influence individual physical and mental health functioning. She carefully walks the reader through each step of the inner workings of addiction and various supportive mechanisms—from traditional treatments to mixtures of modalities formally and other support networks informally— to suggest making reasoned decisions to 'do what we can.' By accepting that the supporters of SUD patients are powerless and cannot control the conditions, Van Vechten helps liberate people from the downward spiral of negativity and shows the path to peace and serenity. This is the most comprehensive book that brings together science and personal connection in the journey of walking the walk with loved ones through chaos, but with the hope of seeing a bright future after the storm."

Philip Hong, PhD
Lucian and Carol Welch Matusak Endowed Professor
Loyola University Chicago School of Social Work
Associate Dean for Research
Director of the Doctoral Program
Director, Center for Research on Self-Sufficiency

ON THE OTHER SIDE OF CHAOS

ELLEN VAN VECHTEN

ON THE OTHER SIDE OF CHAOS

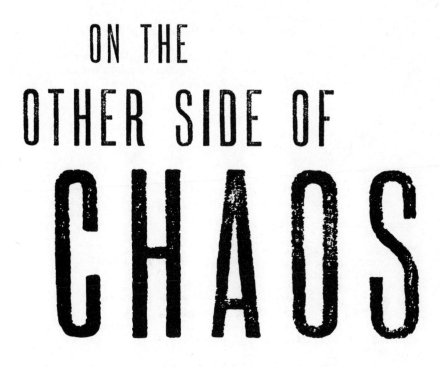

UNDERSTANDING THE ADDICTION OF A LOVED ONE

CENTRAL RECOVERY PRESS

LAS VEGAS

Central Recovery Press (CRP) is committed to publishing exceptional materials addressing addiction treatment, recovery, and behavioral healthcare topics.

For more information, visit www.centralrecoverypress.com.

Publisher: Central Recovery Press
        3321 N. Buffalo Drive
        Las Vegas, NV 89129

23 22 21 20 19 18   1 2 3 4 5

Library of Congress Cataloging-in-Publication Data

Names: Van Vechten, Ellen, author.
Title: On the other side of chaos : understanding the addiction of a loved
    one / Ellen Van Vechten.
Description: Las Vegas : Central Recovery Press, [2018]
Identifiers: LCCN 2018018098 (print) | LCCN 2018034685 (ebook) | ISBN
    9781942094807 (ebook) | ISBN 9781942094791 (pbk. : alk. paper)
Subjects: LCSH: Substance abuse--Treatment. | Addicts--Family relationships.
Classification: LCC RC564 (ebook) | LCC RC564 .V348 2018 (print) | DDC
    362.29--dc23
LC record available at https://lccn.loc.gov/2018018098

Photo of Ellen Van Vechten by Jill Norton, Jill Norton Photography. Used with permission.

Every attempt has been made to contact copyright holders. If copyright holders have not been properly acknowledged please contact us. Central Recovery Press will be happy to rectify the omission in future printings of this book.

Publisher's Note: This book contains general information about addiction, addiction recovery and treatment, and related matters. The information is not medical advice. This book is not an alternative to medical advice from your doctor or other professional healthcare provider.

Our books represent the experiences and opinions of their authors only. Every effort has been made to ensure that events, institutions, and statistics presented in our books as facts are accurate and up-to-date. To protect their privacy, the names of some of the people, places, and institutions in this book may have been changed.

Cover design and interior by Sara Streifel, Think Creative Design.

For all of us

AUTHOR'S NOTE

Faces & Voices of Recovery (facesandvoicesofrecovery.org), an advocacy group for those in recovery and those who love them, has developed language that allows persons in recovery to speak or write about their "experience, strength, and hope" without violating their own anonymity or that of others:

> I'm Ellen and I am a family member in recovery from another's addiction. I am committed to recovery because it has given me new purpose and hope for the future while helping me gain stability in my life. I am speaking out because long-term recovery has helped me change my life for the better, and I want to make it possible for others to do the same. (Adapted from *Advocacy with Anonymity,* a publication of Faces & Voices of Recovery, the Johnson Institute, Join Together, and the National Council on Alcoholism and Drug Dependence.)

This work is not intended as a substitute for professional medical advice. The reader should consult a physician or addiction professional in matters related to health, particularly with respect to any issues or conditions that may require diagnosis or medical attention.

Table of Contents

PART THREE: INFORMED ACTION————————————————————
Bringing It All Together to Support Recovery for Yourself and Your
Loved One

I Know Your Pain Because I Am One of You

INTRODUCTION

We remember how it felt the first time our loved one stayed out on the streets all night. We learned to say, out loud, that he is an addict. We called the police when he was out of control and always refused to bail him out of jail. Even now, we jump every time the phone rings. We found the best treatment we could afford and managed to get him into a program. We did it again and again and again. We had so much hope every time he went into treatment, and we did everything we were advised to do. We walked on eggshells after he came home and tried to avoid our old ways of communicating. Family members and friends stopped asking about him. We learned to see the relapses coming. We thought he would die. We feared that he would hurt someone else. We sought to hide from the world and our responsibilities. Our dreams for the future were shattered.

Finally, we got help for ourselves, worked on our own recovery, moved forward, and lived our own lives.

Grappling with the issue in my own family, I saw that those close to individuals with addictive disease required information and support. The experience prompted my decision to study addiction, and I obtained a Master of Social Work, received certification as an Alcohol and Drug Counselor in the State of Illinois, and counseled those with substance use disorders. The more I learned about addiction and recovery, the better positioned I became to support my loved one's recovery and to move toward serenity in my own life. I have come to believe that knowledge is the key to meaningful action, as long as we act with acceptance of our complete lack of power over the result.

Drug abuse is epidemic in the United States, and its human and societal consequences are overwhelming. The misuse of alcohol accounts for 88,000 deaths annually in the United States.[1] During 2015, over 52,000 people died in the United States from drug overdoses, and more than 33,000 of those deaths arose from the use of opioids.[2] The Centers for Disease Control and Prevention (CDC) estimates that 64,000 people died from drug overdoses during 2016 (which equates to 175 overdose deaths per day), and of those deaths, 20,000 were deemed to be related to synthetic opioids such as fentanyl.[3] In addition to the immeasurable human costs, substance abuse and dependence have serious economic consequences. The expenses related to the cost of healthcare, the administration of criminal justice, law enforcement, and lost productivity arising from the abuse of drugs total over $400 billion a year.[4]

The Substance Abuse and Mental Health Services Administration (SAMHSA), which is part of the US Department of Health and Human Services, conducts a National Survey on Drug Use and Health (NSDUH) annually. The results are based on in-person interviews of a representative, statistical sample of the national population aged twelve and older. The NSDUH survey results provide reliable estimates of the extent of alcohol and other drug use in the United States and identify trends in such use. The data from the most recent survey, the 2016 NSDUH, support the conclusion that over 28.6 million people (about one in every ten Americans age twelve or older) used an illegal drug during 2016. While the largest percentage of respondents who admitted use of an illicit substance reported use of marijuana, the survey also indicates that 11.8 million Americans aged twelve or older misused opioids during 2016. Based on extrapolation of the data derived from the survey sample, in 2016 approximately 20.8 million Americans had a substance use disorder arising from their use of alcohol or other drugs.[5]

The staggering figures reveal there are millions of people like us who struggle while watching family members or friends battle this illness. It is a community of strength and resilience, and one that is willing to share information and support. You are not alone in this fight.

The disease is a great leveler. Addiction knows no boundaries of race, religion, gender, age, background, education, neighborhood, community, class, or economic status. It impacts each of us in similar but distinct ways. The addict is our brother, sister, son, daughter, spouse, partner, parent, grandparent, friend, lover, coworker, and neighbor. Our individual relationship with the user impacts our interaction with him or her. The dynamic between a parent and a minor child is, for example, far different from that of husband and wife. While the circumstances of our connection with the person suffering from addictive disease will impact our decision making, this guide is not written from any single perspective. Rather, its message is intended to apply to all of us who care about someone who has, or may be at risk for, addictive disease. The term *family* is used in the broadest possible context and is not limited to individuals who are related to the person they care about. The universality of the problem has also contributed to the words used to reference our loved ones. They are referred to by different genders and by the roles they have in our lives to illustrate that the same principles apply to all of us.

The havoc brought about by uncontrolled chemical dependence is the same, whether the substance of abuse is legal and commonly used or is an illegal street drug. The text broadly refers to drugs with the understanding that alcohol is a drug and that references to drugs should be read to include alcohol. This book is also based on the principle that substance use or abuse is not addiction, and that the severity of the individual's use is a significant factor in identifying an appropriate response. For purposes of diagnostics, the words *substance abuse* and *dependence* have been replaced by diagnoses of a mild, moderate, or severe substance use disorder (SUD). The terms *addict* and *addiction* are no longer used for diagnostic purposes, but addiction is commonly understood to refer to a severe SUD. The changes in terminology were made, intentionally, to be less judgmental. The terms *substance use, abuse,* and *dependence* do, however, remain relevant as an aid to understanding the progression of the disease and to distinguish the social or habitual use of substances from that which so interferes with a person's life that it becomes problematic and warrants intervention.

The words we use are impactful. Individuals with addictive disorders continue to be stigmatized. While our loved ones may need to self-identify as addicts and/or alcoholics to defeat their own denial and accept their powerlessness over substances, such labels, when routinely applied to individuals, can contribute to feelings of shame and lack of self-worth. This book has been written with the intention of avoiding the use of loaded words such as *addict* and/or *alcoholic.* It refers to persons with addictive disease as individuals, or as clients, in a manner that is consistent with social work practice. The terms *addiction* and *dependence* are used herein to reference severe SUDs.

Like substance abuse, compulsive gambling is disruptive to the family of the person with the problem. Gambling disorders are diagnostically classified as addictive disorders. Gambling disorders are discussed in this guide whose approach and philosophy are applicable to those among us who have loved ones who are engaged in problematic gambling behaviors. As used herein, the term *addictive disease* is intended to reference the progressive, biological process that can lead to addiction to substances or to gambling. In this context, references to drugs can also be read to include gambling.

The lessons I have learned, and the philosophy of this guide, are that before we can help others suffering from the disease, we must first increase our knowledge and understanding of the problem. Part One, Knowledge: Understanding Substance Abuse and Addiction, Treatment, and Recovery, provides detailed information about the different drugs of abuse, the disease of addiction, methodologies of treatment, and what it takes to build a successful recovery program. This part of the book is by far the longest because it is knowledge and understanding of the disease that are the foundation of informed action.

Before we can make reasoned decisions and take meaningful action, however, we must also understand how the disease has impacted us, as the family members or friends of the chemically or behaviorally dependent, and how we can regain control over our lives and move forward despite the continued problems of our loved ones. Part Two, Acceptance: Understanding the Impact That Another's Disease Has on You and the Need for Your Own Recovery, focuses on the impact the disease has on those who are coping with another's use of substances or gambling behaviors. It explores the process by which we recognize and accept our powerlessness over another's behavior and begin to recover from the assault the disease has had on our own well-being. This part of the book also explains how our recovery parallels that of recovery for those dependent on drugs or gambling and how twelve-step family groups support the recovery of those who are powerless over another's addictive behavior.

In Part Three, Informed Action: Bringing It All Together to Support Recovery for Yourself and Your Loved One, the discussion shifts from the academic to the practical. The concluding section of this work addresses the complex problem of how we can use knowledge of the disease to inform decision making and action to support another's recovery while fostering our own serenity. If anyone says this process is easy, they are wholly misinformed or in denial. There is no easy or quick fix to this complex problem. Similarly, the often-quoted slogans "release with love" and "let go and let God" can be misunderstood and misapplied. Acceptance of our powerlessness and lack of control is not an excuse to throw up our hands and rationalize inaction. We love them, so we want to do what is best for their health and recovery. We accept that our actions may not be effective, but at least they can be research-based, logical, reasoned, and purposeful. It has been proven that treatment can and does work. While it does not always succeed, treatment offers the best hope for those we care about. There is no reason to wait to facilitate treatment once it is warranted. If you try to wait until the person is "ready," you have a good chance of losing your loved one forever.

No one can tell you the right choice to make for your own circumstances or the specific situation your loved one is in. Sometimes, every option is bad and there is no right or wrong choice to make. In making decisions, however, it is suggested that you consider three important principles:

1. Act to save a life in a medical emergency and call 911.

2. Take any talk or suggestion of suicide seriously and seek professional help.

3. Act to protect the physical safety of yourself and others.

It is important to take whatever steps are necessary to protect yourself from harm by securing your dwelling, changing locks, removing yourself from contact with your loved one, or calling 911 if you are in immediate danger. Further, while we cannot predict or control the actions of others and are not responsible for their behavior, it is suggested that we consider the safety of others and refrain, for example, from enabling someone who we know may drive under the influence of alcohol or other drugs to gain access to a motor vehicle.

Apart from these rules, however, it is suggested that you gain as much information as you can about the situation and your options, and then make the best possible choice for yourself and your loved one. An appropriate boundary for one person may be wholly unacceptable to someone else with a similar problem. While one person may evict a chemically dependent person from his or her home, another may seek a wholly different solution out of fear of what will happen to that individual on the street. Ultimately, you are the only person who can identify the best option for your situation that is consistent with your own safety, the safety of others, and your needs, abilities, resources, and core beliefs. It is also suggested that you refrain from second-guessing your decisions but remain flexible if you obtain additional information or the situation changes. At times, when we find ourselves without any meaningful choices, the most informed decision may be to take no action at all. In time, however, circumstances may present new opportunities for change. With personal growth and perspective, we may respond to similar situations in different ways. Changes in circumstances may also motivate those with addictive disease to make positive changes in their own lives.

Knowledge coupled with acceptance is the key to any meaningful action. Without a foundation based on knowledge of the facts and acceptance of what is outside of our control, many of us act emotionally and may make decisions based on guilt and fear. Brad Reedy, PhD, one of the founding directors of Second Nature Therapeutic Programs, and now the owner and clinical director of Evoke Therapy Programs, cautions family members to "let go of the outcome." It has taken me many years and lots of practice to understand his wisdom. What I have come to believe is that while you can make informed and reasoned choices to try to help and support another's recovery from addictive disease, you must do so with acceptance of the fact that you are totally powerless over the result.

It takes reflection and practice to accept that we are powerless over whether someone we care about achieves and maintains recovery. With knowledge and hard-won, true acceptance, we can make reasoned decisions as to how to support and encourage those battling the disease, while also preparing ourselves for any future. In this way, we can bring it all together and make the best possible choices to try to support family members in recovery. In so doing, we will also heal ourselves, move forward with our own lives, and find peace and serenity regardless of whether or not our loved ones recover from the disease.

RECOMMENDED RESOURCES

- The National Suicide Prevention Hotline is composed of a network of crisis centers and provides confidential support to people in suicidal crisis or emotional distress free of charge, twenty-four hours a day, seven days a week. https://suicidepreventionlifeline.org; (800) 273-8255

INTRODUCTION NOTES

1   US Department of Health and Human Services (HHS), Office of the Surgeon General, "Facing Addiction in America: The Surgeon General's Report on Alcohol, Drugs, and Health" (Washington, DC, 2016), 1-1, https://addiction.surgeongeneral.gov/.

2   Rose A. Rudd et al., "Increases in Drug and Opioid-Involved Overdose Deaths—United States, 2010–2015," *Morbidity and Mortality Weekly Report* 65, nos. 50 & 51 (December 30, 2016): 1445, https://www.cdc.gov/mmwr/volumes/65/wr/mm655051e1.htm.

3   NIDA, "Overdose Death Rates," last modified September 2017, https://www.drugabuse.gov/related-topics/trends-statistics/overdose-death-rates.

4   HHS, "Facing Addiction in America," 1-2.

5   Center for Behavioral Health Statistics and Quality (CBHSQ), "Key Substance Use and Mental Health Indicators in the United States: Results from the 2016 National Survey on Drug Use and Health" ("2016 NSDUH") (Rockville, MD, 2017), 1-2, https://store.samhsa.gov/shin/content/SMA17-5044/SMA17-5044.pdf.

PART ONE

KNOWLEDGE

Understanding Substance
Abuse and Addiction,
Treatment, and Recovery

*The only fence against the world
is a thorough knowledge of it.*

— JOHN LOCKE —

1

ADDICTION IS A DISEASE, NOT A MATTER OF CHOICE

When we first face the crises of another's addiction and its impact on our lives, we just want the madness to stop. We don't understand why our loved ones are unable to see what is clear to us. The solution seems so simple: they should just stop using drugs. We are confused, frightened, and angry because they don't seem to care that their drug use is destroying their lives, as well as our own. We cannot understand why they won't listen to reason despite the mounting complications and increasingly adverse consequences that arise from their continued use. Our emotions are magnified because we feel responsible for having been unable to prevent their descent into drug abuse. We fear that something we did, or failed to do, has created or contributed to the problem. Our guilt compounds our pain and we may respond emotionally, which only hurts our ability to logically address the problem.

EVOLUTION OF THE SCIENCE OF ADDICTION

Historically, addicts were viewed as morally bankrupt outsiders lacking in character and willpower. It was not until 1956 that the

American Medical Association first identified alcoholism as a disease. In 1957, Alcoholics Anonymous published the "Doctor's Opinion," which describes alcoholism as an allergy to alcohol.[1] Beginning in the 1990s, research and scientific advances in neurobiology, including brain imaging, have enabled scientists to document the disease process of addiction and establish how drugs impact the central nervous system (CNS), which comprises the brain and the spinal cord.

Brain damage caused by chronic use of drugs can be seen on magnetic resonance imaging (MRI), positron-emission tomography (PET), and functional MRI (fMRI) technology. Scientists have also gained a better understanding of biological responses to psychoactive drugs (those substances that interfere with the normal functioning of the CNS) based on scientific research including studies of both animals and humans. Research has established that, over time, drug use reroutes the neural pathways of the brain and changes the way the brain responds to stimuli. These scientific advances laid the groundwork for recognition and acceptance of addiction as a chronic, progressive, relapsing disease that can be fatal if untreated.

In November of 2016, the US Department of Health and Human Services released *Facing Addiction in America,* the surgeon general's report on alcohol, drugs, and health. Among the report's key findings is the conclusion that "[w]ell-supported scientific evidence shows that addiction to alcohol or drugs is a chronic brain disease that has potential for recurrence and recovery."[2] Paraphrasing the *Diagnostic and Statistical Manual of Mental Disorders,* Fifth Edition (*DSM-5*) of the American Psychiatric Association (APA), the report goes on to state that the disease of addiction is characterized by "clinically significant impairments in health, social function, and voluntary control over substance use."[3]

In addition to the Surgeon General of the United States and the APA, many other notable organizations now recognize addiction as a disease. According to the National Institute on Drug Abuse (NIDA):

> Addiction is defined as a chronic, relapsing brain disease that is characterized by compulsive drug seeking and use, despite harmful consequences. It is considered a brain disease because drugs change the brain; they change its structure and how it works.[4]

Similarly, the National Institute on Alcohol Abuse and Alcoholism (NIAAA) references the definition of alcohol use disorder from the *DSM-5,* describing it as "a chronic relapsing brain disease characterized by compulsive alcohol use, loss of control over alcohol intake, and a negative emotional state when not using."[5]

Acceptance of the fact that addiction is an illness and not a personality flaw is the first step in understanding another's disease and in taking informed action to cope with its implications. In its seminal 1987 ad campaign, the Partnership for a Drug-Free America equated a brain on drugs with a raw egg frying in a hot skillet. While the reference is not literal, the powerful symbolism of the image is quite appropriate. Arguably, in simple terms, drugs *do* fry your brain. With chronic use, the brain becomes conditioned to seek drugs, inducing cravings for more drugs, which cause the user to forfeit the ability to exercise free will over the continued use of drugs. In explaining the loss of control, Dr. Nora D. Volkow, Director of the National Institute on Drug Abuse, stated, "[W]hile initial drug experimentation is largely a voluntary behavior, continued drug use impairs brain function by interfering with the capacity to exert self-control over drug-taking behaviors."[6] The person becomes, in the words of twelve-step recovery programs, "powerless" over the use of drugs. In this way, chronic drug use can negate control and transform use from a voluntary choice into a compulsive behavior.

Drugs do not affect every individual in the same way, and numerous factors influence the development and progression of the disease, including heredity, environment, behavior, gender, a person's age at first use, and the presence of any co-occurring mental disorders. It is estimated that about 10 percent of persons who use addictive drugs will develop a severe addiction.[7] Understanding the scientific facts of the disease process and how and why some people become addicted may help us to understand the continued lure of drugs for the user and why they can't stop. The inability of our loved ones to stop using drugs is not because they are weak, and it is not because of anything we did. Rather, they can't easily stop the behavior because their drug use has profoundly changed their brain chemistry and structure.

DRUGS OF ABUSE CHANGE THE REWARD PATHWAYS OF THE BRAIN

Basic knowledge about brain function is necessary to an understanding of why addiction is considered to be a brain disease. Communications between the cells within the CNS control all human function and activity. The brain contains billions of nerve cells (neurons) that send electrical and chemical messages to other neurons both within the CNS and throughout the rest of the nervous system, which is called the peripheral nervous system (PNS). These chemical messages control basic bodily functions such as breathing and digestion, as well as all human thought and emotion.

Messages are relayed between neurons by chemical neurotransmitters. A neuron in the brain releases a chemical (the neurotransmitter) into the space between the releasing neuron and an adjacent neuron. The spaces between neurons are called synapses. Neurotransmitters cross synapses and bond with protein receptors on receiving neurons to deliver these chemical messages.

Adrenaline (a natural stimulant) provides a burst of energy to respond to a crisis or perceived danger. One of the most important chemicals essential to the functioning of the reward circuits in the brain is dopamine. Dopamine is released by the brain to reward activities necessary to survival such as eating, exercise, sex, and social interaction. The pleasurable feelings and mood elevation caused by the release of dopamine in response to these activities encourages humans to repeat essential, life-affirming behaviors.

Addictive drugs interfere with the brain's production and processing of dozens of these essential chemical neurotransmitters.

These include dopamine, gamma-aminobutyric acid (GABA) (which controls impulses and generally slows down the brain), serotonin (which controls mood, including anxiety and depression), endorphins and enkephalins (naturally produced opioids), and norepinephrine and epinephrine (stimulants). Drugs produce artificial stimuli that cause the brain to release an abundance of these and other essential chemicals.

Different drugs interfere with different receptors. For example, opioids, such as heroin, interfere with the receptor sites for naturally produced opioids. Drug use conditions the brain to respond to the user's preferred substances (his or her drugs of choice). A user's brain will also respond to other drugs of the same type or class as the user's preferred substance. In other words, since heroin is an opioid, the brain of a heroin user will automatically respond to all opioids, including other illegal synthetic opioids, such as fentanyl and prescription pain relievers.

Certain drugs cause the brain to produce up to ten times the amount of dopamine occurring in the natural state. The amount of dopamine released in response to the normal pleasures of living pales in comparison to the amount of dopamine that floods the system when drugs are ingested. When a person first starts using a drug, they experience a euphoric high that signals the brain to seek more of the drug. In other words, the euphoric feelings caused by use of a drug positively reinforce its continued use.

In response to the artificial introduction of elevated levels of dopamine, the brain seeks to protect itself and return to a state of equilibrium by slowing down the production of dopamine in the presence of the drug (or other drugs in the same class). In other words, when a psychoactive drug is first experienced, huge quantities of dopamine are released, but with their repeated use, the brain becomes less sensitive to the substance used and releases smaller amounts of dopamine in response to its presence. Due to this desensitization, the user requires more and more of a substance to feel the same effects. This is known as tolerance. With increased tolerance for a drug, use typically escalates in a doomed attempt to recreate the euphoria experienced when the drug was first used.

In addition to reduction in the natural production of dopamine, the brain defends itself from excess amounts of dopamine by shutting down the number of receptor neurons that can accept dopamine. This fact has been established by brain imaging, which shows that addicted individuals have fewer D2-type dopamine receptors compared to individuals with no history of addictive disease.[8] The combined effect of lessened production of dopamine and reduction of the number of dopamine receptors is impairment of the user's ability to feel pleasure from either natural experiences or drug use.

The sights, sounds, smells, objects, locations, and people connected with a pattern of drug use cause the brain to anticipate receipt of the drug and induce cravings for the substance. For example, if a person passes by a park where he or she habitually used drugs, the person's brain associates that location with drug use and is primed to receive the drug. The user's brain may also automatically respond to the smell of his or her drug of choice or the sight of drug paraphernalia associated with its use. Similarly, if an individual used when stressed, angry, or when feeling isolated, that individual's brain may also have been conditioned to associate those feelings with drug use. For that person, stress and feelings of anger or isolation may activate his or her brain to expect the drug. These internal and external reminders of drug use were typically referred to as triggers. Since the word *trigger* is associated with gun violence, the nomenclature is changing, and references are now made to stimuli (or cues) that "activate" cravings, rather than to triggers.[9] For those with addictive disease, while cravings will be activated by similar things, specific cues are unique to individuals and are based on the user's personal history.

When the brain is activated by cues to expect a drug, it releases dopamine in anticipation of the high. This surge of dopamine does not satiate the user's desire for the substance. Rather, the anticipatory release of dopamine produces strong cravings for the actual substance. This is basic biology, familiar to us from Pavlov's well-known experiments with dogs. Similarly, cooking aromas trigger our anticipation, make our mouth water, and increase our desire for the meal.

Over time, the brain releases more dopamine in response to the stimuli that it associates with the drug than upon ingestion of the drug itself. While drug consumption causes additional dopamine to be released, it does not satisfy the user; rather, it fuels continued craving. Clinically, craving is identified as such a strong urge to use the drug that the individual cannot think of anything else.[10] A user's brain is so conditioned to respond to his or her internal and external stimuli or cues that the compulsion to continue to use the substance is automatic and not willful. The reaction to stimuli occurs even after prolonged periods of abstinence. This biological response and the resultant craving is one of the factors that challenge those in recovery and contribute to relapse.

THE SYMPTOMS OF WITHDRAWAL PROMOTE CONTINUED DRUG USE

Prolonged drug use may cause the body to adapt to the presence of the drugs. Withdrawal occurs as the brain attempts to rebalance, that is, return to a point of homeostasis, and function without the artificial stimulus of drugs. While dependence on substances can be psychological, in some cases the body's tissues and organs become dependent on drugs to function. This biological response to chronic use is called tissue dependence or physical dependence. When a person becomes physically dependent on a substance, the absence of that substance or chemically similar substances will cause the individual to suffer symptoms of withdrawal.

The specific symptoms of withdrawal differ by substance and range from mild to life-threatening. The negative feelings associated with withdrawal arise from the lowered levels of dopamine and other chemicals. Symptoms of withdrawal are generally the opposite of the symptoms of intoxication for the same class of drug and vary between classes based on the specific substance used. For example, heroin and other opioids cause feelings of euphoria. In withdrawal from opioids, the user may experience anxiety or depression. Opioids also reduce blood pressure and bring about a reduced heart rate and shallow breathing. In withdrawal, an opioid-dependent person experiences high blood pressure, a rapid heartbeat, and coughing.

The pain experienced due to the absence of the drug causes the user to crave more of the substance to alleviate his or her discomfort. Thus, when an individual first starts to use drugs, the high creates positive reinforcement for continued use, that is, the drug seeker initially uses to experience euphoria. Over time, the euphoria is lessened, and the body becomes dependent on the substance. With dependence, the pain and severe discomfort that come with withdrawal negatively reinforce drug use as the user seeks out the drug to stop the pain. In addition to conditioning the brain to compulsively crave the drug of choice, a pattern of drug use makes individuals more sensitive to stress. Repeated use of psychoactive drugs causes individuals to feel stress more acutely and for longer periods of time. The heightened reaction to stress increases negative moods and contributes to the motivation to use drugs to relieve the distress. The euphoria is gone, and the drug is necessary to merely survive.

After binge and intoxication, and as the effect of the drug wanes, the user experiences withdrawal symptoms that cause physical discomfort, as well as negative feelings and emotions that induce the desire for more drugs. The craving leads to consumption and intoxication. The biological process thus creates a cycle with three recurring phases:

1. Binge and intoxication

2. Withdrawal

3. Anticipation and craving

This cycle is self-perpetuating and drug-seeking compulsions override rational thought, resulting in continued use at any cost and regardless of the attendant consequences.

PSYCHOACTIVE DRUGS IMPACT COGNITIVE FUNCTION AND DECISION MAKING

When triggered by normal life activities, the brain recognizes a satiation point and stops releasing dopamine, thus ending the desire or craving for more. For example, when we are hungry, the brain releases dopamine as a chemical message to cause us to desire or crave something to eat. After we have eaten enough food and are no longer hungry, the brain stops releasing dopamine and our desire to consume additional food abates. The brain does not react to psychoactive drugs in the same way. This has been explained by reference to an "on" and "off" switch. The brain turns off the switch that releases the chemicals that signify hunger when sufficient food has been consumed. In contrast, the mechanism activated by stimuli that predict a drug high will be forthcoming remains stuck in the "on" position and will not turn off even after drugs are consumed.

Chronic drug use also damages the circuitry of the prefrontal cortex (PFC) of the brain that regulates decision making and the ability to control impulses. The degradation of the circuitry of the PFC impairs the user's cognitive function, lessening his or her ability to make reasoned decisions. At the same time, damage to the PFC caused by drug use increases the user's impulsivity and weakens inhibitory controls. The user thus becomes unable to resist the chemical messages to continue to seek drugs despite negative consequences. The deterioration of function in the PFC brought about by repeated usage contributes to the compulsive use of drugs.

GAMBLING CHANGES THE REWARD PATHWAYS OF THE BRAIN AND IMPAIRS BRAIN FUNCTION

Scientific studies have shown that gambling produces the same type of chemical responses in the brain as the use of psychoactive drugs. Like drug use, gambling activity causes the release of chemical messengers, including dopamine, serotonin, natural opioids, glutamate, norepinephrine, and adrenalin. As with substance use, over time the brain releases less dopamine in response to the same level of gambling. The gambler thus develops tolerance for the activity and may be motivated to increase the stakes or assume more risk in an effort to recreate the same level of excitement previously obtained from the activity. The stimuli associated with gambling, such as the lights and sounds of the casino, are cues that activate release of reward chemicals and induce craving for the activity. When not gambling, problem gamblers will also experience withdrawal from the pleasures associated with gambling and will return to the behavior in an effort to alleviate those negative feelings. Just as the chronic use of substances impairs the function of the PFC, individuals with gambling disorders have also been shown to have decreased cognitive function, reduced decision-making abilities, and lessened inhibitory controls. Thus, in a self-fulfilling cycle, the user continues gambling regardless of the consequences, and the compulsion to use overpowers reason and logic.

While additional research is warranted, the science supporting the role of brain chemistry in the development of both SUDs and gambling disorders resulted in the classification of problem gambling as an addictive disease. In 2013, under the *DSM-5*, the diagnostic criteria related to problem gambling were significantly changed. What had been identified as the impulse control disorder of pathological gambling is now classified as gambling disorder, which is a type of addictive disorder.

WHY IT MATTERS: THE SIGNIFICANCE OF THE DISEASE MODEL OF ADDICTION

While science explains why the dependent drug user or compulsive gambler can't simply stop, and neurobiology defeats the argument that addiction is merely a behavioral choice, the prevailing view is not without naysayers. Some argue that addiction is a choice and that it is based on repeated voluntary actions rather than a disease mechanism. This argument ignores the physical symptoms of tolerance and withdrawal, as well as the identifiable and measurable changes to the brain resulting from chronic drug use or gambling. Rejection of the disease model is also inconsistent with the fact that many other chronic medical conditions have behavioral components. For example, the fact that the development of lung cancer has been linked to the behavior of smoking does not negate the fact that lung cancer is a disease and that the disease requires medical treatment.

Treatment emphasizes abstinence and behavioral modifications to help heal and retrain the brain to break the cycle of addiction. Just as patients with other chronic diseases, such as heart disease or diabetes, learn to modify their behavior to include better nutrition, more exercise, and other lifestyle changes, individuals with addictive disorders learn to avoid environmental cues and make choices to help them manage their cravings. Thus, while the development of addictive disease has environmental and behavioral components, the resulting disease requires medical intervention and treatment, just like other behaviorally based conditions.

Some critics also question the disease model on the basis that not everyone who uses mind-altering substances or gambles becomes addicted. The same is true of other behaviorally based diseases. For example, not everyone who uses tobacco develops cancer. To some commentators, the disease model's characterization of a dependent user's lack of control over a substance or behavior gives them an excuse to continue to use. In fact, however, the disease theory provides individuals suffering from the disease with an explanation for their unmanageable desires. In early recovery, many people suffer remorse and self-loathing. Science explains their continued desire for drugs or gambling as a matter of biology rather than a character flaw or personal weakness.

The disease model of addiction is the foundation for our understanding of treatment and recovery. It supports empathy for the addict. This knowledge also allows us to let go of guilt based on the misperception that we somehow allowed or contributed to another's dependence on a substance or gambling. Similarly, an understanding of the science of addiction may help us let go of anger because a family member or friend will not stop using alcohol or other drugs or continues to gamble despite all the harm he has caused to himself and others.

Identification of addiction as a chronic medical condition that requires treatment is also important for the development of laws and policies promoting prevention, treatment, and recovery. The disease model of addiction forms the foundation for the advancement of public policies that provide access to quality medical care and mandate the availability of adequate insurance coverage for treatment of addictive disorders. For example, the Mental Health Parity and Addiction Equity Act of 2008 (MHPAEA) is a federal law requiring group health plans and providers to afford benefits for mental health and substance disorders that are on par with the benefits provided for medical and surgical services. Developed in response to the implications of the opioid epidemic, the Comprehensive Addiction and Recovery Act of 2016 (CARA) contains numerous provisions to support the prevention and treatment of SUDs, including expansion of access to overdose-reversal medications. Acknowledgment that addiction is a chronic illness rather than a behavioral choice is necessary to continue public support for the development and enforcement of such laws protecting the rights of those suffering from the disease.

Recognition of the biological process of addiction aids in defeating stereotypes about those dependent on substances and may help to lessen the stigma that impacts our loved ones. Further, the disease model of addiction supports policies ensuring that those suffering from the disorder are guaranteed their workplace rights. When addiction is recognized as a disease, it must be treated like any other medical condition. Employees with addictive disease will thus have the same rights to medical leave and excused absences for medical treatment as coworkers suffering from other diseases or conditions. Similarly, the disease model of addiction protects individuals from discriminatory action in the workplace. An employer should not, for example, make negative decisions relating to the hiring, firing, or promotion of individuals based on their medical condition.

We have come too far in protecting the rights of individuals suffering from addictive disease to allow the dialogue to be dominated by those claiming that addiction is merely a choice. As the family and friends of those battling this illness, we can stand by them as advocates for prevention initiatives, continued scientific research, better access to affordable and scientifically based treatment interventions, the lessening of stigma, and prevention of discrimination.

RECOMMENDED RESOURCES

- National Institute on Alcohol Abuse and Alcoholism (NIAAA), https://niaaa.nih.gov/.

- National Institute on Drug Abuse (NIDA), https://www.drugabuse.gov/.

- Substance Abuse and Mental Health Services Administration (SAMHSA), https://www.samhsa.gov/.

CHAPTER 1 NOTES

1   Alcoholics Anonymous, *Alcoholics Anonymous,* 4th ed. (New York: Alcoholics Anonymous World Services, Inc., 2001), xxv–xxxii.

2   HHS, "Facing Addiction in America," 2-1.

3   Ibid., 2-2.

4   National Institute on Drug Abuse (NIDA), "The Science of Drug Abuse and Addiction: The Basics," in "Media Guide," last modified October 2016, https://www.drugabuse.gov/publications/media-guide/science-drug-abuse-addiction-basics.

5   National Institute on Alcohol Abuse and Alcoholism (NIAAA), "Alcohol Use Disorder," https://niaaa.nih.gov/alcohol-health/overview-alcohol-consumption/alcohol-use-disorders.

6   Nora D. Volkow and Marisela Morales, "The Brain on Drugs: From Reward to Addiction," *Cell* 162 (August 13, 2015): 712, doi: 10.1016/j.cell.2015.07.046.

7   Nora D. Volkow, George F. Koob, and A. Thomas McLennan, "Neurobiologic Advances from the Brain Disease Model of Addiction," *New England Journal of Medicine* 374 (2016): 367, doi: 10.1056/NEJMra1511480.

8   HHS, "Facing Addiction in America," 2-13-14.

9   Pamela K. Williams, "Creating a 'Trauma Informed' Treatment Setting" (Seminar, Haymarket Center, Chicago, IL, September 30, 2017).

10 American Psychiatric Association (APA), *Diagnostic and Statistical Manual of Mental Disorders,* 5th ed. (DSM-5) (Arlington, VA: APA, 2013), 483.

"He Must Be on Something, but What Is It?"

2 DRUGS OF ABUSE AND THEIR EFFECTS ON THE BODY

When first confronted by drastic changes in the behavior of someone dear to us, we may suspect drugs, but remain fearful and uncertain about what should be done. We may jump to conclusions and assume the worst or simply retreat into a shell of denial. Neither reaction is productive. An understanding of the different drugs of abuse, the physical signs of their use, and the short- and long-term effects on the body lays the foundation for identification and understanding of the scope of another's problem.

While the variety and range of drugs of abuse may at first be overwhelming, drugs fall into only a few main categories. Although they vary widely in strength, different drugs in the same class generally impact the body in the same or similar ways. For example, while vastly different, both alcohol and heroin are depressants, and they have some similar effects on bodily functions, such as the slowing of respiration and heart rate. Given the commonalities within classes, it is helpful to classify drugs by type and to examine how each class affects the body.

Drugs taken for their psychoactive effects include illegal street drugs as well as legal prescription and over-the-counter medications that are misused by taking them in a manner other than as prescribed or directed. Drugs of abuse also include illegally produced analogs, which are designer drugs or copycat formulations intended to mimic the effect of prescription and nonprescription drugs. Some products (such as paint thinners and aerosol household products) are sold legally and, while they have legitimate uses apart from human consumption, they are misused for their psychoactive effects. Other products are manufactured with the intent that they be used for their psychoactive effects but are labeled as innocuous substances such as "plant food" to disguise their purpose and to skirt the laws controlling the distribution of controlled substances.

It should also be noted that users may combine different drugs to enhance their individual effects or may use a depressant to "come down" off a stimulant-induced high. Use of drugs in combination or sequentially is called polydrug or polysubstance use. Drugs sold on the street are often adulterated, or cut with other drugs or cheaper substances to stretch the product. These additives may be dangerous, and/or may cause symptoms and effects distinct from what the user anticipated. These factors may complicate efforts to identify the substance or substances that are being used by a loved one.

While we should not jump to conclusions about a specific drug problem, basic information about how drugs impact the body and the risks presented by different classes of drugs may help to identify situations that require an immediate emergency response. This information may also help us to recognize problematic behaviors that require further investigation in consultation with experts. Understanding the distinct effects of different classes of drugs will also help us recognize the specific issues presented by the consumption of different substances. Users often have a drug or drugs of choice, but they may also gravitate toward other substances that have the same effect, that is, other drugs in the same classification. For this reason, study of the classes of drugs aids understanding of a user's progression from one substance to another.

It is also important to remember that drugs go in and out of style. Fads may also be specific to geographic regions. Trends are, in some cases, cyclical. While a drug may have faded from use due to a growing reputation for bad trips, accidents, violence, or suicide, it may experience renewed popularity decades later among users who have no familiarity with its history. Moreover, drug traffickers continue to produce new formulations of drugs and develop designer drugs that mimic the effects of other substances.

While print media cannot keep pace with evolving trends and concerns, NIDA is an excellent source for timely and accurate information about new risks and patterns in the street sale of adulterated drugs. The NIDA website contains a page on emerging drug trends and alerts (see https://www.drugabuse.gov/drugs-abuse/emerging-trends-alerts). Another source for up-to-date information about drug trends is the website of the National Drug Early Warning System (NDEWS), published by the Center for Substance Abuse Research at the University of Maryland (see https://ndews.umd.edu/).

HOW DRUGS ENTER THE SYSTEM HAS AN IMPACT ON THEIR EFFECTS

The speed at which a drug impacts the user varies by the method of administration. The fastest way for drugs to reach the brain is by smoking or other inhalation (e.g., vaping or "huffing" chemicals). When smoked or inhaled, drugs are absorbed by the capillaries in the lungs and enter the bloodstream, where they are pumped to the brain and the organs. When drugs are inhaled, they reach the brain within seven to ten seconds. Smoking drugs presents respiratory risks like those of smoking tobacco.

The second-fastest means of administration is the intravenous injection of the drug into a vein (IV injection). When injected directly into the bloodstream, the drug reaches the brain in fifteen to thirty seconds and produces an intense reaction or "rush." IV injection also avoids loss of some of the substance through smoke evaporation. Drugs can also be injected into the muscle mass or under the skin (subcutaneously). The latter methods of injection, which cause the drug to reach the brain within three to five minutes, create a slower buildup of the chemicals in the brain, leading to euphoria but not the intensified rush of IV injection.[1] The IV injection of drugs, regardless of class, presents risks of HIV and hepatitis C.

When powdered drugs (or pills that have been crushed) are snorted through the nose, they are absorbed into the mucous membranes and reach the brain in about the same time as those injected into muscle or subcutaneously (about three to five minutes). Oral administration is a less efficient means of administering drugs to the system. When a substance is swallowed, in either pill or liquid form, it must pass through the stomach and into the small intestine before it is absorbed. The substance must then be partially metabolized by the liver before being released into the bloodstream and pumped throughout the body. When the drugs are taken orally, their impact is not felt for twenty to thirty minutes after ingestion. The slowest method for drugs to reach the brain is through contact with the skin by means of transdermal patches, like nicotine patches or patches for pain management, which may take days for effective absorption of a therapeutic dose.[2] Patches can be abused by chewing pieces of the patch, rolling and smoking the patch, or removing the liquid content for IV injection.

With progression of the disease, users may change from a less efficient to a more efficient means of administration of the substance. For example, a heroin user may progress from snorting the drug to IV injection to increase the speed and intensity of the high and avoid loss of any of the substance during administration. Thus, the method of administration of a substance may provide clues as to where the user is on a continuum from experimentation to dependence.

CLASSIFICATION OF DRUGS OF ABUSE

Drugs are classified differently for legal and medical purposes. The federal Comprehensive Drug Abuse and Control Act of 1970 (the Controlled Substances Act) identifies five schedules of substances for purposes of managing their control, sale, import, and export. Criminal penalties for federal drug offenses are based on the scheduled classification of the drug involved in the crime. Generally, states adopt the federal classifications for purposes of state drug offenses. The law provides procedures whereby substances can be reclassified, that is, moved to a different schedule.

Since the schedules are designed for legal purposes related to the control of drugs, they are not used for diagnostic or treatment purposes and are not based on the chemical nature of the substance or its effects on the body. Rather, substances are classified based upon the potential for abuse and dependence weighed against the medical value of the drug. These classifications do, however, provide clues as to the perceived dangers of specific drugs and how access to drugs is controlled. For example, some dangerous drugs may be in your medicine cabinet, garage, or basement; others are available for your teen to purchase at the market or on the internet; and some are sold on the street after production in clandestine labs.

The most dangerous drugs, those placed on Schedule I, are seen to have the highest potential for abuse and a recognized lack of safety for use even under medical supervision, and are perceived to be without any medical value. Schedule I drugs currently include heroin, marijuana, and LSD. While medical and recreational use of marijuana is legal in some states, it remains illegal under federal law and is classified as a Schedule I drug. Schedule II drugs are substances that have a high potential for abuse and, while it is recognized their abuse may lead to severe psychological or physical dependence, each of the substances on Schedule II has a currently accepted medical use in the United States. This criterion is met even if use of the drug is severely restricted. Schedule II drugs currently include cocaine, methadone, hydrocodone, fentanyl, and methamphetamine.

Schedule III drugs are those that are considered to have less potential for abuse than the substances on Schedules I and II, and have a currently accepted medical use in the United States. It is recognized that abuse of Schedule III substances may lead to low or moderate physical dependence or high psychological dependence. Schedule III drugs currently include anabolic steroids. Schedule IV substances are drugs that have a lower potential for abuse compared to drugs on Schedule III, and have an accepted medical use in the United States. It is recognized that abuse of Schedule IV drugs may lead to limited physical dependence or psychological dependence. Schedule IV drugs include the prescription drug clonazepam, a sedative-hypnotic benzodiazepine (tranquilizer). Schedule V substances are those considered to have a low potential for abuse compared with substances on Schedule IV, and have an accepted medical use in the United States. Abuse of these drugs may lead to limited physical dependence or psychological dependence compared to that of the substances on Schedule IV. Prescription cough medications containing codeine are currently listed as Schedule V drugs.

While the schedule on which drugs are listed is informative, the impact of psychoactive drugs on the body is better understood by differentiating drugs into classes based on the way they affect the body. There are a number of different systems for the classification of drugs. The *DSM-5*, for example, divides several of the main classes of drugs into subclasses. For our purpose, that of understanding the way different types of drugs affect the user, the commonly abused psychoactive drugs are grouped into four main classes:

1. Stimulants

2. Depressants

3. Hallucinogens

4. Inhalants

While the effects vary with the specific drug used, stimulants generally speed up the function of the CNS, increasing respiration and heart rate. Stimulants, or uppers, energize the body, increase feelings of confidence, decrease appetite, and may cause sleeplessness. Stimulants include cocaine, amphetamines, methamphetamine, nonamphetamine medicines such as those used to treat attention disorders, and synthetic cathinones (e.g., bath salts).

Generally, in direct contrast to stimulants, depressants (downers) slow down the functions of the CNS, suppressing respiration and slowing heart rate. The symptoms vary with the specific substance used, but signs of depressant intoxication include drowsiness or coma, lowered pulse and respiration rate, insensitivity to pain, lowered blood pressure, confusion, impaired attention or memory, slurred speech, and/or slowed coordination. Alcohol is the best-known depressant. Many other substances also act as depressants. Notably, opioids are depressants. Opioids include naturally occurring opiates (opium) and synthetic opioids (painkillers such as hydrocodone, oxycodone, and fentanyl). Sedative hypnotics fall within the broader class of depressants. These include benzodiazepines (e.g., Xanax and Valium), barbiturates (e.g., Seconal and Amytal), and GHB (gamma-hydroxybutyrate).

After stimulants and depressants, the third class of drugs discussed herein is hallucinogens (psychedelics). Hallucinogens alter or intensify perception of outside stimuli and may cause hallucinations and delusions.

The fourth and final class of drugs is composed of inhalants. Inhalants include a wide variety of substances that do not fall within the three other broad categories of drugs. Inhalants produce psychoactive effects and are drugs of abuse.

The term *club drug* does not identify any specific class of drugs. Rather, club drugs are those which, at a particular time, are favored as party drugs. Generally, they are drugs that may reduce inhibitions, elevate mood, and increase social interaction. They can include hallucinogens like LSD, stimulants such as methamphetamine or cocaine, and ecstasy (MDMA), which has both stimulant and hallucinogenic effects. Some club drugs include depressants, such as flunitrazepam (Rohypnol), and dissociative anesthetics, such as ketamine, that cause feelings of disconnection with reality, an inability to control the situation, and impaired recall of events while under the influence, and that have been associated with sexual assaults.

STIMULANTS (UPPERS)

Stimulants vary widely in strength, ranging from mild legal stimulants to dangerous Schedule I controlled substances. Some plant-based substances have long been used as stimulants, including the leaves of the coca plant, khat (the leaves of a shrub found in East Africa), and betel nuts (seeds of the areca palm tree). The caffeine present in coffee, chocolate, and energy drinks, as well as the nicotine in tobacco products, are considered to be mild stimulants. Attention medications and diet pills have been classified as moderate stimulants. At the far end of the spectrum, cocaine and amphetamines, including methamphetamine, are extremely strong stimulants and are classified as Schedule II controlled substances.

Generally, stimulants increase energy, self-esteem, and confidence, as well as physical and mental performance. They can produce feelings of euphoria, exhilaration, and well-being. Uppers typically raise blood pressure and heart rate. They also increase wakefulness and may contribute to talkativeness, hyperactivity, and gregariousness. Stimulants can impair judgment, can decrease appetite and thirst, and may cause the user to be anxious, irritable, and restless. Signs of stimulant intoxication include dilated pupils, sweating, and nausea, and may include chest pain. Abuse of stimulants may reduce appetite and cause weight loss. Stimulants can be consumed orally, dissolved in water and injected intravenously, snorted, or smoked. Over time, prolonged abuse of stimulants can result in paranoia, auditory and visual hallucinations, and aggression.

As discussed in Chapter One, drugs stimulate and interfere with the production of chemicals in the brain. Uppers target the brain's production of epinephrine, which affects physical energy, and norepinephrine, which contributes to feelings of confidence. This class of drugs also impacts release and absorption of the feel-good chemicals of serotonin and dopamine. Users develop tolerance and suffer symptoms of withdrawal from stimulants. In stimulant withdrawal, the symptoms are the opposite of those of stimulant intoxication, generally resulting in fatigue, increased sleepiness, or extended sleep. Stimulant withdrawal is also associated with feelings of sadness, isolation, loneliness, and depression.

Stimulants block neural receptor sites, preventing the absorption of the drugs and thereby allowing them to continue to cycle through the brain and body. This sustained energy depletes and exhausts the body, ultimately resulting in a "crash." The crash brought about by withdrawal from strong stimulants such as methamphetamine can plague the user with deep fatigue and depression for days. Consistent with the disease mechanism of addiction, stimulant withdrawal also induces craving for renewed stimulant use and intoxication. Use of strong stimulants such as cocaine or methamphetamine may lead to the development of an SUD in as short a period as a week and, when the drug is administered by smoking or IV use, the disorder can progress to a severe stimulant use disorder in as little as weeks or months.[3]

Cocaine

Cocaine is a powerful Schedule II stimulant made from the leaves of the coca plant, which is native to South America. Historically, native peoples chewed coca leaves to increase energy and defeat hunger, as well as for social and religious purposes. Most of the cocaine entering the United States originated in South America, primarily Colombia. The leaves are processed to extract the chemical, cocaine hydrochloride. Although not a common practice, cocaine can be used medically as a topical local anesthetic.

On the street, powdered cocaine is a fine, white, crystallized powder that dissolves in water. It is sometimes cut with other substances, including cornstarch, flour, or talcum powder, to stretch the product. Other amphetamines may also be mixed into the powder for street sales. Cocaine mixed with heroin is called a "speedball." The powder can be snorted, rubbed on gums, or dissolved and injected intravenously.

Cocaine can also be processed into rock crystals (known as freebase or crack), which look like whitish chunks or small rocks. This type of cocaine is produced by dissolving the crystals in an alkaline solution and heating it to create lumps or rocks of cocaine. The solid form of the drug combusts at a lower temperature than the powder, so crack can be smoked in a pipe. The term *crack* comes from the sound the chunk of cocaine makes when it is heated and smoked. Street names for cocaine include blow, bump, C, candy, coca, coke, Charlie, crack, flake, rock, snow, soda sot, and toot.

While the effects of cocaine intoxication and the symptoms of withdrawal from cocaine are consistent with those associated with the use of other stimulants, due to its strength cocaine has a magnified impact on the body and the mind. As a result, cocaine produces more aggravated symptoms and is far more dangerous than mild or moderate stimulants. Cocaine use has, for example, been associated with aggressive behavior and violence. Cocaine users may experience chest pain, causing the user to think he or she is experiencing a heart attack. In fact, users can overdose on cocaine. A cocaine overdose is typically manifested by rapid heartbeat and hyperventilation. While overdose is not usually fatal, cocaine-related deaths do occur from cardiac arrest, seizure, stroke, and respiratory failure.

Cocaine is rapidly metabolized or absorbed in the body. When inhaled, cocaine reaches the brain in five to eight seconds, and when injected into a vein, it takes between fifteen and thirty seconds to reach the brain. When inhaled or injected, cocaine produces an immediate and intense, but short-lived, high. The faster the drug enters the bloodstream, the faster the high is achieved and the more intense the high. Similarly, the more intense the rush, the faster and more profound the crash. Given cocaine's fast absorption rate, cocaine users experience rapid cycles (from binge, intoxication, crash, and craving to binge). In some cases, these binge cycles can occur every twenty minutes.[4] The rapid cycle contributes to the fact that cocaine use can rapidly progress to addiction.

Over time, cocaine can damage the user's heart, cardiovascular system, brain, gastrointestinal tract, lungs, and nasal membranes. Cocaine can cause inflammation of the heart muscle and increase the risk of stroke, seizures, infection, and tears in the aorta.[5] Cocaine abuse has also been associated with bleeding in the brain, cerebral atrophy, and blockages in blood vessels in the brain. Cocaine can decrease blood flow in the intestines, causing tears and ulcers.[6] Cocaine abuse can result in weight loss and malnutrition.

Chronic users can develop paranoia and, in some cases, psychosis involving visual, auditory, or tactile hallucinations.[7] High-dose or long-term use of cocaine can cause sensory disruptions that make the user feel as if bugs are crawling under his or her skin. This is known as formication, and the user may develop sores from scratching the skin. Studies have also indicated that long-term use of cocaine impairs cognitive functions (reasoning and decision-making abilities) as well as the brain's inhibitory controls, memory, and motor skills.[8] Snorting cocaine temporarily constricts the capillaries in the nose. When the constriction subsides, the tissues swell, causing the symptoms of sniffling that are associated with snorting cocaine. Repeated snorting can destroy nasal tissues, cause bleeding, impair the sense of smell, and, in some cases, result in a perforated nasal septum.

The prevalence of cocaine use is lower than during the epidemic of the 1980s and 1990s, but it remains problematic. Recent data reflect that in the United States there were 1.6 times the number of deaths due to cocaine overdose in 2015 than in 2010.[9] Data from the 2016 NSDUH survey indicate that 1.9 million Americans over age twelve (representing 0.7 percent of the population) used cocaine during 2016. The survey also showed that 0.2 percent of Americans used crack cocaine during 2016. Based on the survey data, approximately 0.3 percent of the population aged twelve or older had a cocaine abuse disorder[10] in 2016.[11]

In contrast to the height of the epidemic, the average age of those entering treatment for cocaine abuse has increased. The 2016 NSDUH survey reflects that cocaine use is currently most prevalent among Americans aged eighteen to twenty-five when compared with other age groups.[12] Monitoring the Future (MTF) surveys are conducted annually and are based on interviews of eighth, tenth, and twelfth graders in public and private schools in the United States. The results of the 2016 MTF survey indicate that the number of respondents who admitted use of cocaine at some time during the year prior to the survey was at the lowest point ever reported by the survey, which began in 1975. The study concluded that the percentages of eighth, tenth, and twelfth graders reporting cocaine use during the year prior to the survey were 0.8 percent, 1.3 percent, and 2.3 percent, respectively.[13] The results of the 2017 MTF survey suggest that the annual use of cocaine (in the twelve months prior to the survey) by eighth graders remained steady at 0.8 percent, with slight increases in annual use by tenth and twelfth graders to 1.4 and 2.7 percent.[14]

Amphetamines Including Methamphetamine

Cocaine and amphetamines are considered to be the strongest stimulants. While cocaine is plant based, amphetamines are synthetic, that is, they are manufactured chemicals. The Combat Methamphetamine Epidemic Act of 2005 restricted the sale of nonprescription products containing the ingredients that can be used to make methamphetamine, notably pseudoephedrine, to control the diversion of those products for methamphetamine production. The effects produced by amphetamines are like those of cocaine. Cocaine produces a more intense high, but the effects of amphetamines are longer-lasting.

Traditionally, amphetamines have been produced as tablets often referred to as crosstops, black beauties (biphetamine), beans or dexys (Dexedrine), and bennies (Benzedrine). Methamphetamine (meth) is a Schedule II drug with limited medical uses. It is a white powder or pill that can be swallowed, snorted, or dissolved in water or alcohol and injected. Crystal meth, or crystal methamphetamine, looks like shards of glass or crystals and is white or bluish white. Crystal meth can be smoked in a process similar to smoking crack. Most of the meth currently used in the United States is manufactured and distributed by Mexican drug trafficking organizations.[15] Street names for meth include chalk, chicken feed, crank, crystal, ice, glass, poor man's cocaine, shabu, shards, speed, stovetop, Tina, trash, tweak, yaba, and yellow bam.

Pronounced tolerance is associated with amphetamine use.[16] The energy drain and the stress on the cardiovascular system caused by amphetamines are like those of cocaine. Due to their comparable properties, overdosing on amphetamines, including meth, creates the same types of cardiovascular risks, including death, as those related to cocaine use. At high doses, amphetamine use can cause irregular heartbeat, seizure, and heart failure. Chronic use of amphetamines can also result in heart problems, exhaustion, anger, violent behavior, paranoia, and psychosis. As with cocaine, chronic use of strong amphetamines can lead to formication, resulting in skin sores from scratching. General health risks, such as malnutrition, are common to cocaine, amphetamine, and meth users.

Meth has a disastrous effect on the body and mind of the user, especially the brain. Studies show that heavy meth users have lost over 11 percent of gray matter, particularly in the hippocampus, which is associated with emotions, mood, and memory. Reduction in cognitive function is found to be common in meth users. Prolonged use of meth can cause amphetamine psychosis, which includes loss of contact with reality and hallucination.[17] Poor dental hygiene and severe oral dehydration can result in rotting of teeth and receding and infected gums (referred to as "meth mouth").

Data from the 2016 NSDUH indicate that approximately 667,000 people aged twelve or older (about 0.2 percent of the population) used methamphetamine in the thirty days prior to the survey (which equates to "current use" as defined in the survey). The 2016 data also indicate that about 0.3 percent of Americans had a methamphetamine use disorder at some time during 2016. Prior to the 2015 survey, the interviewers did not inquire separately about methamphetamine use; rather, meth was included in a group of prescription stimulants. For this reason, the survey does not provide long-term data regarding trends in meth use.[18]

Synthetic Cathinones, Including Bath Salts

Bath salts are synthetic (man-made) stimulants that have no relationship to products for the bath or to salt. Cathinones are natural stimulants found in khat, a bush native to East Africa and the Arabian Peninsula. Historically, khat leaves have been chewed for their stimulant effect, and khat remains a drug of abuse. Bath salts include one or more synthetic chemicals that are produced to mimic the effect of natural cathinones, other stimulants such as cocaine and meth, and MDMA (which has both stimulant and hallucinogenic effects). These preparations commonly include mephedrone, methylone, or 3,4-methylenedioxypyrovalerone (MDPV). MDPV produces effects like those of cocaine but is ten times more powerful.[19] Synthetic cathinones are not controlled substances and can be sold in the United States for purposes other than human consumption. The Synthetic Drug Abuse Prevention Act of 2012 (SDAPA) classified additional substances, including two synthetic cathinones—mephedrone and MDPV—as Schedule I controlled substances.

Synthetic cathinones are usually a white, pink, or brown, crystal-like powder. They may be marketed in plastic bottles or foil packets labeled as bath salts, plant food, or cleaners for jewelry or cell phones. They are sold online and can be found in retail stores such as smoke shops, head shops, and convenience markets. These synthetic stimulants can be orally ingested, sniffed, snorted, smoked, vaporized (heated to release gases without combustion), or dissolved in liquid and injected. These synthetic products are referred to on the street as bath salts, or by the brand names under which they are marketed, including Bloom, White Lightning, and Vanilla Sky. The formulations are subject to change, and new products with different names regularly appear on the street.

Synthetic cathinones produce euphoria and alertness, and increase socialization and sex drive. This group of stimulants also increases heart rate and blood pressure. Intoxication is further manifested by dilated pupils. The drug has also been associated with grinding of the teeth, anxiety, aggression, violent behavior, hallucinations, the breakdown of muscle tissue, and kidney damage. The most serious symptoms occur when a user reaches a state of excited delirium as demonstrated in hyperstimulation, paranoia, hallucinations, and aggressive behavior. These man-made stimulants are exceptionally strong and have, in some cases, resulted in death. Symptoms of withdrawal from synthetic cathinones include anxiety, depression, sleep problems, and tremors.[20]

Attention Medications

Attention deficit disorder (ADD) and attention hyperactivity disorder (ADHD) are often medically managed with stimulants. Methylphenidate (Ritalin and Concerta) is an amphetamine congener, which means that it is chemically different from, but has the same effects as, amphetamines. The amphetamines Adderall and Dexedrine are also prescribed to manage attention disorders. ADD and ADHD are thought to be related to dopamine deficiencies. The prescribed stimulant causes the release of dopamine and prevents its reabsorption. These medications also cause the release of serotonin, a pleasure chemical that is thought to have a calming effect. The drugs prescribed for attention disorders can be abused. Pills can be swallowed or crushed and smoked, snorted, or injected. The symptoms of intoxication and withdrawal, as well as the risks associated with the abuse of these medicines, are like those of amphetamines.

DEPRESSANTS (DOWNERS)

Depressants have the opposite effects of stimulants. While stimulants speed up bodily systems and energize the body, depressants slow the functions of the CNS. Depressants can relax muscles, lessen anxiety, and induce sleep. They slow heart rate, blood pressure, pulse, and breathing. High concentrations of these drugs significantly slow a user's respiration and heart rate. This depression of essential life functions is what causes the risk of death from overdose of depressants such as alcohol and heroin. There are three major types of depressants:

1. Alcohol

2. Opiates/opioids

3. Sedative hypnotics

Alcohol

Alcohol is the most commonly used psychoactive drug. Alcohol dissolves in water and does not require digestion. For this reason, it is easily absorbed into the bloodstream and circulated to the brain and throughout the body. The absorption of alcohol into the bloodstream begins in the mouth and continues in the stomach and intestinal tract. The concentration of alcohol in the bloodstream is called the blood alcohol concentration (BAC). A person with a BAC of at least 0.08 is legally intoxicated.

Many factors impact BAC. The rate of absorption is affected by the concentration of the alcoholic beverage. Thus, for example, even though an ounce and a half of liquor and a twelve-ounce beer have the same amount of alcohol, the alcohol in the liquor is more concentrated, that is, there is more alcohol in an ounce of liquor than an ounce of beer. Due to its higher concentration, a shot of alcohol will be absorbed more quickly than a glass of beer. The rate of absorption of alcohol into the bloodstream is also affected by the user's body weight. A larger body mass spreads out or dilutes the impact of the same amount of alcohol. Food slows the rate of absorption in the stomach and delays the speed at which alcohol enters the bloodstream. When alcohol is consumed on an empty stomach, it is more rapidly absorbed into the bloodstream and its impact is felt more quickly.

Gender also impacts the concentration of alcohol in the blood. Alcohol is partially broken down in the stomach by an enzyme known as alcohol dehydrogenase (ADH). Women have lower amounts of the enzyme. As a result, men break down (eliminate) more alcohol in the stomach. In contrast, in women a greater percentage of alcohol passes through the stomach to the intestines, where it is then absorbed into the bloodstream. Women also have a lower percentage of water in their bodies than men. Thus, when men and women of the same weight consume the same type and amount of alcohol over the same period, the greater water content of the man's blood will dilute the concentration of alcohol in his blood compared to that of his female counterpart. For these reasons, alcohol consumption has a greater impact on women compared to men.

A drink is generally considered to be an alcoholic beverage containing 1.5 ounces of alcohol. A 1.5-ounce shot of whiskey, a mixed drink containing 1.5 ounces of liquor, five ounces of wine, and twelve ounces of beer each contain the same amount of alcohol.[21] It is important to remember that while a 1.5-ounce shot of straight liquor will be absorbed into the bloodstream more quickly than a twelve-ounce glass of beer, the shot and the glass of beer both contain the same amount of alcohol. Thus, other factors (such as gender and weight) being equal, drinkers who consume the same number of drinks, whether in the form of whiskey, wine, or beer, will ultimately reach the same BAC.

The body reacts to alcohol as a toxin and seeks to eliminate it from the body. Small amounts of alcohol are excreted from the body through breathing and in sweat, urine, and saliva. The rest of the alcohol is processed (metabolized) by the liver. While a variety of factors influence the rate at which BAC is increased, the elimination of alcohol from the body occurs at a constant rate. It takes about one hour to eliminate each alcoholic drink. The remaining alcohol stays in the bloodstream while it awaits elimination. It will take six hours for an individual to eliminate alcohol from the bloodstream after drinking either a six-pack of beer or six vodka tonics. The process is not hastened by a cold shower or drinking coffee. Such efforts will only result in person who is cold, wet, awake, *and* intoxicated.

Alcohol interacts with many different chemical neurotransmitters, including the feel-good chemicals, dopamine and serotonin. Alcohol consumption initially elevates mood by a release of serotonin, but is followed by a drop in serotonin that has a depressive effect. Alcohol causes the release of met-enkephalin, which reduces pain. Alcohol consumption also reduces the level of GABA, which controls behavior and thus lessens the user's inhibitions.

At low to moderate doses, and when BAC is increasing, alcohol can elevate mood, stimulate appetite, calm and relax the user, reduce inhibitions, and increase social confidence and talkativeness. At higher doses, however, and particularly when BAC is falling, the depressive effects of alcohol become more apparent. The user's blood pressure lowers, his or her speech may become slurred, and coordination and balance may be impaired. Intoxication may lead to mental confusion, mood swings, memory loss, and loss of control over emotions. A high BAC may also cause the user to fall asleep. Alcohol intoxication may result in blackout. While the user is conscious during a blackout, he or she cannot later remember what happened. At higher concentrations, alcohol continues to depress respiration and heart rate. The user may become unconscious and enter a coma, which may result in death. While death can occur at a lower concentration, a BAC of 0.40 is the threshold for alcohol poisoning and a BAC of 0.50 is fatal.

Hangovers can occur after a period of alcohol use regardless of whether the user is first experimenting with alcohol or is dependent on it. Hangovers may include nausea, vomiting, headache, dizziness, sleep disruption, sensitivity to noise and light, dry mouth, thirst, and feelings of depression. Over time, users develop tolerance and may suffer symptoms of withdrawal from alcohol. More pronounced withdrawal symptoms occur when the user is a chronic drinker.

In withdrawal from alcohol, the depressive effects of alcohol intoxication wear off, which may result in a period of hyperactivity. Symptoms of withdrawal from alcohol are generally the opposite of alcohol intoxication, including increased pulse, rapid heart rate, increased blood pressure, and insomnia. Alcohol withdrawal may also cause craving, agitated movements, hand tremors, nausea, vomiting, hallucinations, and anxiety. Acute alcohol withdrawal can result in a state of hyperarousal, in which the user experiences anxiety, insomnia, and irritability and may exhibit shaking or trembling (i.e., "the shakes"). A person in withdrawal from alcohol may also experience auditory or visual hallucinations, a condition known as alcoholic hallucinosis. The most serious complication of withdrawal from alcohol is delirium tremens (otherwise known as "the DTs"). The condition is characterized by hallucinations, confusion, and disorientation accompanied by frenzied motor activity (such as agitation), increased pulse, shakiness, and tremors. In its most severe forms, withdrawal is life-threatening and should be medically managed.[22]

Alcohol abuse has high social costs, including alcohol-related accidents, and alcohol-fueled aggression and violence result in death and injury. Chronic alcohol abuse also affects the major organs of the body. Most of the alcohol consumed passes through the liver, and chronic high use damages the liver. The condition of fatty liver, in which fatty acids accumulate in the liver, can occur after even short periods of heavy drinking. While the process is reversible, continued heavy drinking can lead to alcoholic hepatitis or cirrhosis. Cirrhosis, which is irreversible, occurs when liver cells die and scar the organ, rendering it unable to perform its function.

Chronic drinking can also cause damage to the stomach, including ulcers, inflammation, bleeding, and cancer. It also causes inflammation of the esophagus, pancreas, and intestines. Alcohol abuse presents risks of cardiovascular disease and can result in an enlarged heart, cardiac arrhythmias (irregular heartbeats), high blood pressure, and increased risk of stroke. Chronic high-dose use of alcohol can impair mental capacity and can cause memory loss and dementia. Heavy use of alcohol has been linked to the development of breast cancer in women. An increased risk of other cancers such as those of the mouth, throat, esophagus, and larynx is also presented.

The accepted definition of binge drinking is the consumption of five or more alcoholic drinks on the same occasion for men and four or more drinks on the same occasion for women. Heavy drinking is generally accepted to mean binge drinking on five or more days within a thirty-day period. The NSDUH survey asks participants about the use of alcohol during the thirty days prior to the interview (current use). Based on data from the 2016 NSDUH, an estimated 65.3 million Americans were binge drinkers and 16.3 million people were heavy drinkers. The survey data also support the conclusion that 15.1 million Americans aged twelve or older (5.6 percent of the population) had an alcohol use disorder in 2016. The 2016 survey further indicates that 19.3 percent of underage Americans (between the ages of twelve and twenty) drank alcohol at least once in the month prior to the interview, 12.1 percent of underage Americans engaged in binge drinking, and 2.8 percent were heavy drinkers during the month prior to the survey. Moreover, based on the survey results, in 2016 about 2.5 percent of American adolescents aged twelve to seventeen met the criteria for diagnosis of an alcohol use disorder. The survey also supports the conclusion that one out of every ten young adults (aged eighteen to twenty-five) was a heavy drinker in 2016.[23]

Opioids

Opioids (also known as "narcotics") are the second of the three types of depressants. This classification includes naturally occurring opiates and their derivatives as well as synthetically produced opioids. Opiates are processed from the opaque, milky-white sap of the poppy plant (*Papaver somniferum*), which turns black when it is exposed to air. This sap contains morphine and codeine. Heroin, which is derived from morphine, is also considered an opiate. Opioids are like opiates, but they are produced in a lab. The term *opioid* is commonly used to refer to both opiates and opioids. As such, the term *opioid* as used in this book refers to both natural opiates and synthetic opioids.

Generally, opioids relieve physical, mental, and emotional pain and create euphoria, that is, a rush. Medically, opioids are used for pain management and to control coughing and diarrhea. These legal prescription opioids include morphine, codeine, and painkillers such as oxycodone (Oxycontin), hydrocodone (Vicodin), and certain cough suppressants. Opioids interfere with the receptor sites in the brain for natural opioids. Users can develop tolerance for opioids, become physically and psychologically dependent on them, and suffer withdrawal symptoms after cessation of opioid use. Like other depressants, opioids slow the functions of the CNS, lowering blood pressure and reducing respiration. For this reason, they create the risk of death from overdose. These risks are increased when opioids are used with alcohol and other drugs.

Heroin and other opioid overdoses can be reversed with an injection of an opioid antagonist, naloxone (Narcan), which blocks the effect of the drug. Naloxone is available in an injectable form and as a nasal spray. The drug works by displacing opioids from receptors in the brain and stops their suppression of breathing and heart rate. Emergency responders typically carry naloxone, and some schools have the drug on hand for emergency use. While regulations vary by state, efforts are being made to make the drug available to individuals at risk for opiate overdose and to their family members.[24] If you have a loved one at risk for an opioid overdose, it is recommended that you contact your loved one's treatment provider, another provider who treats opioid addiction, your pharmacist, or a local prevention group to obtain information on how to obtain access to the drug and training in its use.

Symptoms of opioid intoxication include constricted (tiny) pupils. Speech may be slurred, and the user's voice may become hoarse. The user's physical coordination may be impaired, his limbs may feel heavy, and his skin may become itchy. There may also be impairment of attention, judgment, or memory. After the initial rush, the opioid user may become drowsy. The user's eyelids may droop and the head nod forward. While under the influence of opioids, a user may be insensitive to pain or injury. Initial feelings of euphoria may be followed by apathy, agitation, and lowered mood. Opioids can cause severe constipation.

The symptoms of withdrawal from opioids include symptoms that are the opposite of those of opioid intoxication. These include insomnia, anxiety, diarrhea, high blood pressure, rapid pulse, coughing, dilated pupils, and lowered mood. Withdrawal symptoms may also include pain in the bones, muscles, or joints; muscle cramps; sweating; runny nose; stomach cramps; vomiting; fever; chills; and goose flesh.

• HEROIN

Heroin has no medical use in the United States and is a Schedule I narcotic. Street names for heroin include H, hell dust, horse, junk, brown sugar, skunk, skag, smack, and Mexican black tar. Heroin, which is usually a white or brown powder, may be cut with flour, starch, sugar, or other materials. In its pure form, powdered heroin can be snorted and smoked. Most of the powdered heroin, which is prevalent on the East Coast of the United States, is from South America, but some of the product originates in Southeast Asia.[25] Most of the heroin found west of the Mississippi River originated in Mexico. A type of Mexican heroin known as black tar or tar is a potent form of the drug that is sold as a gummy paste or a hard, coal-like substance. It is less pure than powdered heroin. Both powdered and black tar heroin dissolve in liquid and the liquid is often injected into veins or muscles, or under the skin. The paste can also be smoked.

Heroin is an opioid depressant and, as such, its effects are like those of other depressants and other opioids. Given the pronounced strength of heroin, however, the symptoms of heroin intoxication are often more obvious than those following the use of other opioids. Pinpoint pupils that do not react to light are characteristic of heroin intoxication. Drooping eyelids and the nodding forward of the head (referred to as "nodding off") are also associated with heroin use. Further signs of heroin intoxication include slurred, slow, or raspy speech and lack of physical coordination.

Overdose of heroin presents a significant risk of death. One of the factors contributing to the high potential for overdose is that the purity of street heroin varies, and its strength can be unpredictable. When users abstain from heroin, their tolerance is reduced. For this reason, they may overdose if they pick up and use what they had previously considered a normal dose of heroin. In overdose, death occurs when the respiratory and cardiovascular systems become so depressed that the user passes out, enters a coma, and ultimately stops breathing. An overdose may be evidenced by blue lips and pale or bluish skin, labored breath, irregular heartbeats, and convulsions. These effects can be reversed with an injection of Narcan.

Since heroin is a short-acting drug, withdrawal symptoms may occur within six to eight hours after use.[26] Withdrawal can also begin in response to administration of Narcan. The first stage of withdrawal from heroin and other powerful opioids is acute withdrawal or detoxification. The symptoms include bone, joint, and muscular pain; insomnia; depressed mood; anxiety; sweating; runny nose; nausea, vomiting, and diarrhea; high blood pressure; rapid pulse; coughing; yawning; dilated pupils; teary eyes; hyperactive reflexes; muscle cramps; and fever, chills, and/or goose flesh. With heroin, while withdrawal symptoms become milder over time, the abstinent user may continue to experience physical symptoms of withdrawal, including sleep problems and mood swings during a post-acute withdrawal period of weeks or months. Post-acute withdrawal symptoms (PAWS) may continue for as many as eighteen months as the brain seeks to recover from the drug's impact on its pathways.[27] These extended withdrawal symptoms also induce craving and a present risk of relapse to users in recovery.

In addition to the potential for overdose, heroin users are at risk for numerous health problems. Those who inject heroin are at risk for hepatitis C and HIV transmitted by shared and dirty needles. Collapsed veins, skin abscesses, infections, and ulceration are also common among injection users. Injection also presents a risk of an infection of the valves of the heart. Heroin use may cause severe constipation and stomach cramps, as well as diseases of the liver and kidney.

Data from the 2016 NSDUH indicate that approximately 0.4 percent of Americans aged twelve and over used heroin at some time during the prior year. Generally, the study supports the conclusion that the percentage of Americans using heroin in 2016 was higher than estimates for the years 2002 to 2013, but similar to the estimates of use in 2014 and 2015. Based on the 2016 NSDUH, approximately 0.2 percent of the American population met the criteria for diagnosis of a heroin use disorder. The survey also supports the conclusion that approximately 0.4 percent of Americans between the ages of eighteen and twenty-five qualified for a diagnosis of a heroin use disorder.[28]

Data from the 2017 MTF survey indicate that heroin use among secondary school students has declined since its peak in the late 1990s and the year 2000. The percentage of eighth-, tenth-, and twelfth-grade students who admitted use of heroin at least once in the year prior to the survey interview continued to decline, from 0.8 percent in 2010 to 0.3 percent in 2017.[29]

• PRESCRIPTION PAIN RELIEVERS

Many different types of prescription pain relievers are subject to abuse or misuse. Misuse of drugs is defined as any use other than what is prescribed or as directed, including use more often, in larger amounts, or for a longer period of time than prescribed, as well as any use by a person to whom the drug was not prescribed. Some people become dependent upon painkillers that were originally prescribed for medical reasons, even if used as directed. Some users manipulate the system to obtain the drugs by prescription. In some cases, legitimately produced drugs are stolen or otherwise diverted for street sale. Generally, prescription painkillers are abused by oral ingestion, snorting crushed pills, or dissolving the substance for injection. The effects, signs of intoxication, symptoms of withdrawal, and health risks presented by the abuse of prescription opioids are consistent with those of the other opioids. Sadly, those who become dependent on pain relievers may progress to the use of less expensive illegal opioids such as heroin.

Morphine is a Schedule II narcotic that is used medically for pain management. Traditionally, it was injected; however, it is now available in a variety of forms, including tablets, capsules, suppositories, and drinkable liquid. Street names for morphine include dreamer, emsel, first line, hows, M.S., mister blue, morf, morpho, and unkie.

The widely prescribed pain reliever hydrocodone, which is sold under the names Vicodin, Hycodan, Tussend, and Norco, is also subject to abuse. Another commonly abused prescription painkiller is oxycodone, which is marketed under the names OxyContin and Percocet. It has been referred to on the street as hillbilly heroin, ocs, oxy, and o'cotton. Oxycodone has a time-release feature that was intended to reduce abuse. Users have, however, overridden this safeguard by chewing the pills or by crushing them and snorting or injecting the substance. Hydromorphone (Dilaudid) is a prescription pain reliever that is up to ten times more potent than morphine. Street names for hydromorphone include D, dillies, dust, and juice. The drug can be taken orally or crushed and injected. Other pain medications that are subject to abuse include meperidine (Demerol) and oxymorphone, which has the brand name Opana.

Codeine is a moderate prescription pain reliever that is sometimes combined with acetaminophen, a more moderate pain reliever that increases its effect. A side effect of codeine is nausea. Some of these medicines also contain antihistamines, which have sedative effects. Prescription cough syrups containing codeine and promethazine HCl, an antihistamine, are abused after being mixed in a drink with soda, alcohol, and/or hard candies. These beverages, which originated in Houston in the 1990s and were associated with some hip-hop musicians and referenced in lyrics, are known as purple drank, syrup, or sizzurp. Their use can cause respiratory arrest and death.

The 2016 NSDUH gathered data about the misuse of pain medications. The survey results indicate that in 2016 approximately 11.5 million Americans aged twelve or over (4.3 percent of the population) misused pain relief medications. The data further reflect that 3.5 percent of adolescents aged twelve to seventeen and 7.1 percent of young adults aged eighteen to twenty-five misused prescription drugs. The survey supports the conclusion that in 2016, an estimated 2.1 million people aged twelve or over (0.8 percent of the population) had an opioid use disorder based on the abuse of painkillers. For about 0.6 percent of adolescents, the misuse of pain medicine rose to the level of an opioid use disorder.[30]

• FENTANYL

Fentanyl, a Schedule II synthetic narcotic, is the most powerful known opioid. It is one hundred times stronger than morphine and fifty times stronger than heroin.[31] First introduced in 1968, fentanyl has been used intravenously during and after surgery for pain management. Fentanyl is legally produced for medical purposes in various forms, including liquids for intravenous use, oral lozenges (fentanyl lollipops), tablets that can be swallowed or dissolved under the tongue, oral and nasal sprays, and transdermal patches. Pharmaceutical fentanyl is diverted for abuse. The pills can be swallowed, but fentanyl can also be injected, snorted, and smoked. Fentanyl patches are abused by removing the gel content and injecting it, as well as by freezing them and cutting them into pieces to be placed under the tongue or on the cheek.

Fentanyl and numerous fentanyl analogs— pharmacologically like fentanyl—are also produced illegally. Acetyl fentanyl, also known as desmethyl fentanyl, is a fentanyl analog that has been linked to numerous deaths in the United States. The analog has been sold as tablets that look like pharmaceutical fentanyl, spiked onto blotter paper, and as a powder. At times, fentanyl analogs are mixed into or sold as heroin. This occurs more often on the East Coast, where powdered heroin is more common than on the West Coast.[32] The sale of fentanyl as heroin presents a huge risk of overdose because the drug is far stronger than heroin. The concentration of the powdered form of the analog also presents a significant risk to emergency responders because exposure to even a few grains of fentanyl can be fatal. Street names for fentanyl include apache, China girl, Chinatown, China white, dance fever, friend, goodfellas, great bear, he-man, jackpot, king ivory, murder 8, tango & cash, and TNT.

The symptoms of intoxication and withdrawal, as well as the risks associated with fentanyl, are like those of heroin. The risks presented by fentanyl and its analogs are magnified by their potency. Since much of the drug that is sold on the street is manufactured in clandestine labs, its purity varies widely and is unknown to the user. It is important to recognize that those trafficking drugs continue to change formulations and that other dangerous synthetic opioids with different names and different compositions will continue to appear on the street.

• METHADONE

Methadone is a long-acting synthetic opioid that is used in medication-assisted treatment or the medical management of addiction to heroin and other opioids. When administered in controlled therapeutic doses, methadone alleviates the symptoms of opioid withdrawal and cravings without producing a high. Methadone is often administered in liquid form that is swallowed, but it is also produced as a tablet. The drug can be abused, producing the same type of euphoria as other opioids. Even when it is administered for maintenance purposes, users will suffer withdrawal symptoms when the drug is discontinued.

Sedative-Hypnotics

Sedative-hypnotics are the third type of depressants in addition to alcohol and opioids. These calming drugs include tranquilizers, sleep medications, antianxiety medications, and certain antidepressants. Generally, sedatives (benzodiazepines) calm and hypnotics (barbiturates) induce sleep, although many drugs in this category have both sedative and hypnotic effects. Drugs of this type are generally marketed as tablets, pills, or capsules, although some medications manufactured in liquid form are abused by injection. Drugs used for anesthesia, such as propofol, would also fall within this general category.

The effects of drugs in this class are like those of alcohol because they interfere with the brain's production of the neurotransmitter GABA, which reduces anxiety and lessens inhibitions. The drugs in this class are, however, stronger than alcohol. Initially, sedative-hypnotics cause euphoria before their sedative effects become overwhelming. Sedative-hypnotics relax the body, cause drowsiness, lower inhibitions, and depress bodily functions, including breathing. They can result in slurred speech, confusion, dizziness, poor concentration, and memory problems.

A person under the influence of a sedative-hypnotic may be prone to accidents, injuries, aggression, and physical altercations. Drugs in this class have been used to facilitate sexual assaults. Since they depress the CNS, the symptoms of overdose from sedative-hypnotics are like those of other depressants, and overdose presents a risk of coma and death. Users can develop tolerance for the drugs and experience severe withdrawal symptoms when use of the substance is discontinued.

The 2016 NSDUH survey inquired about the misuse of tranquilizers and sedatives. The findings indicate that approximately 0.7 percent of Americans misused tranquilizers in 2016 and 0.2 percent of the same population misused sedatives. For adolescents aged twelve to seventeen, 0.5 percent are estimated to have misused tranquilizers in 2016, but only 0.1 percent misused sedatives.[33]

• BARBITURATES

Barbiturate pills, tablets, and capsules are manufactured in a variety of colors and are known by street names including barbs, barbies, red birds, reds & blues, yellow jackets, and yellows. Barbiturates were very popular in the 1940s and 1950s and were commonly abused in the 1950s through the 1970s. There are twelve types of barbiturates in medical use, ranging from short-acting to long-acting drugs. Short-acting barbiturates that take effect quickly and are of shorter duration, such as amobarbital (Amytal) and secobarbital (Seconal), are more often diverted for abuse because the longer-acting drugs sedate the user for longer periods of time.[34]

As depressants, barbiturates affect the body in a way much like alcohol, inducing euphoria and reducing inhibitions. High-dose or chronic use can result in personality changes, mood disturbances, or depression. Withdrawal symptoms include anxiety and agitation, increased heart rate, nausea and vomiting, sweating, stomach cramps, and tremors. A dependent user may experience severe withdrawal symptoms that present the risk of convulsions and death.[35] As such, withdrawal from barbiturate use should be managed by a physician.

• BENZODIAZEPINES

Benzodiazepines are the most widely prescribed sedative-hypnotic medications in the United States. They became popular in the 1960s because they are deemed safer than barbiturates. The perceived safety arises from the fact that a fatal dose of a barbiturate is ten times the amount of a therapeutic dose, while a fatal dose of a benzodiazepine is 700 times that of a therapeutic dose.[36] While death from overdose tends to be uncommon, the risks increase dramatically when benzodiazepines are used with alcohol.

Benzodiazepines are intended for short-term use due, in part, to the fact that physical dependence can occur at low doses and the symptoms of withdrawal from extended use are severe. Dependent users may need to taper down their use of the drug, under the care of a physician, for several months. Without medical monitoring, withdrawal from benzodiazepines can result in seizures that can be fatal. Symptoms of benzodiazepine withdrawal include craving for the drug, headaches, nausea and vomiting, muscle twitches, anxiety, high blood pressure, and sleep problems.[37] The most commonly prescribed benzodiazepines are alprazolam (Xanax), lozarazepam (Ativan), clonazepam (Klonopin), diazepam (Valium), and temazepam (Restoril). Of these, alprazolam and diazepam can be found on the street.[38] Benzodiazepines are known on the street as benzos, trans, BDZs, and downers. They may be used in combination with other drugs. For example, cocaine and meth addicts may use benzodiazepines to come down from the stimulant effects of their drugs of choice.

Benzodiazepines lower inhibitions, disrupt memory, sedate, and incapacitate users. Rohypnol, the trade name for flunitrazepam, is a benzodiazepine that is associated with sexual assaults. The drug is not used medically, nor is it sold legally in the United States. It is used in other countries for the treatment of insomnia and smuggled into the United States. Street names for Rohypnol include forget-me pill, roach, roofies, roapies, and rufies. Prior to 1997, the drug was manufactured as a white tablet that when dissolved did not change the color of the liquid. It was reformulated by the manufacturer for safety reasons and is now sold as an olive-green tablet that when dissolved in liquid turns the liquid blue. It is reported, however, that generic formulations of the drug do not change the coloration of the liquid in which they are dissolved.[39]

• GHB

Gamma hydroxybutyrate (GHB) is a strong, fast-acting depressant that targets the GABA receptors of the brain. GHB is a colorless liquid or a white powder that is often mixed with alcohol or water. Reportedly, it is mixed in bottled water so that it can be brought into events undetected. GHB gained a reputation as a club drug in the 1990s and has been used in association with sexual assaults. Street names for GHB include easy lay, Georgia homeboy, grievous bodily harm, and liquid ecstasy.

GHB is a Schedule I controlled substance. The generic form of the drug (sodium oxybate) is sold as Xyrem and is FDA approved for treatment of narcolepsy. Analogs of GHB (drugs manufactured to mimic GHB) are sold legally as industrial solvents and are used in the production of pesticides, plastics, polyethene, and other products.[40] GHB creates feelings of euphoria, lowers inhibitions, slows heart rate and breathing, reduces anxiety, and inhibits memory. Symptoms of withdrawal are generally opposite to those of GHB intoxication, and include increased heart rate and blood pressure, anxiety, sweating, insomnia, tremors, and psychotic thoughts.[41] Potential side effects of GHB include nausea, vomiting, depression, delusions, hallucinations, and seizures. Use also presents risks of respiratory depression and coma.[42]

HALLUCINOGENS

Hallucinogens, also known as psychedelics, are both found in natural plant materials and synthetically produced. This class of drugs includes a diverse group of drugs that produce similar effects despite having different chemical structures. Generally, hallucinogens alter the user's perception of reality, thoughts, mood, and feelings. The most commonly used drug in this category is marijuana (cannabis). Other drugs in the class of hallucinogens or psychedelics are LSD, psilocin mushrooms, MDMA (ecstasy), ketamine, PCP, *Salvia divinorum,* peyote (mescaline), and dextromethorphan (DXM).

Hallucinogens stimulate the CNS and impact many of the brain's essential neurotransmitters, notably serotonin, dopamine, and norepinephrine. The drugs cause a surge in these chemicals that overwhelms, and thus distorts, the senses. This process may cause a mingling of sensory perceptions, such that a person may see, rather than hear, music. Hallucinogenic drugs may also distort the user's sense of time. Further, hallucinogens may cause users to feel separated or disassociated from themselves or their surroundings.

The user may suffer illusions, which are mistaken perceptions of real things, such as when a hose is perceived to be a snake. Users may also suffer delusions, which are erroneous beliefs unrelated to logic, such as a person's conviction that he or she can fly. Illusions and delusions are commonly experienced while under the influence of psychedelic drugs. Hallucinations are visual, auditory, or tactile experiences that have no connection with external things, such as seeing an animal that is not present in the room. Hallucinations are more common with certain of the drugs in this class, such as mescaline (peyote), psilocybin, and PCP.[43] Severe overdoses of hallucinogens have resulted in respiratory failure and death. Other fatalities occur due to accidents related to altered perception, for example, jumping off a roof based on a user's delusion that he can fly.

A person's individual experience when taking this type of drug is influenced by his or her emotional health, as well as by the setting or context in which the drug is taken and the user's mood at the time of ingestion. Generally, this class of drugs causes an increase in pulse rate and blood pressure. Use of hallucinogens may also result in dilated pupils, loss of appetite, tremors, dry mouth, sweating, nausea, loss of coordination, panic, or paranoia. Hallucinogens are generally taken orally, but some can be smoked.

A condition known as hallucinogen persisting perception disorder (HPPD) may cause users to experience flashbacks in which they reexperience the effects of the drug long after its use. HPPD may also cause long-term visual disturbances, such as seeing light trails or halos around objects. In other rare cases, use of hallucinogens has been associated with the development of long-term psychosis involving visual disturbances, paranoia, mood disorders, and confused thinking. This category of drugs may cause memory loss and may either aggravate or hasten the manifestation of preexisting mental disorders.

Use of hallucinogens is not as prevalent as the use of other drugs. While the *DSM-5* establishes criteria for hallucinogen use disorder, it states that it is one of the rarest forms of addictive disease.[44] The 2016 NSDUH survey indicates that approximately 1.4 million Americans (0.5 percent of the population) were current users of hallucinogens in 2016. Approximately the same percentage of adolescents aged twelve to seventeen are estimated to have been current users of hallucinogens in 2016.[45]

LSD

Lysergic acid diethylamide (LSD) is a semisynthetic form of a fungus toxin. It is a Schedule I controlled substance and is produced in illegal laboratories in the United States. LSD is generally sold on the street in the form of tablets or capsules. It is often added to decorated absorbent paper—the paper is marked by a grid or images to designate doses. This form of the drug is ingested by placing a dose-sized piece of the paper in the mouth, where the chemicals are absorbed. LSD is also sold in liquid form. Street names include acid, blotter acid, dots, and windowpane.

LSD heightens sensations and causes changes in sensory perceptions. It may raise blood pressure and heart rate, increase temperature, and cause dizziness, dilated pupils, sweating, and impaired judgment that give rise to risk-taking behavior and injury. LSD does not have recognized withdrawal symptoms but may make the user feel emotionally drained. Users may experience acute anxiety reactions and panic, which are referred to as "bad trips." LSD is not associated with physical dependence or chemically compelled efforts to seek the drug such as those associated with dependence on other drugs, but it may become psychologically habit-forming.

Psychedelic Mushrooms

Certain mushrooms contain the psychedelic components psilocybin and psilocin. These mushrooms have long been used in some cultures for religious purposes. They are now Schedule I controlled substances. Psychedelic mushrooms are known on the street as shrooms or magic mushrooms. The mushrooms may be fresh or dried; have long, slender stems and caps with dark ribs on the underside; and vary widely in strength. The stems and caps of the psychedelic mushrooms are eaten either fresh or dried to achieve a high. They may also be brewed to make tea.

Psychedelic mushrooms cause hallucinations, alter sensual perceptions (vision, auditory, taste, and touch) and undermine the user's ability to tell fantasy from reality. Ingestion of mushrooms often causes nausea before the psychedelic effects are felt. There are no known symptoms of withdrawal from psilocybin and psilocin. Short-term risks are presented by the fact that poisonous mushrooms may be mistaken for psychedelic mushrooms. Users may also become nervous or suffer from panic attacks or paranoia.

Peyote (Mescaline)

The small peyote cactus contains the hallucinogen mescaline. Mescaline can also be synthetically manufactured. Peyote has long been used for religious and cultural purposes in the Americas. The fresh or dried crowns (buttons) of the cactus are bitter and have a bad taste. They may be mixed with liquids, chewed, ground into a paste and stuffed into capsules, or added to another substance and smoked. The buttons can also be boiled to make a tea. Mescaline is a Schedule I controlled substance. The street names for peyote include button, peyo, and cactus. Mescaline may cause illusions, colorful visual hallucinations, and altered perception of time. It typically produces intense nausea and vomiting. Mescaline intoxication manifests by dilated pupils and increased blood pressure, heart rate, and body temperature that causes sweating.

DMT

While originally found in certain South American plants, DMT is synthetically produced. It presents as a white, yellow, or brown powder that, while most often smoked, can be snorted or injected. It is not taken orally because digestive juices neutralize it.[46] DMT is a Schedule I controlled substance. Street names for DMT include businessman's special, Dimitri, and DMT. DMT creates a short period of intoxication (about thirty to sixty minutes) that is characterized by visual hallucinations and loss of connection with reality. Symptoms of intoxication also include agitation, increased heart rate, high blood pressure, dilated pupils, rapid eye movements, dizziness, and lack of physical coordination. Coma and respiratory arrest have occurred at high doses.[47]

MDMA (Ecstasy)

MDMA (3,4-methylenedioxy-methamphetamine) is a synthetic drug that has both stimulant and psychedelic effects. It is a Schedule I controlled substance that is produced in illegal laboratories both within and outside the United States. MDMA is most often distributed as a pill, but it can appear as powder, as capsules containing powder, or in liquid form. It is generally swallowed, but the powder can be snorted. The pills, which are manufactured in assorted colors, often contain an imprinted logo such as "E." Street names for MDMA include Adam, E, ecstasy, Molly, and X. Molly is often used to refer to the powdered or capsule form of the drug.

Originally popular as a club drug, MDMA is now used in various settings. About thirty minutes after ingestion, MDMA produces muscle tightness and muscle spasms before the psychedelic effects are felt. MDMA is taken to increase energy, self-awareness, and empathy; lower inhibitions; and promote feelings of happiness. As such, it encourages human interaction, touching, and sexual activity. It makes the user more sensitive to visual stimuli and tactile sensations. It also distorts perceptions and sense of time. MDMA is often used with other drugs, including alcohol, marijuana, LSD, and pain medications.

Significant risks are presented by the fact that drugs sold as MDMA often contain other drugs, such as PCP, ketamine, meth, and bath salts. For this reason, use of drugs identified as MDMA may present unanticipated risks, making the drug wholly unpredictable. MDMA causes increases in blood pressure, heart rate, and motor activity. Use of MDMA causes a rise in body temperature that has, in rare cases, been associated with organ failure and death. Use of the drug has been associated with anxiety, confusion, depression, and long-term memory impairment.

PCP

Phencyclidine (PCP) was originally in use as a dissociative general anesthetic for humans, but its use was discontinued because of its severe hallucinogenic effects. PCP is illicitly sold as a white or colored powder with a dry, crystallized, or gummy consistency. It is also produced as a tablet or capsule and in a liquid form (PCP dissolved in ether). It can be smoked, snorted, dissolved in liquid, swallowed, or injected. PCP has been added to marijuana, tobacco, and herbs (mint, parsley, or oregano) and then smoked. Street names for PCP include angel dust, dust, hog, ozone, and peace pill. Fry and sherm are among the street names for tobacco or marijuana cigarettes that have been dipped in liquefied PCP or embalming fluid.

PCP deadens pain and causes the user to lose connection with reality. PCP may cause hallucinations. Use of the drug initially increases blood pressure and pulse and manifests in flushing and sweating. At higher doses, blood pressure, respiration, and heart rate are lowered, creating a risk of coma and death. The user may also become violent, angry, or suicidal. Individuals under the influence of PCP may experience nausea, vomiting, rapid eye movements, and blurred vision. They may lose balance or become dizzy. Users may also appear to walk in a zombie-like manner because they cannot feel the bottoms of their feet. PCP use has been associated with injuries and violent altercations because it causes the user to dissociate from reality while feeling anger and the absence of pain. While withdrawal symptoms are not well established, long-term effects include memory loss, anxiety, weight loss, and depression. For certain individuals, hallucinogenic effects may continue for weeks and may create a persistent psychotic episode.[48]

Ketamine

Ketamine is an anesthetic that is used for medical procedures on humans and animals. It is of a short-acting duration (about sixty minutes). Since it has legitimate veterinary uses, ketamine is often stolen from veterinary clinics. Ketamine is produced as a clear liquid or as a white powder. The liquid can be mixed with liquids and swallowed or injected. Powdered ketamine can be snorted or added to tobacco or marijuana and smoked. Street names for ketamine include cat Valium, K, and special K.

Ketamine causes hallucinations, alters visual and audio perceptions, sedates, and may immobilize the user. It is referred to as a dissociative anesthetic because it makes the user feel disconnected with or disassociated from reality and unable to control the situation. The user may lack memory of events while under the influence. Given these properties, ketamine has been used to facilitate sexual assaults. Signs of intoxication may include dilated pupils, involuntary eye movements, stiff muscles, and difficulty moving. In some cases, ketamine use can result in respiratory arrest and death. Withdrawal symptoms have not been scientifically established. Long-term risks include depression, flashbacks, and memory problems. They may also include stomach pain, ulcers, bladder pain, and kidney problems.[49]

DXM

Dextromethorphan (DXM) is a cough suppressant that has some hallucinogenic effects when used at higher-than-recommended doses. DXM, along with other drugs such as pain relievers, is contained in some cough medicines (syrups, tablets, and capsules) that are sold over the counter (OTC), for example, Robitussin DM. Street names for DXM include dex, DXM, orange crush, and robo (a.k.a. robo tripping).

At quantities far above the recommended dosage, medicines containing DXM cause stimulation, euphoria, and dissociation from reality, as well as visual and auditory hallucinations. Symptoms of intoxication may include excitability, slurred speech, increased heart rate and blood pressure, dizziness, nausea, vomiting, loss of coordination, confusion, and involuntary eye movements. DXM presents a risk of overdose, coma, and death, particularly when combined with alcohol, antidepressants, or other drugs. Accidental injuries or death may also result due to dissociative effects and impaired perception of reality. The other medicines contained in DXM formulations can cause liver damage.

Salvia

Salvia divinorum (salvia) is a perennial plant in the mint family that has hallucinogenic and dissociative effects. It originated in the Sierra Mazatecan region of Oaxaca, Mexico, but can be grown in humid climates or indoors. Currently, salvia is not a controlled substance in the United States. While it is not against the law to sell salvia, it is illegal to sell it for human consumption. Given this legal status, however, salvia is available for purchase online. Street names include Sally-D and salvia.

Fresh or dried leaves of the plant can be chewed, smoked, or vaporized, causing out-of-body sensations, a dreamlike state, and hallucinations. Salvia can cause the user to experience visions of bright lights or overlapping objects, as well as physical sensations of motion or being pulled. Salvia may also cause uncontrollable laughter, slurred speech, the inability to speak or move, loss of coordination, dizziness, mood swings, and sweating. Neither symptoms of withdrawal nor health risks associated with salvia use have been scientifically established.

INHALANTS

There are other substances used for their effects on the body that do not fall within the broad categories of uppers, downers, or hallucinogens. These include inhalants, which are abused for their psychotic effects and are fast acting and widely available. A wide variety of products from prescription medicine and anesthetics to household chemicals fall within the broad category of inhalants. Inhalants are referred to by many different street names, including gluey, huff, laughing gas, poppers, snappers, and whippets.

Various liquids that produce fumes can be inhaled. These include petroleum-based products such as certain glues, gasoline, spray paint, hairspray, nail polish remover, keyboard cleaners, and felt-tip markers. Anesthetics, such as nitrous oxide (laughing gas) and ether, have also been used as inhalants. Nitrites are a different type of inhalant that dilate blood vessels, increasing blood flow, and relax muscles. Amyl nitrite inhalant is a prescription medicine used to treat chest pain. It is known on the street as poppers because the prescription medication used to be sold in glass vials that had to be cracked and popped. Nitrites continue to be sold illegally in small bottles with innocuous labels such as "cleaners." Nitrites are used to obtain a high and are considered to enhance sexual performance.

Inhalants are abused in a variety of ways. These include sniffing, which is breathing in the fumes of the inhalant, and huffing, which is placing a rag or other material that has been soaked into the toxic substance over the nose and mouth or directly in the mouth. The term *huffing* is also used more generically for all forms of inhalant abuse. The inhalant or material soaked in the inhalant may be placed into a plastic bag to allow the fumes to be inhaled from the bag. This technique is known as bagging. Pins or other implements can be used to puncture cans containing inhalants. The gases released from the can are captured in a balloon from which the gas is inhaled. Balloons may also be filled with nitrous oxide for purposes of inhalation. Inhalants can also be used to soak collars or sleeves of clothing that are then sniffed. It is particularly dangerous to spray toxic substances directly into the mouth or nose. Heating the substances is also highly dangerous and has resulted in injuries from burns and explosions.

Initially, inhalants provide stimulation, reduce inhibitions, and elevate mood. These feelings are followed by dizziness, slurred speech, sleepiness, and lack of coordination. At higher doses, hallucinations, illusions, and delusions may occur. Inhalants are toxic to many of the body's systems. Inhalant use can cause sudden cardiac arrest or result in coma or death even when used for the first time. Use of inhalants in a closed space can lead to death by suffocation. Symptoms of withdrawal may include nausea, sleep problems, and mood changes, but withdrawal symptoms are mild and are not considered for diagnostic purposes.[50] Inhalants also cause damage to the brain, heart, lungs, and liver. Chronic use impairs memory and impacts cognitive function.

Data from the 2016 NSDUH indicate that approximately 0.2 percent of the population aged twelve and over use inhalants for their intoxicating effects. Inhalant use is most common among adolescents, with approximately 0.6 percent of those aged twelve to seventeen estimated to have used inhalants at least once in the thirty days prior to the survey.[51] The MTF surveys indicate that inhalant use is most common among eighth graders, but decreases as students age. The authors of the report theorize that this pattern may be due to the low cost and wide availability of inhalants and that use lessens when older students have increased access to other drugs.[52] The results of the 2017 MTF survey indicate that 4.7 percent of eighth graders, 2.3 percent of tenth graders, and 1.5 percent of twelfth graders reported they had used inhalants in the year prior to the survey.[53] While the incidence of inhalant use by secondary school students had been in decline for decades, a 0.9 percent increase in use by 2017 eighth graders over the 2016 results suggests "a possible reversal of that trend and bears watching" in the opinion of the authors of the MTF reports.[54]

RECOMMENDED RESOURCES

- Center for Substance Abuse Research, *National Drug Early Warning System (NDEWS)*, University of Maryland, https://ndews.umd.edu/.

- National Inhalant Abuse Coalition, http://www.inhalants.org/about.htm.

- NIDA, Drugs of Abuse, https://www.drugabuse.gov/drugs-abuse.

- NIDA, Emerging Trends and Alerts, https://www.drugabuse.gov/drugs-abuse/emerging-trends-alerts.

CHAPTER 2 NOTES

1   Darryl S. Inaba and William E. Cohen, *Uppers, Downers, All-Arounders: Physical and Mental Effects of Psychoactive Drugs,* 8th ed. (Medford, OR: CNS Productions, Inc., 2014), 2.4.

2   Ibid.

3   APA, DSM-5, 563 and 565.

4   Inaba and Cohen, *Uppers, Downers, All-Arounders,* 3.16.

5   Suraj Maraj, Vincent M. Figueredo, and D. Lynn Morris, "Cocaine and the Heart," *Clinical Cardiology* 33 no. 5 (5) (2010): 264–65, doi: 10.1002/clc.20746.

6   NIDA, "What Are the Long-Term Effects of Cocaine Use?" in *Research Report on Cocaine* (2016), https://www.drugabuse.gov/publications/research-reports/cocaine/what-are-long-term-effects-cocaine-use.

7   Inaba and Cohen, *Uppers, Downers, All-Arounders,* 3.15.

8   Desiree B. Spronk et al., "Characterizing the Cognitive Effects of Cocaine: A Comprehensive Review," *Neuroscience and Behavioral Reviews* 37 (2013): 1853–54, doi: 10.1016/j.neubiorev.2013.07.003.

9   NIDA, "Overdose Death Rates."

10   The NSDUH bases its estimates of whether individuals qualify for diagnosis of the criteria for substance abuse or dependence as determined by the outdated *DSM-IV.* Despite the difference in diagnostic terminology between the *DSM-IV* and *DSM-5,* the NSDUH estimates are a relevant measure of the prevalence of the SUDs based on the use of different classes of drugs.

11   CBHSQ, "2016 NSDUH," 17, 27.

12   Ibid., 17.

13 Richard A. Miech et al., *Monitoring the Future, National Survey Results on Drug Use, 1975–2016: Vol. I, Secondary School Students ("2016 MTF, Vol. I")* (Ann Arbor: The University of Michigan Institute for Social Research, 2017), 162–63, http://www.monitoringthefuture.org/pubs/monographs/mtf-vol1_2016.pdf.

14 Richard A. Miech et al., ""National Adolescent Drug Trends in 2017: Findings Released." National press release, Ann Arbor, MI: December 14, 2017, Table 6, http://monitoringthefuture.org/press.html. Tables at http://monitoringthefuture.org/data/17data.html#2017data-drugs.

15 Drug Enforcement Administration (DEA), *Drugs of Abuse, A DEA Resource Guide.* Drug Enforcement Division, US Department of Justice, 2017, 54, https://www.dea.gov/pr/multimedia-library/publications/drug_of_abuse.pdf#page=51DEA.

16 Inaba and Cohen, *Uppers, Downers, All-Arounders,* 3.27.

17 Ibid., 3.26, 3.28.

18 CBHSQ, "2016 NSDUH," 19–20 and 29.

19 NIDA, "Synthetic Cathinones ('Bath Salts')," in "Drug Facts," last modified January 2016, https://www.drugabuse.gov/publications/drugfacts/synthetic-cathinones-bath-salts.

20 NIDA, "Synthetic Cathinones (Bath Salts)" in "Commonly Abused Drug Charts," last modified July 2017, https://www.drugabuse.gov/drugs-abuse/commonly-abused-drugs-charts#synthetic-cathinones-bath-salts.

21 NIAA, "What Is a Standard Drink?" https://niaaa.nih.gov/alcohol-health/overview-alcohol-consumption/what-standard-drink.

22 Jean Kinney, *Loosening the Grip: A Handbook of Alcohol Information,* 10th ed. (New York: McGraw-Hill Education, 2012), 188.

23 CBHSQ, "2016 NSDUH," 11–13, 25.

24 HHS, *Facing Addiction in America,* 4–11–12.

25 NIDA, *Research Report on Heroin* (2014), https://www.drugabuse.gov/publications/research-reports/heroin/what-heroin.

26 APA, DSM-5, 548.

27 Inaba and Cohen, *Uppers, Downers, All-Arounders,* 4.20.

28 CBHSQ, "2016 NSDUH," 20–21 and 28.

29 Lloyd D. Johnston et al., 2017 MTF Key Findings, 27.

30 CBHSQ, "2016 NSDUH," 1, 15, 21, and 30.

31 DEA, *Drugs of Abuse,* 40.

32 Center for Substance Abuse Research, "Fentanyl and Fentanyl Analogs," *National Early Drug Warning News (NEDWN)* 10 (2015), http://pub.lucidpress.com/NDEWSFentanyl/#0uATvewBep_i.

33 Ibid., 17.

34 DEA, *Drugs of Abuse,* 58.

35 Inaba and Cohen, *Uppers, Downers, All-Arounders,* 4.41.

36 Ibid., 4.40.

37 Ibid., 4.39–4.40.

38 DEA, *Drugs of Abuse,* 59.

39 Ibid., 61.

40 Ibid., 60.

41 NIDA, "GHB," in "Commonly Abused Drug Charts," last modified July 2017, https://www.drugabuse.gov/drugs-abuse/commonly-abused-drugs-charts#ghb.

42 Inaba and Cohen, *Uppers, Downers, All-Arounders,* 4.43.

43 Ibid., 6.50.

44 APA, *DSM-5,* 525.

45 CBHSQ, "2016 NSDUH," 19.

46 Inaba and Cohen, *Uppers, Downers, All-Arounders,* 6.12.

47 NIDA, *Research Report on Hallucinogens and Dissociative Drugs* (2015), https://www.drugabuse.gov/publications/research-reports/hallucinogens-dissociative-drugs/director, and NIDA, "DMT," in "Commonly Abused Drug Charts," last modified July 2017, https://www.drugabuse.gov/drugs-abuse/commonly-abused-drugs-charts#hallucinogens.

48 APA, *DSM-5,* 521.

49 NIDA, "Ketamine," in "Commonly Abused Drug Charts," last modified July 2017, https://www.drugabuse.gov/drugs-abuse/commonly-abused-drugs-charts#ketamine.

50 NIDA, "Inhalants," in "Commonly Abused Drug Charts," last modified July 2017, https://www.drugabuse.gov/drugs-abuse/commonly-abused-drugs-charts#inhalants, and APA, *DSM-5,* 535.

51 CBHSQ, "2016 NSDUH," 19.

52 Johnston et al., 2017 MTF, Key Findings, 15.

53 Ibid., 68.

54 Ibid., 1.

3 DEBUNKING THE MYTHS: THE FACTS ABOUT MARIJUANA

There have been significant changes in societal attitudes about marijuana, and many people support widened legislation based on their perception that the drug has value with negligible risk. For those of us concerned about the use of mind-altering substances by children, adolescents, and young adults, there is no policy dilemma. The science is definitive: marijuana use by children and adolescents detrimentally impacts their minds and bodies, producing life-altering, long-term effects. Similarly, marijuana use by adults, which so interferes with their ability to function as to meet the criteria for an SUD, is a disease that warrants medical intervention. In these contexts, it does not matter whether the drugs being used by our loved ones are legal or illicit. For our purposes, however, widened legalization raises at least two major concerns. First, legalization generally makes a formerly illegal drug more accessible to all, including the most vulnerable underage population. Second, the growing misperception that marijuana is not dangerous tends to increase its use, including use by children and teenagers. Arguably, these arguments outweigh other interests and tip the balance against further legalized access to the drug.

Janice E. Gabe, an Indianapolis-based licensed clinical social worker and licensed clinical addictions counselor specializing in the treatment of adolescents and young adults, has said that debates about legalization "fog the real and present danger of youth marijuana use."[1] Similarly, due to the risks of marijuana to children and adolescents, the American Academy of Pediatrics (APA) opposes legalization and is against the use of marijuana for medical purposes outside of the formal FDA-approval process. The APA supports the decriminalization of marijuana-related offenses and advocates for additional research on the potential medical benefits of cannabinoids. Its position statement also recognizes the potential need for compassionate use of the marijuana-based medicines for treatment of children with debilitating or life-limiting diseases.[2]

THE BASICS: THE PLANT, THE DRUG, AND ITS USES

Cannabis, the most widely used illegal psychoactive drug in the United States, is derived from plants. There are a variety of plants in the cannabis family. The term *marijuana* is generally used to refer to the species of cannabis that have high concentrations of psychoactive chemicals. Some species, generally referred to as hemp, do not produce psychoactive effects, but contain fibrous material that is used in the production of rope and other products. Marijuana contains hundreds of constituent elements and dozens of cannabinoids that may contribute to the plant's effects. The chemical component primarily associated with the psychoactive properties of marijuana is delta-9-tetrahydrocannabinol, commonly referred to as THC. THC is present in the leaves, buds, and flowers of marijuana plants. The flowering tops of the plants, or buds, contain more THC than the smaller leaves and stems. THC is also concentrated in resins produced by the plants.

There are two main species of marijuana plants, *Cannabis sativa* and *Cannabis indica,* but growers have cultivated hundreds of hybrid varieties. The most common species of the plant is *Cannabis sativa,* a species that was originally grown in tropical, subtropical, and temperate regions but is now cultivated indoors and in a variety of conditions. On average, the plant reaches heights of between five and twelve feet, but it can grow as high as twenty feet. Its leaf structure is easily recognized: five thin serrated leaves on a stem with two smaller leaves at the base of the leaf cluster. The other main species of the plant, *Cannabis indica,* which is shorter and bushier, originated in India, Pakistan, Afghanistan, and the Himalayas. Some hybrids from the cross-pollination of *Cannabis indica* and *Cannabis sativa* produce marijuana with a stronger odor, resulting in the street name skunk or skunk weed.

Advances in growing techniques have dramatically increased the potency of THC in the final product. One of these techniques is the cultivation of a seedless variety of marijuana called sinsemilla (a Spanish word that means "without seeds"). The growing technique involves separation of the male and female plants before pollination. The female plants produce more of the psychoactive resin than the male plants, particularly before pollination and the production of seeds. The seedless buds of the female sinsemilla plants contain high concentrations of THC. Marijuana can also be grown hydroponically, without soil, using mineral nutrients in a water solution.

Dried marijuana looks like the plant-based material it is, presenting as shredded leaves, stems, and flowers that may be green, gray, or brown and may look like tobacco. Dried marijuana can be crushed and rolled into cigarettes or joints. It can also be rolled in tobacco leaves (cigar wrappers) or placed into hollowed-out cigars, producing thick marijuana cigars known as "blunts." The dried product can also be smoked in a pipe or water pipe (a bong or hookah), used to make tea, or vaporized in a dry herb vaporizer or compatible vape pens that are similar to e-cigarettes. When a drug such as marijuana is vaporized (also referred to as vaping), it is heated to the point that the psychoactive ingredients are released as a vapor (as distinct from the release of smoke that results from the combustion of the product). There are many different street names for plant-based marijuana, including blunt, bud, bloom, dope, gangster, ganja, grass, green, hash, hemp, herb, hydro, joint, Mary Jane, pot, reefer, sinsemilla, skunk, smoke, reefer, weed, and yerba.

Hairlike growths (trichomes) on marijuana buds and flowers contain a THC-rich resin that is used to produce more concentrated forms of the drug. Hash has been produced from the resin of marijuana plants for centuries. In more recent decades, the resin has been compressed into cakes or balls known as hash or hashish. Pieces of the solid cakes can be broken off and smoked in a bong, vaporized, or added to dried marijuana to increase its potency. Hash can also be eaten alone or mixed with food. Hash oil, which is extracted from resin of the cannabis plant, has also been in use for decades. It can be spread on rolling papers or dripped onto leafy marijuana and smoked or added to food.

Most hash is extracted from plants in the *Cannabis indica* species. Resin has long been derived from the plants through manual, mechanical processes. Processing has become more efficient and solvents are now used to remove the plant material and isolate concentrated resins. A volatile extraction process involving butane has resulted in explosions and injuries. In recent years, the University of Colorado burn center has reported an increased number of marijuana-related burns attributed to the butane extraction process.[3] After extraction from the plant material, the end products range from sticky, black, or golden oils and golden or brown soft solids with the texture of wax, honey, or butter, to brittle solids.

The DEA refers to resin-based concentrates as THC concentrates or THC extractions. NIDA uses the term *marijuana extracts* to refer to THC-rich concentrates, including those in hard brittle, soft solid, and liquid forms. Recently, there has been an increase in the practice of smoking the concentrated forms of THC, a method known as "dabbing." Dabbing refers to taking a "dab" of concentrate, heating it on a metal surface, and then inhaling the vapors. THC concentrates can also be vaped using a vape pen or vaporizer. Street names for these concentrates include budder, butane hash oil, butane honey oil, ear wax, wax, and 710 (because it resembles the word *oil* upside down and spelled backward). In its hard, resinlike form, the concentrate may be referred to on the street as black glass or shatter.

THC-rich oils are used in the manufacture of edible marijuana products. These "edibles" include brownies, cookies, and candy. The psychoactive impact of edibles is slowed by the digestive process, and therefore it takes much longer for that impact to reach the brain. It may take from thirty minutes to several hours to feel the full impact of edibles. During the delay, users may continue to consume THC-laden edibles to prompt the expected effects. Unintended overconsumption, coupled with the fact that once they are digested the effects of edibles last longer than when the product is smoked, can result in adverse reactions and overdose. The problem is also complicated by inconsistences in THC concentration and portion size, or dosage, in edible products.

Ingestion of high-potency products, including edibles, has resulted in increased emergency room visits in Colorado. There have been increases in admissions for marijuana intoxication (as manifested in vomiting, anxiety, and panic attacks) and cyclic vomiting syndrome (characterized by severe abdominal pain, vomiting, and excessive sweating). There have also been reports of increased emergency room admissions for accidental ingestion of edible marijuana products by children.[4]

Marijuana remains a Schedule I controlled substance and is illegal under federal law. With the relaxation of state laws governing the sale of marijuana for medical or recreational purposes, the federal government has largely deferred regulation and enforcement to the states except in areas of federal interest such as preventing the sale of marijuana to minors and cultivation of marijuana on federal land.

Medical marijuana products are derived from marijuana plants and sold for medicinal purposes under state law. Medical marijuana is generally more potent than plant-based street products.[5] While laws vary by state, medical marijuana can generally be obtained with a doctor's prescription for conditions enumerated under state law. Some states allow use of medical marijuana for subjective symptoms such as generalized pain. In many cases, states have failed to establish a medically based professional protocol for use or delivery of medical marijuana.

Plant-based medical marijuana is not FDA-approved, and no medicines derived from the marijuana plant are FDA-approved. There are, however, two synthetic cannabinoid drugs approved by the FDA: dronabinol (Marinol) and nabilone (Cesamet) are used for treatment of nausea and vomiting induced by chemotherapy and for weight loss and loss of appetite in AIDS patients.

SYNTHETIC CANNABINOIDS

Synthetic cannabinoids are designer drugs with brand names such as K2 and Spice that are manufactured to mimic the effects of THC. These products have a different molecular structure than marijuana, and users may not test positive for THC. Most synthetic cannabinoids are manufactured in Asia. Despite a plant base, the psychoactive ingredients are chemical and are not derived from marijuana, even though they may be advertised as "natural." Typically, powdered chemicals are dissolved in acetate and sprayed on absorbent plant materials. When manufactured in this way, the chemicals may not be evenly distributed, resulting in a wide variety of potency, even within a single batch. The fact that they are produced illicitly, with no regulatory control, and the imprecise method of how they are manufactured render these products highly unpredictable. In other words, both their chemical content and potency are wholly unknown to the user. These drugs may be far more potent than marijuana and can be life-threatening. Overdose deaths from heart attack have occurred following use of synthetic cannabinoids.[6] During 2016, increases in emergency room visits related to ingestion of synthetic cannabinoids were reported. Some patients present with symptoms of suppressed respiration, as with opioid overdoses, while others are agitated and violent.[7] In 2018, synthetic cannabinoids were identified as the source of emergency room admissions for excessive bleeding, and some deaths are believed to have been related to the adulteration of the products with rat poison.[8]

Like bath salts (synthetic stimulants), synthetic cannabinoids are widely available in stores and online. They are often sold in colorful foil packets under misleading labels (such as "potpourri" or "herbal essence") and may be labeled as "not for human consumption." These synthetic drugs were not designated as controlled substances and were not illegal prior to the enactment of SDAPA in 2012. Manufacturers continue to change the chemical composition of the products to avoid criminal prosecution. The Controlled Substance Analogue Enforcement Act of 1986 allows prosecution of individuals for the manufacture and sale of drugs chemically similar to those on Schedule I of the Controlled Substances Act. The DEA reports that this law has been used to prosecute those trafficking variations of synthetic cannabinoids that mimic the effects of marijuana, a Schedule I controlled substance.[9]

Synthetic cannabinoids are used in the same way as plant-based marijuana; they are smoked using rolling papers, pipes, and water pipes, and can be vaporized or brewed in a tea. Synthetic cannabinoids are also produced as liquids that can be vaporized. In addition to K2 and Spice, other brand and street names for these synthetic drugs include Black Magic, Blaze, Cloud 9, Demon, Joker, Kush, Liquid Essence, Fake Weed, Mojo, Ninja, Paradise, Sence, Serenity, Smacked, Spike, and Yucatan.

INCREASED POTENCY

Some who smoked marijuana in their youth without adverse consequences may minimize the impact of today's drug. Such comparison fails to account for the dramatic and steady increases in the potency of the drug since the 1970s, 1980s, and 1990s due to advances in the cultivation of THC-rich plants and the extraction of THC concentrates. In the 1960s, the average concentration of THC in marijuana was between 1 and 3 percent.[10] Based on the concentration of drugs seized by the DEA, the average concentration of THC in marijuana was 3 percent in the 1980s; it increased to 4 or 5 percent in the 1990s and was 12 percent in 2012.[11] The DEA estimated that in 2017, high-grade, plant-based marijuana contained about 20 percent THC and that THC extractions contained 40 to 80 percent THC.[12]

EFFECTS, SYMPTOMS OF INTOXICATION, AND IMMEDIATE HEALTH RISKS

While marijuana is generally classified as a hallucinogen, it can also act like a depressant or a stimulant. The *DSM-5* describes cannabis as having hallucinogenic effects but diagnoses cannabis use disorders separately from those related to use of other hallucinogens because of what it refers to as significant differences in the psychological and behavioral effects of cannabis.[13] The effects of marijuana depend upon a variety of circumstances, including the specific substance used, the dosage taken, and its potency. Further, marijuana, like other hallucinogens, impacts individuals in different ways. The effect of the drug on a specific user is influenced by environmental factors such as an individual's prior history of use, emotional well-being, and mood at the time of ingestion. The environment or context in which the drug is consumed (such as whether the user is alone or with other people) also influences the experience.

Marijuana activates and disrupts natural cannabinoid neurotransmitters in the brain, including anandamide, that regulate many functions of the CNS including sensory perception, emotion, memory, concentration, sense of novelty, appetite, anxiety, and motor coordination. Marijuana prompts the brain to release natural anandamides that stimulate the amygdala, which is the part of the brain that judges the emotional importance and novelty of stimuli. For that reason, while under the influence of marijuana, commonplace things may take on enhanced significance. Marijuana causes the user to perceive even the mundane as novel or exciting. Marijuana also impacts the dopamine receptors in the brain that regulate pleasure and reward life-affirming activities. As the brain acts to protect itself from overstimulation by the chemicals contained in psychoactive drugs, it slows or blocks the natural transmission of feel-good chemicals such as natural cannabinoids and dopamine. This process is referred to as downregulation. In chronic cannabis users, the protective downregulation of natural chemicals inactivates receptors for anandamides, diminishing the user's perception of normal stimuli and making normal things seem uninteresting and boring.[14]

When marijuana is smoked, intoxication occurs within minutes and lasts three or four hours. When it is consumed orally, it takes thirty minutes to an hour to feel the effects of the drug, but the effects generally last longer than with inhalation. Marijuana often produces an initial high, with feelings of euphoria and grandiosity, which may be accompanied by inappropriate laughter or giddiness. These feelings may be followed by relaxation, drowsiness, and lethargy. The drug may cause the user to feel separated from the environment or aloof. Marijuana may also create feelings of familiarity, or déjà vu, and exaggerate mood as well as personality. The drug may also cause the user to become more suggestible or to feel more empathy for others. Users may also feel less inhibited and more sociable. In contrast, some users experience fear, anxiety, panic, paranoia, and detachment from self while under the influence of the drug.

Marijuana increases appetite, a symptom that is commonly referred to as the munchies. Marijuana hinders judgment, disrupts focus and concentration, and interferes with the perception of time and the ability to track moving objects. The drug also disrupts short-term memory. Because of its impact on concentration and memory, marijuana impairs the ability to learn and complete tasks. It also impacts balance, coordination, motor skills, and reaction time. At higher doses, marijuana use can produce greater alertness, distortion of color and sounds, illusions, and hallucinations. Higher doses can also result in a temporary acute psychosis, manifested in hallucinations, delusions, and loss of the sense of self. In addition to the changes in sensory perception and motor coordination, the signs of marijuana intoxication may include increased heart rate and appetite, redness in the whites of the eyes (bloodshot eyes), and dry mouth. Other signs of use may include odor on clothing, the practice of burning incense to hide odors, a chronic cough, and an unusual appetite or craving for specific foods.

Marijuana is generally not associated with death from overdose, although deaths have occurred following use of synthetic cannabinoids and overdose of edibles. The immediate consequences of marijuana use include impaired concentration and short-term memory, which makes it difficult to study and learn. Marijuana impairs the ability to track moving objects, lessens reaction time, and interferes with motor coordination. For these reasons, drivers under the influence of marijuana have been found to be twice as likely to be involved in automobile accidents than nonintoxicated drivers. When marijuana is used with alcohol, the accident risk is increased. The drug also impairs decision making, increasing the potential for risky behaviors.

TOLERANCE, WITHDRAWAL, AND ADDICTION POTENTIAL

According to the *DSM-5*, regular use of marijuana can lead to the development of tolerance for the substance, which is lost if use is stopped for a period of at least several months. Sudden cessation of daily or almost-daily use of cannabis can result in cannabis withdrawal syndrome as defined in the *DSM-5*. Under the *DSM-5*, symptoms of withdrawal from cannabis may include irritability, anger or aggression, nervousness or anxiety, restlessness, sleep disturbances, loss of appetite, weight loss, or depressed mood. Withdrawal may also cause "significant distress" from at least one of the following symptoms: abdominal pain, shakiness/tremors, sweating, fever, chills, or headache.[15] The symptoms of withdrawal from marijuana may also include craving for the drug and general aches and pains. The existence of demonstrated symptoms of tolerance and withdrawal illustrate the addictive properties of marijuana and other cannabinoids. The *DSM-5* recognizes diagnoses of mild, moderate, and severe cannabis use disorders. Cannabis use disorders typically develop during adolescence or young adulthood but can occur in older adults.[16] Cannabis use disorder may occur alone or in combination with other SUDs.

Studies have shown that about 8.9 percent of marijuana users (or about one in eleven) will become dependent.[17] The *DSM-5* calls early onset of use (prior to age fifteen) a "robust predictor of the development of cannabis use disorder and other types of substance use disorders and mental disorders during young adulthood."[18] Studies have shown that one in six (17 percent) of those who first use marijuana as teenagers are statistically likely to become dependent on marijuana.[19] The risk of addiction is higher for adolescents than for individuals who start using the drug as adults. Those who start using cannabis as adolescents are two to four times more likely to develop an addiction within two years than those who first start to use the drug as an adult.[20] The risks are also compounded by daily use and the potency of the drug used. Early use of marijuana, as well as the early use of alcohol and tobacco (nicotine), has been shown to condition the brain to respond to psychoactive drugs, thereby reinforcing the use of other drugs.

ADOLESCENT VULNERABILITY TO MARIJUANA AND OTHER DRUGS

Teenagers are thought to be more vulnerable than adults to the development of addiction and long-term cognitive impairments from the use of psychoactive drugs, including marijuana. This vulnerability is due to the fact that the prefrontal cortex of the brain remains in an active stage of development until the mid-twenties. During this period of development, the brain is more vulnerable to the effects of psychoactive drugs than the mature adult brain. Early in adolescence, there is significant nerve growth in the frontal lobe of the brain. Over the next ten to twelve years, those nerve connections (synapses) that are reinforced by external stimuli are strengthened, while those that are unused will weaken and break. This process, which is called pruning, reduces the amount of gray matter in the brain and streamlines the neural connections to make the process of communication between the brain and the rest of the body more efficient. The cannabinoids in marijuana, including THC, interfere with the brain's endocannabinoid system (ECS), which is thought to be important to the pruning process.

SERIOUS LONG-TERM RISKS LINKED TO HEAVY USE THAT BEGINS IN ADOLESCENCE

In addition to the risk of addiction to marijuana and other substances, heavy consumption of marijuana in adolescence presents other very serious long-term health risks. While further research is needed, studies have shown that heavy use with an early onset correlates to impairment of brain development, changes in the structure of the brain, loss of IQ, and long-term cognitive, attention, and memory problems. The impairment of attention and memory in adolescent users has been associated with school failure, the inability to pursue educational and career opportunities, and reduced life satisfaction. Chronic marijuana users may also suffer impaired mental health and be at risk for the development of respiratory and cardiac problems.

Effects of Marijuana on the Adolescent Brain

The most profound effects on the brain produced by marijuana use occur when chronic use begins in childhood or adolescence and lasts for a period of years. Imaging and other brain studies have shown that individuals with a history of chronic marijuana use that began in adolescence have more gray matter in the PFC, indicating that the pruning of excess neural connections (synapses) has not been efficiently completed.[21] Brain studies of individuals who smoked marijuana regularly during adolescence also reveal deficiencies in the regions of the brain that are important to executive function, memory, learning, concentration, awareness, inhibitory control, and the fostering of habits and routines.[22] More specifically, several studies have shown that the size of the hippocampus—a part of the brain important to the processing of information and memory—is smaller in adult chronic marijuana users.[23] While some studies show that cognitive impairments improve with prolonged abstinence, other research indicates that cognitive deficits are long-lasting, despite abstinence.[24]

A 2012 study found an 8 percent drop in IQ between the ages of thirteen and thirty-seven among subjects who started using marijuana in adolescence and continued using it, consistently, into adulthood. These users were also found to have problems with attention and memory. The same study concluded that neuropsychological functioning among adolescent-onset persistent cannabis users did not fully recover after cessation of use. Similar deficits were not identified in subjects that began marijuana use in adulthood.[25]

Learning and Lifetime Achievement

Because marijuana interferes with learning, attention, and memory and these deficits last for days after use, even occasional marijuana use has a negative effect on school performance and academic success. With chronic use over a period of years during high school, the ongoing and persistent effects of these impairments on learning ability often result in academic failure and the decision to drop out of school before graduation. Given its association with school failure and the continuing inability to pursue further educational and career aspirations, scientists have a high degree of confidence that chronic marijuana use beginning in adolescence correlates to "diminished lifetime achievement."[26]

The *DSM-5* recognizes a diagnosis of avoidant personality disorder. The essential feature of the disease is "a pervasive pattern of social inhibitions, feelings of inadequacy, and hypersensitivity to negative evaluation that begins by early adulthood."[27] Janice E. Gabe has treated many avoidant young adult males in her practice. These passive young men, who are generally between the ages of eighteen and twenty-four, typically retreat from interaction with the world, are reluctant to leave the house, are nonproductive, and are unwilling or unable to move forward toward self-sufficiency. In her seminar, aptly entitled "The Young Avoidant Adult: Peter Pan Is Alive and Well and

Living in His Parents' Basement," she estimates that 90 percent of these young male patients have a history of chronic marijuana use with an onset in early adolescence, while the remaining 10 percent have a chronic gaming history.[28]

Anxiety, Depression, and Mental Health

While research is ongoing, there are many other serious long-term health risks associated with chronic marijuana use that began in adolescence, including impairments to mental health. Marijuana use has been associated with the development or worsening of anxiety and depression. While further research is needed, it also appears that chronic and early use of marijuana by individuals with a genetic predisposition to schizophrenia may advance the manifestation of symptoms of the disease.[29]

Cardiovascular and Respiratory Impairments

Marijuana use has been associated with heart and vascular problems that increase the risk of heart attack and stroke. Cardiac risks also include increased angina, arrhythmia (irregular heartbeat), cardiomyopathy (a chronic disease of the heart muscle), and sudden cardiac death. Further, smoking marijuana may give rise to cannabis arteritis, a serious peripheral vascular disease that may cause plaque and blockages in the blood vessels supplying the legs and feet.[30]

Marijuana smokers experience adverse effects like those associated with smoking tobacco cigarettes. Due to the number of chemicals contained in marijuana and the irregular, harsh, and unfiltered nature of the product, it is thought to be more toxic to the user than commercial tobacco products. Respiratory problems have been associated with marijuana use, including coughing, increased sputum production, increased rates of bronchitis and frequency of medical visits for respiratory problems, and shortness of breath.[31]

Marijuana smoke contains the same type of carcinogens as tobacco smoke and is believed to present cancer risks, but additional studies are needed to isolate the impact of smoking marijuana from that of concurrent smoking of tobacco.[32] Research results are mixed, and while there is some evidence that heavy long-term use presents a cancer risk, a link between moderate marijuana use and cancers of the lung or upper airway has not been established.[33] While vaporization is considered to be less harmful to the lungs because the product is inhaled as water vapor and not smoke (which also includes tar and other harmful properties), use of a water pipe does not remove toxins from the smoke.[34] The greatest damage to the lungs is found in those who smoke both tobacco and marijuana.[35]

While the known impact of chronic marijuana use beginning in adolescence is serious, it is important to note that much of the research on the health effects of marijuana was done when the average concentration of THC in plant-based marijuana was much lower than it is today and prior to the higher incidence of THC extracts and concentrates. This fact highlights the need for additional research and heightens concerns about the adverse effects of concentrated, high-potency cannabis and related products. To date, however, it has been conclusively established that serious health risks are associated with long-term, heavy, or chronic use (daily or almost daily use) of marijuana, particularly when such use began in adolescence.

PREVALENCE OF USE

Marijuana is the most commonly used illicit drug in the United States. The results of the 2016 NSDUH indicate that twenty-four million Americans (8.9 percent of the population) were current marijuana users. The 2016 survey also supports the conclusion that approximately four million Americans aged twelve or older in 2016 (1.5 percent of the population) qualified for a diagnosis of a cannabis use disorder. The survey results regarding the prevalence of adolescent and young adult use of marijuana are troubling. The survey indicates that about 6.5 percent of adolescents between the ages of twelve and seventeen were current users of marijuana in

2016. As discussed above, significant brain development occurs not only in the teen years but until the mid-twenties. The 2016 NSDUH projected that 20.8 percent of eighteen-to-twenty-five-year-olds currently used marijuana. Similarly, in 2016 about 2.3 percent of Americans aged twelve to seventeen and 5 percent of young adults between the ages of eighteen and twenty-five would satisfy the criteria for diagnosis of a cannabis use disorder.[36]

The 2017 MTF study supports the finding that 10.1 percent of eighth graders, 25.5 percent of tenth graders, and 37.1 percent of twelfth graders reported use of marijuana or hashish at least once in the year prior to the survey. In 2017, daily use of marijuana, that is, use of marijuana on at least twenty days during the prior thirty-day period, was reported by 0.8 percent of eighth graders, 2.9 percent of tenth graders, and 5.9 percent of twelfth graders.[37] The 2016 MTF survey confirmed that chronic marijuana use often has an early onset. Seven percent of all 2016 twelfth graders reported that they started daily use (current or past) before they entered tenth grade. These results may underestimate the use of marijuana by those of high school age because the survey population is limited to students attending school. The survey does make an adjustment for absenteeism among students, but the authors state that they cannot adjust for students who have dropped out of school (even though they recognize that dropouts typically have higher rates of drug use than students). The 2016 MTF study of young adults concluded that approximately 7.5 percent of Americans between the ages of nineteen and twenty-eight were daily marijuana users.[38]

LEGALIZATION CONTRIBUTES TO THE PERCEPTION THAT MARIJUANA IS NOT HARMFUL, RESULTING IN INCREASED USE

According to the authors of the MTF reports, one of the most important conclusions derived from their annual surveys is that "changes in beliefs and attitudes about drugs are important determinants of trends, both upward and downward, in the use of many drugs."[39] Drug use generally occurs in inverse proportion to perceived risk. That is, use increases when a drug is perceived to involve insignificant risks and declines when a substance is perceived to present high risks to users.

The inverse relationship between the perception of risk and the prevalence of use is aptly demonstrated by MTF data regarding declines in the use of synthetic marijuana between 2012 and 2016. Over that time period, the percentage of twelfth graders who thought using synthetic marijuana once or twice presented a risk of great harm increased from 23.5 to 35.6 percent. The increased perception of risk corresponded to decreased use as the number of twelfth graders reporting that they had used synthetic marijuana at some time during the last year decreased from 11.3 to 3.5 percent during the same time period.[40]

Perceptions of the harmfulness of drugs ebb and flow over the years and are impacted by numerous factors, such as media reports and public education campaigns. The theory that decreased perception of harm from using marijuana has corresponded to increased use is generally borne out by the results of the MTF surveys.[41] The authors of the MTF studies concur that media reports concerning legalization of marijuana and the fact of its legalization in some states have driven recent declines in the perception that marijuana is harmful.[42] In essence, a snowball effect is created when decreased perception of risk leads to broadened legalization, which increases availability and further reduces the perception of harm, resulting in further increases in use by all segments of the population.

The MTF surveys document that the percentage of adolescents who think marijuana is harmful has been steadily declining and is now at its lowest level in decades, and that this reduced perception of harm has corresponded to increased use.[43] The MTF survey questions are designed to ask about levels of use: experimental use (trying the substance once or twice), occasional use, and regular use. In 2009, 69.8 percent of eighth graders reported that they considered the regular use of marijuana to present a great risk of harm. By 2017, however, only 54.8 percent of eighth graders held that belief. The trend is similar for twelfth graders. In 2009, 52.4 percent of twelfth graders considered the regular use of marijuana to present great harm, while by 2017, only 29.0 percent thought so.[44]

While continued declines in the perception of risk foreshadow continuing increases in use, the authors of the 2016 and 2017 MTF survey reports note that increases in marijuana use by secondary students have not kept pace with the continued declines in perceived risk. They associated this finding with a reduction in the smoking of tobacco by adolescents, which they correlate to a reduced prevalence of smoking marijuana.[45] Data from the 2017 MTF survey, however, indicate a "statistically significant" increase of 1.3 percent (to 24 percent) of eighth, tenth, and twelfth graders combined who reported use of marijuana at some time over the last year.[46]

In 2017, for the first time, the MTF survey included inquiries about the prevalence of vaping marijuana among secondary school students. In 2017, according to the survey, 3 percent of eighth graders, 8 percent of tenth graders, and 10 percent of twelfth graders vaped marijuana in the prior year.[47] Data are not yet available to determine whether secondary school students consider vaping marijuana to be less harmful to the user than smoking the drug and whether growth in the popularity of vaping will further increase marijuana use among secondary school students, including those who do not smoke tobacco.

The 2016 MTF survey of young adults aged nineteen to twenty-eight showed similar declines in the perception that regular use of marijuana is harmful. In 2004, for example, 57.2 percent of the population of young adults thought the regular use of marijuana presented a great risk. In 2016, however, only 30 percent of this age group reported that they thought regular use of marijuana presented a great risk. This change in perception correlates to increased use among this population. In 2016, 7.6 percent of respondents aged nineteen to twenty-two reported daily marijuana use. The authors of the study indicate that the 2016 figures represent the highest level of such use by this population in the more than thirty years in which it has been tracked by the survey. Thus, based on this study, decreased perception of risk of marijuana use has correlated to increased use of the drug by young adults.[48]

RECOMMENDED RESOURCES

- National Institute on Drug Abuse (NIDA), *Marijuana: Facts Parents Need to Know* (2016), https://d14rmgtrwzf5a. cloudfront.net/sites/default/files/parents_mj_ brochure_2016.pdf.

- NIDA, *Marijuana: Facts for Teens* (2013), https://www. drugabuse.gov/sites/default/files/teens_brochure_2013. pdf.

CHAPTER 3 NOTES

1   Janice E. Gabe, "Marijuana Use in Teens and Young Adults" (Online seminar, ATTP, 2016), http://aatpofillinois.com/.

2   American Academy of Pediatrics, "American Academy of Pediatrics Reaffirms Opposition to Legalizing Marijuana for Recreational or Medical Use," last modified January 26, 2015, https://www.aap.org/en-us/about-the-aap/aap-press-room/pages/American-Academy-of-Pediatrics-Reaffirms-Opposition-to-Legalizing-Marijuana-for-Recreational-or-Medical-Use.aspx.

3   Andrew A. Monte, "The Implications of the Marijuana Legalization in Colorado," *JAMA* 313, no. 3 (2015): 241–42, doi: 10.1001/jama.2014.17057.

4   Ibid., 242.

5   Gabe, "Marijuana Use in Teens."

6   DEA, *Drugs of Abuse*, 88.

7   NIDA, "Emerging Trends and Alerts," in *Drugs of Abuse*, posted July 16, 2016, https://www.drugabuse.gov/drugs-abuse/emerging-trends-alerts#spice.

8   NIDA, "Emerging Trends and Alerts," in *Drugs of Abuse*, last updated April 6, 2018, https://www.drugabuse.gov/drugs-abuse/emerging-trends-alerts.

9   DEA, *Drugs of Abuse*, 88.

10 Darryl Inaba and William Cohen, *Uppers, Downers, All Arounders: Physical and Mental Effects of Psychoactive Drugs*, 6th ed. (Medford, OR: CNS Publications, 2007), 285.

11 Volkow et al., "Adverse Health Effects of Marijuana Use," *The New England Journal of Medicine* 370 (2014): 2222–2223, doi: 10.1056/NEJMra1402309.

12 DEA, *Drugs of Abuse*, 54.

13 APA, *DSM-5*, 524.

14 Inaba and Cohen, *Uppers, Downers, All-Arounders*, 8th ed. (2014), 6.36.

15 APA, *DSM-5*, 518.

16 Ibid.

17 Catalina Lopez-Quintero et al., "Probability and Predictors of Transition from First Use to Dependence on Nicotine, Alcohol, Cannabis, and Cocaine: Results of the National Epidemiologic Survey on Alcohol and Related Conditions (NESARC)," *Drug and Alcohol Dependence* 115, no. 1-2 (2011): 120, doi: 10.1016/j.drugalcdep.2010.11.004.

18 APA, *DSM-5,* 513.

19 Wayne Hall and Louisa Degenhardt, "Adverse Health Effects of Non-Medical Cannabis Use," *The Lancet* 374 (2009): 1386, doi: 10.1016/S0140-6736(09)61037-0.

20 Chuan-Yu Chen, Carla L. Storr, and James C. Anthony, "Early-Onset Drug Use and Risk for Drug Dependence," *Addictive Behaviors* 34, no. 3 (2009): 320, doi: 10.1016/j.addbeh.2008.10.021.

21 Seth Ammerman et al., "The Impact of Marijuana Policies on Youth: Clinical, Research, and Legal Update," *Pediatrics* 135, no. 3 (2015): e771, doi: 10.15421/peds.2014-4147.

22 Volkow et al., "Adverse Health Effects of Marijuana Use," 2220.

23 Albert Batalla et al., "Structural and Functional Imaging Studies in Chronic Cannabis Users: A Systematic Review of Adolescent and Adult Findings," *PLOS ONE,* 8, no. 2 (2013): e55821, 4, doi: 10.1371/journal.pone.0055821.

24 Wayne Hall and Louisa Degenhardt, "The Adverse Health Effects of Chronic Cannabis Use," *Drug Testing and Analysis* 6 (2014): 41, doi: 10.1002/dta.1506.

25 Madeline H. Meier et al., "Persistent Cannabis Users Show Neuropsychological Decline from Childhood to Midlife," *Proceedings of the National Academy of Sciences of the United States of America (PNAS)* 109, no. 40 (2012): E2661–662, doi: 10.1073/pnas.1206820109.

26 Volkow et al., "Adverse Health Effects of Marijuana Use," 2225, table 2.

27 APA, *DSM-5,* 676–673.

28 Janice E. Gabe, "The Young Avoidant Adult: Peter Pan Is Alive and Well and Living in his Parents' Basement" (Online seminar, ATTP, 2016), http://aatpofillinois.com/.

29 Marta Di Forti et al., "Daily Use, Especially of High-Potency Cannabis, Drives the Earlier Onset of Psychosis in Cannabis Users," *Schizophrenia Bulletin* 40, no. 6 (2014): 1509, doi: 10.1093/schbul/sbt181.

30 Grace Thomas, Robert A. Kloner, and Shereif Rezkalla, "Adverse Cardiovascular, Cerebrovascular, and Peripheral Vascular Effects of Marijuana Inhalation: What Cardiologists Need to Know," *American Journal of Cardiology* 113, no. 1 (2014): 187–89, doi: 10.1016/j.amjcard.2013.09.042.

31 Donald P. Tashkin, "Effects of Marijuana Smoking on the Lung," *Annals of the American Thoracic Society* 10, no. 3 (2013): 240, doi: 10.1513/AnnalsATS.201212-127FR.

32 Hall and Degenhardt, "Chronic Cannabis Use," 40.

33 Tashkin, "Effects of Marijuana Smoking on the Lung," 239.

34 Ammerman et al., "The Impact of Marijuana Policies on Youth," e772.

35 Inaba and Cohen, *Uppers, Downers, All-Arounders,* 6.37.

36 CBHSQ, "2016 NSDUH," 27.

37 Miech et al., "National Adolescent Drug Trends in 2017: Findings Released," tables 2 and 4.

38 John E. Schulenberg et al., "Monitoring the Future: National Survey Results on Drug Use, 1975–2016: Vol. II, College Students and Adults Aged 19–55" (2016 MTF, Vol. II) (Ann Arbor: The University of Michigan Institute for Social Research, 2017), 117, table 4-5, http://www.monitoringthefuture.org/pubs/monographs/mtf-vol2_2016.pdf.

39 Miech et al., 2016 MTF, Vol. I, 377.

40 2017 MTF, Key Findings, tables 6 and 12.

41 Volkow et al., "Adverse Health Effects of Marijuana Use," 2225, figure 2.

42 Miech et al., 2016 MTF, Vol. I, 383.

43 Miech et al., "National Adolescent Drug Trends in 2017: Findings Released."

44 Ibid., tables 5 and 7.

45 Miech et al., 2016 MTF, Vol. I, 383–84.

46 Miech et al., "National Adolescent Drug Trends in 2017: Findings Released."

47 Ibid.

48 Schulenberg et al., 2016 MTF, Vol. II, 141 and 255, table 6-1.

4 THE CRITERIA FOR DIAGNOSIS OF ADDICTIVE DISORDERS

Denial of a problem is a hallmark of addictive disease. We hear loved ones responding to our concerns with declarations that they do not have a problem, and that they are not addicts, alcoholics, or compulsive gamblers. It is not in any way suggested that we should attempt to diagnose those we are concerned about or confront them with the facts in an effort to convince them that they have a problem. Logic will not convince an individual who is in denial about his or her own substance abuse or behavioral compulsion, and an unplanned attempt at intervention by untrained family members or friends may have serious consequences or merely serve to escalate existing problems. The diagnostic information in this chapter is, instead, provided to help the reader to:

1. Identify potential problems and seek professional help

2. Better understand the disease

3. Comprehend the meaning of a professional diagnosis, once made

4. Understand the severity of another's condition, as well as the corresponding recommended level of care

Historically, addiction professionals have discussed the evolution of the disease as progressing through a continuum of levels. In *Loosening the Grip: A Handbook on Alcohol Information*, a treatise on alcoholism, Jean Kinney outlines the development and progression of the disease through stages of experimentation, use, abuse, and dependence. Kinney explains that as the disease of alcoholism advances, individuals develop tolerance for alcohol and require more and more of it to achieve the desired effect. Tolerance for other drugs of abuse develops the same way. When a drug is used over time, more and more of the same substance must be ingested for the user to experience the same result. When the pattern of use is disrupted and a dependent person stops using his or her drug of choice, that person generally suffers physical symptoms of withdrawal from the substance. The objective and measurable symptoms of tolerance and withdrawal not only are evidence that addiction is a biological process, they are also among the criteria used in the diagnosis of substance-related addictive disorders.

An assessment of whether an individual has an addictive disorder is not based on these physical symptoms alone. Rather, the diagnosis of a mental disorder, including an SUD or a gambling disorder, must be made by a qualified professional and should be made in the context of a full biopsychosocial evaluation, including the client's medical history. A biopsychosocial evaluation is a holistic evaluation that considers the totality of the person's physical, mental, and emotional health in the context of the subject's environment and his or her functionality in that environment.

The *Diagnostic and Statistical Manual of Mental Disorders*, 5th Edition details specific diagnostic criteria for mental disorders, including SUDs and gambling disorders. The fifth edition of the manual, published in 2013, significantly changed the way in which addictive disorders are categorized and diagnosed based on advances in scientific research.[1] The prior edition of the manual, the 1994 *DSM-IV*, identified criteria for diagnoses of substance "abuse" and "dependence." While the terms *substance abuse* and *dependence* are no longer used in a diagnosis, they remain relevant to an understanding of the progression of the disease. In other words, the scientific explanation of the development and progression of the disease remains unchanged despite the change in diagnostic terminology.

Instead of using the terms *abuse* or *dependence*, the *DSM-5* provides criteria for the diagnosis of "substance use disorders" (SUDs) and gambling disorders that are classified as mild, moderate, or severe. In fact, apart from the title of the chapter, "Substance-Related and Addictive Disorders," the *DSM-5* does not even refer to "addiction." Rather, the *DSM-5* is premised on the authors' conclusion that the term *substance use disorder* is more neutral than the term *addiction* and that the severity qualifiers (mild, moderate, or severe) identify where the client is within a wide range encompassed by the disorder.[2] While not used in the *DSM-5*, the term *addiction* is used, synonymously, to refer to a severe SUD as diagnosed under the *DSM-5*.[3]

The *DSM-5* explicitly cautions that "[c]linical training and experience are needed to use the *DSM* for determining a diagnosis" and that clinical expertise is required to differentiate diagnostic criteria from conduct that falls within the range of normal behavior.[4] This discussion of the criteria for SUDs is not intended as a substitute for professional advice or as grounds for declaration that any person has an SUD. Further, this chapter does not attempt to summarize the material in the *DSM-5*, which consists of over 800 pages and is written for clinicians, not the public. Rather, the purpose of this chapter is to provide information and objective criteria to help family members better understand when another's substance use or gambling has become problematic and inform their response to it.

SUBSTANCE USE DISORDERS UNDER THE *DSM-5*

According to the *DSM-5*, determination of the existence of an SUD relates to the examination of "a pathological pattern of behaviors" based on the use of a substance "despite significant substance-related problems."[5] The *DSM-5* identifies ten classes of drugs:

1. Alcohol

2. Caffeine

3. Cannabis

4. Hallucinogens

5. Inhalants

6. Opioids

7. Sedative-hypnotics and anxiolytics

8. Stimulants

9. Tobacco

10. Other or unknown substances

Under the guidelines of the *DSM-5*, with the exception of caffeine, a diagnosis of an SUD can be based on the use of any of the other nine classes of drugs. This book is intended to address situations where a loved one's use of psychoactive drugs has caused significant disruption in our own lives. While caffeine is a drug, it does not present significant problems to the family and friends of a user and will not be discussed in this work. Similarly, while tobacco products are addictive and the source of serious health risks to the user, the problems associated with their use are also outside the intended scope of this book and will not be addressed.

The *DSM-5* defines eleven symptoms as indicative of an SUD. These eleven symptoms fall within four distinct categories: impaired control, social impairment, risky use, and pharmacological criteria. While the presence of only two or more of the eleven symptoms identifies the existence of an SUD, the number of criteria satisfied determines the severity of the disease. The criteria are largely the same for identification of various SUDs and differ by identification of the specific drug of choice. The diagnostic criteria for alcohol use disorder, for example, are based on the use of alcohol, while the criteria for the diagnosis of cannabis use disorder are dependent upon the use of cannabis. While the diagnostic criteria are largely the same, evaluation of the symptoms of withdrawal for each class of drug is based on the specific symptoms of withdrawal for that drug class.

These concepts are more readily understandable based on an examination of specific diagnostic criteria. As detailed in the *DSM-5*, the following criteria are used for the diagnosis of an alcohol use disorder.

Alcohol Use Disorder

DIAGNOSTIC CRITERIA

A. A problematic pattern of alcohol use leading to clinically significant impairment or distress, as manifested by at least two of the following, occurring within a 12-month period:

[Impaired Control]

1. Alcohol is often taken in larger amounts or over a longer period than was intended.

2. There is a persistent desire or unsuccessful efforts to cut down or control alcohol use.

3. A great deal of time is spent in activities necessary to obtain alcohol, use alcohol, or recover from its effects.

4. Craving, or a strong desire or urge to use alcohol.

[Social Impairment]

5. Recurrent alcohol use resulting in a failure to fulfill major role obligations at work, school, or home.

6. Continued alcohol use despite having persistent or recurrent social or interpersonal problems caused or exacerbated by the effects of alcohol.

7. Important social, occupational, or recreational activities are given up or reduced because of alcohol use.

[Risky Use]

8. Recurrent alcohol use in situations in which it is physically hazardous.

9. Alcohol use is continued despite knowledge of having a persistent or recurrent physical or psychological problem that is likely to have been caused by or exacerbated by alcohol.

[Pharmacological Criteria]

10. Tolerance, as defined by either of the following:

    a. A need for markedly increased amounts of alcohol to achieve intoxication or desired effect.

    b. A markedly diminished effect with continued use of the same amount of alcohol.

11. Withdrawal, as manifested by either of the following:

    a. The characteristic withdrawal syndrome for alcohol (refer to Criteria A and B of the criteria set for alcohol withdrawal).

    b. Alcohol (or a closely related substance, such as a benzodiazepine) is taken to relieve or avoid withdrawal symptoms.[6]

Criteria 1 through 4 relate to the person's impaired control over use of the substance. As explained scientifically by the disease model of addiction, the chronic use of alcohol has changed the brain and conditioned it to seek alcohol such that the continued use of alcohol is a compulsion rather than a choice. In lay terms, and in the parlance of Alcoholics Anonymous (AA), an individual has become powerless over the use of the drug. Criteria 5 through 7 relate to the impairment of the individual's ability to function socially and to fulfill the obligations of daily life. Criteria 8 and 9 relate to the individual's continued involvement in risky behaviors despite the consequences and impairments arising from use of the substance.

Criteria 10 and 11 are pharmacological criteria. Pharmacology is the scientific study of drugs and their effects. Thus, these criteria relate to tolerance and withdrawal. Criterion 11 must be read with the criteria for withdrawal of the specific drug of abuse at issue. Therefore, in evaluating the potential for an alcohol use disorder, criterion 11 is assessed based on two of the *DSM-5*'s diagnostic criteria for alcohol withdrawal. While four criteria must be satisfied to support a diagnosis of alcohol withdrawal under the *DSM-5*, only the following two criteria are relevant to the determination of criterion 11 for the diagnosis of an alcohol use disorder:

Alcohol Withdrawal

DIAGNOSTIC CRITERIA

A. Cessation of (or reduction in) alcohol use that has been heavy and prolonged.

B. Two (or more) of the following, developing within several hours to a few days after the cessation of (or reduction in) alcohol use described in Criterion A:

1. Autonomic hyperactivity (e.g., sweating or pulse rate greater than 100 bpm).

2. Increased hand tremor.

3. Insomnia.

4. Nausea or vomiting.

5. Transient visual, tactile, or auditory hallucinations or illusions.

6. Psychomotor agitation (unintentional motions without purpose, including pacing, restlessness, tapping of fingers, wringing of hands, and rapid speech).

7. Anxiety.

8. Generalized tonic-clonic seizures.[7]

The number of criteria met by a subject determines the severity of the disorder. If the subject has any two or three of the eleven diagnostic criteria for an SUD, regardless of the category under which the criteria fall, the resulting diagnosis will be that of a mild SUD. If the subject manifests four or five of the eleven criteria from one or more categories, the diagnosis will be a moderate SUD. Finally, if the subject has any six or more of the eleven symptoms, the appropriate diagnosis will be a severe SUD. A diagnosis will include both a code and a narrative description identifying the drug used and whether the diagnosis is mild, moderate, or severe. For example, diagnoses of alcohol use disorders are identified as follows: 305.00, mild alcohol use disorder; 303.90, moderate alcohol use disorder; or 303.90, severe alcohol use disorder.[8] Under this protocol, the severity of the subject's condition is objectively determined based on the number of symptoms presented.

Problematic use of any substances from any of the nine classes of drugs can form the basis of an SUD under the *DSM-5*. While distinct classes of drugs affect the body differently, the same criteria are used to diagnose the presence of a substance use disorder based on the problematic use of substances in any of those nine classes of drugs. Thus, the diagnosis of a cannabis use disorder will be based on a problematic pattern of cannabis use, and criterion 11 will be evaluated based on the diagnostic criteria for withdrawal from cannabis. For example, criterion 1 will be applied to address whether "[c]annabis is often taken in larger amounts or over a longer period than was intended." Similarly, the *DSM-5* criteria for the diagnosis of withdrawal from cannabis will be considered in determining whether the pharmacological criteria for withdrawal have been satisfied. In the same way, a diagnosis of an opioid use disorder will be made based on application of the eleven diagnostic criteria to the problematic use of opioids and diagnostic criteria for withdrawal from opioids. The number of criteria satisfied will determine whether the disorder is mild, moderate, or severe, regardless of the individual's drug of choice.

The traditional model of the progression of the disease from experimentation to dependence helps to explain the severity qualifiers of the *DSM-5*. The severity of the disorder also impacts determination of the appropriate level of care. For example, a person with a mild alcohol use disorder may benefit from counseling or outpatient services. In contrast, a diagnosis of severe alcohol use disorder would likely support a recommendation for inpatient treatment.

Under the *DSM-5*, while the evaluation is based on criteria for the class of drug used, the diagnosis will identify the specific substance used. Thus, the evaluation of a person with a history of heroin use is based upon the criteria for identification of an opioid use disorder, but the narrative diagnosis identifies the specific drug of choice, that is, heroin. The numerical codes for opioid use disorders are the same, regardless of the specific opioids used.[9] For example, a heroin user who satisfies the criteria for an opioid use disorder will be diagnosed with 305.50, mild heroin use disorder, 304.00, moderate heroin use disorder, or 304.00, severe heroin use disorder. Similarly, a person who misuses various prescription pain medications such as oxycodone and hydrocodone and who meets the criteria for an opioid use disorder may be diagnosed with 305.50, mild prescription opioid use disorder; 304.00, moderate prescription opioid use disorder; or 304.00, severe prescription opioid disorder.

According to the *DSM-5*, the physical symptoms of withdrawal are marked and easily measured for alcohol, opioids, sedatives, hypnotics, and anxiolytics, but the symptoms of withdrawal from stimulants, while present, may be less apparent. The *DSM-5* states that research has not documented withdrawal from prolonged use of some drugs, including certain hallucinogens and inhalants, and for this reason the manual does not include withdrawal as a diagnostic criterion for evaluation of an SUD related to the use of those substances.[10]

Tolerance and withdrawal may occur in connection with the use of a prescription opioid even when it is used as prescribed. A person recovering from an injury may, for example, have developed tolerance for opioid pain relievers and experience symptoms of withdrawal from opioid pain medications after he or she stops using the medications. These symptoms would satisfy criteria 10 and 11 of the diagnostic criteria for opioid use disorder. While physical symptoms are present in this situation, the individual lacks the cognitive and behavioral symptoms associated with substance use disorders. For this reason, the *DSM-5* provides that tolerance and withdrawal alone should not be the basis for a diagnosis of an SUD when they arise in the context of "appropriate medical treatment with prescribed medical medications."[11] Prescribed medicines can certainly be misused and abused. Thus, if criteria other than tolerance and withdrawal are satisfied, a person may be correctly diagnosed with an SUD even if his or her drug use began with a legitimate prescription.

The *DSM-5* distinguishes tobacco from other stimulants, classifies cannabis in a separate category from other hallucinogens, and divides hallucinogen use disorders into two groups: (1) phencyclidine (PCP and similar compounds like ketamine), and (2) other hallucinogens (including LSD, mescaline, psilocin, MDMA, DMT, and salvia). Benzodiazepines and barbiturates, including all prescription sleeping medicines and most antianxiety prescription medicines, are grouped together in the category of sedative, hypnotic, or anxiolytic use disorders.[12] On this basis, the *DSM-5* defines criteria for the following types of SUDs: (1) alcohol use disorders; (2) cannabis use disorders; (3) phencyclidine use disorders; (4) other hallucinogen use disorders; (5) inhalant use disorders; (6) opioid use disorders; (7) sedative, hypnotic, or anxiolytic use disorders; (8) stimulant use disorders; (9) tobacco use disorders; and (10) other or unknown substance use disorders.

The final category of other or unknown SUDs is used for anabolic steroids. While use of anabolic steroids presents the potential for serious health risks and may form the basis for an SUD, they are not taken for their psychoactive effects on the CNS, but for enhanced athletic performance and appearance. For these reasons, discussion of the abuse of steroids is also outside the context of this work. The category of unknown SUDs is also used for new designer-type drugs. The codes for other or unknown SUDs are 305.90 (mild), 304.90 (moderate), and 304.90.[13] The narrative description will identify the substance used, such as anabolic steroids, to the extent known.

According to the *DSM-5*, if a person satisfies the criteria for a disorder based on more than one substance, each disorder should be separately diagnosed. A loved one's diagnosis may include a qualifier, which is an explanation of special circumstances relevant to the diagnosis. For example, the qualifier "on maintenance therapy" is used when an individual is in remission from the nonmanaged use of opioids, but is receiving opioids as part of the medical management of his or her disease (such as methadone maintenance, which may be used in the treatment of opioid addiction). The qualifier "in early remission" means that while the full criteria for the disorder were previously met, they have not been met for at least three months but not more than twelve months. The qualifier "in sustained remission" means the full criteria were previously met, but they have not been met for a period of twelve months or longer. The qualifier "in a controlled environment" is used to designate the fact that the client is in a setting such as an inpatient treatment program where access to substances is prevented. Thus, a client may be diagnosed with a severe alcohol use disorder in early remission in a controlled environment. The references to remission highlight the fact that the disorder is a disease and that the disease is not gone, but is merely in remission. These qualifiers also distinguish the remission of clinical symptoms from the broader and more holistic concept of recovery.

In many cases, a person suffering from an SUD has other co-occurring mental disorders. In the past, individuals with more than one mental disorder were said to have a "dual diagnosis." While the disorders that commonly co-occur with substance abuse vary depending on the substance of abuse, they often include depressive disorders, bipolar disorders, trauma and stress-related disorders, anxiety disorders, and attention deficit disorders. The presence of co-occurring disorders complicates the diagnosis of the individual's condition. The symptoms of drug use may make it more difficult to make an initial diagnosis of a mental disorder. An accurate diagnosis may only be possible if the person has ceased using substances for a period of time so that the symptoms of substance intoxication or withdrawal can be distinguished from symptoms of a co-occurring mental disorder.

GAMBLING DISORDERS UNDER THE *DSM-5*

Problem gambling is sometimes referred to as a process addiction arising out of a pattern of behavior rather than a pattern of substance use. The *DSM-IV* identified what was referred to as pathological gambling as impulse control disorder. In the *DSM-5*, the condition has been renamed gambling disorder and is now included in the same section as SUDs. As such, it is considered an addictive disorder and is listed under the heading Substance-Related and Addictive Disorders. The National Center for Responsive Gaming reports that about 1 percent of the adult population of the United States has a severe gambling disorder.[14]

As demonstrated by the disease model of addiction, compulsive gambling, like substances of abuse, has been scientifically shown to impact and change the reward pathways of the CNS. These changes, like those brought on by chemical substances, can therefore be identified based on measurable, objective criteria. These symptoms of a gambling disorder mirror the characteristics of tolerance, lack of control, social isolation, and dependence that are used to evaluate SUDs. Thus, the criteria for diagnosis of gambling disorder are similar to those for diagnosis of substance-related addictive disorders:

Gambling Disorder

DIAGNOSTIC CRITERIA

A. Persistent and recurrent problematic gambling behavior leading to clinically significant impairment or distress, as indicated by the individual exhibiting four (or more) of the following in a 12-month period:

1. Needs to gamble with increasing amounts of money in order to achieve the desired excitement.

2. Is restless or irritable when attempting to cut down or stop gambling.

3. Has made repeated unsuccessful efforts to control, cut back, or stop gambling.

4. Is often preoccupied with gambling (e.g., having persistent thoughts of reliving past gambling experiences, handicapping or planning the next venture, thinking of ways to get money with which to gamble).

5. Often gambles when feeling distressed (e.g., helpless, guilty, anxious, depressed).

6. After losing money gambling, often returns another day to get even ("chasing" one's losses).

7. Lies to conceal the extent of involvement with gambling.

8. Has jeopardized or lost a significant relationship, job, or educational or career opportunity because of gambling.

9. Relies on others to provide money to relieve desperate financial situations caused by gambling.

B. The gambling behavior is not better explained by a manic episode.[15]

Like the criteria for substance abuse, these symptoms are based upon persistent and recurrent maladaptive behavior that continues despite its impact on the subject's life. In this case, the maladaptive behavior is gambling and is not substance related. Notably, the criteria for identification of a gambling disorder do not include withdrawal symptoms. Clinicians have, however, reported that compulsive gamblers exhibit an intense desire to resume gambling and other symptoms of withdrawal similar to those of alcohol withdrawal, including irritability, anger, restlessness, abdominal pain, headaches, cold sweats, diarrhea, insomnia, and general apprehension.[16] While not identified as withdrawal symptoms in the *DSM-5*, symptoms of restlessness or irritability when attempting to reduce or stop gambling satisfy criterion A.2 of the diagnostic criteria for gambling disorder.

The codes for gambling disorder are mild gambling disorder (four to five of the criteria met), moderate gambling disorder (six to seven of the criteria met), and severe gambling disorder (eight to nine of the criteria met). All three levels of severity are identified by a single code (312.31) rather than one of the three separate codes associated with diagnosis of an SUD.[17] The *DSM-5* includes specifiers for a gambling disorder. In the gambling context, "episodic" is used when the subject meets the diagnostic criteria "at more than one time point, with symptoms subsiding between periods of gambling disorder for at least several months." The specifier "persistent" is used in connection with a gambling disorder when the subject is "[e]xperiencing continuous symptoms to meet the diagnostic criteria for multiple years." The specifier "in early remission" means that while the subject had previously satisfied the criteria for a disorder, none of the criteria have been met for at least three months but not more than twelve months. Finally, the specifier "in sustained remission" means that while the subject had previously satisfied the criteria for the disorder, none of the criteria have been met for twelve months or more.[18]

Other repetitive compulsions, which some refer to as addictions, include obsessive exercise, sexual behaviors, gaming, use of the internet, and shopping. The *DSM-5* does not include these compulsions as behavioral addictions because, according to the manual, at the time of publication "there is insufficient peer-reviewed evidence to establish the diagnostic criteria and course descriptions needed to identify these behaviors as mental disorders."[19] Notably, the *DSM-5* suggests that the addictive characteristics of internet gaming is an area for further study and provides potential diagnostic criteria for identification of an internet gaming disorder under the category of substance-related and addictive disorders.[20]

In contrast, the *DSM-5* includes hoarding disorder in the section on obsessive-compulsive and related disorders. Thus, hoarding is clinically distinct from addictive disorders under the *DSM-5*. Eating disorders, including anorexia nervosa and bulimia nervosa, are discussed in a separate chapter of the *DSM-5;* they are referred to as feeding and eating disorders and are clinically distinct from addictive disorders.

CHAPTER 4 NOTES

1   APA, DSM-5, 5.

2   Ibid., 485.

3   Nora Volkow et al., "Neurobiologic Advances from the Brain Disease Model of Addiction," 374.

4   APA, DSM-5, 5.

5   Ibid., 483.

6   Ibid., 490–91.

7   Ibid., 499–500.

8   Ibid., 491.

9   Ibid., 485.

10   Ibid., 484.

11   Ibid.

12   Ibid., 552.

13   Ibid., 578.

14   National Center for Responsible Gaming (NCRG), "Prevalence of Gambling Disorders," http://www.ncrg.org/discovery-project/prevalence-gambling-disorders.

15   Ibid., 585.

16   Inaba and Cohen, *Uppers, Downers, All-Arounders,* 9.49.

17   APA, *DSM-5,* 585–86.

18   Ibid., 586.

19   Ibid., 481.

20   Ibid., 795–98.

5 UNDERSTANDING RISK FACTORS AND ACCEPTING THAT CAUSATION IS "NO FAULT"

Some of the first things said in programs for the family members of those in treatment for substance abuse are "You didn't cause it," "You can't control it," and "You can't cure it." While the simplistic concept of the "three C's" can be understood cognitively, it is difficult to take to heart and accept. To promote clear thinking, however, it is necessary for us to release our personal guilt for the problems of our loved ones. To promote the understanding that we are not responsible for another's disease, this chapter goes beyond simple slogans to provide information on risk factors that have been shown to influence development of the disease.

While addiction impacts families of all types and in all neighborhoods, many risk factors have been found to influence substance use and the later development of addictive disease. There is no simple cause and effect. As explained by the Surgeon General of the United States, there is no single reason why some individuals develop a substance abuse problem and others do not.[1] Causation is based on the complex interaction of genetic, physiological, developmental, environmental, and experiential factors and may be influenced by the existence of co-occurring mental disorders.

Known risk factors for substance use and abuse and the development of addictive disease are not discussed to lay fault or blame on any person or circumstance. Rather, the underlying events and factors that have led a person to turn to drugs and contributed to the development of a disease are the keys to his or her recovery. The factors underlying a person's history of substance abuse should be identified, addressed, and processed by individuals in a treatment program where staff has the expertise (i.e., is culturally competent) to address the issues presented and meet the needs of the specific populations to which the patient belongs (e.g., veterans, adolescents, or female victims of trauma). The individual needs of the client will inform the development of a personalized treatment plan and identification of coping skills and support systems to sustain the client's long-term recovery after treatment. An understanding of the factors that contributed to the development of the disease also helps us to let go of guilt and see with greater clarity how to help our loved ones move forward from the burdens of their past.

GENETIC AND BIOLOGICAL FACTORS

Addiction has a genetic component, and heredity has a significant role in the development of the disease. In other words, heredity may predispose some individuals to become dependent on psychoactive substances. While heredity is one of those things over which we have utterly no control, recognition of its role in the development of the disease does contribute to our understanding of the risks that may be faced by our loved ones.

NIDA reports that as much as 50 percent of the risk for developing an addictive disease is based on genetic factors.[2] The Surgeon General concludes that genetic factors account for between 40 and 70 percent of the risk for developing an SUD.[3] According to the *DSM-5*, between 40 and 60 percent of the risk of developing an alcohol use disorder is based on genetic influences. For individuals who have a close relative with an alcohol use disorder, the risk increases to three or four times the average. The degree of risk increases in relationship to the closeness of an individual's familial relationship to a relative with the disease, the number of other relatives with the disease, and the severity of the disease among family members. According to the *DSM-5*, research has identified a risk of three to four times the average for development of an alcohol use disorder among children born to parents with an alcohol use disorder who were adopted and raised by parents who did not have the disorder.

Science has shown us that addiction develops over time based on the brain's response to the presence of psychoactive substances. An individual's biological makeup influences the way he or she responds to substances, making some people more vulnerable to the impact of drugs. The characteristic of a low response or low sensitivity to alcohol (the individual can consume larger quantities of alcohol without feeling its impact) is cited by the *DSM-5* as a risk factor for the development of an alcohol use disorder.[4] Further, as discussed above, the method by which the user delivers a drug to the system and the potency of the substance used can contribute to the rapid development of addiction.

EARLY ONSET OF USE AND DEVELOPMENTAL FACTORS

The search for a personal identity distinct from one's parents is part of the normal process of maturation and development. While self-growth, development of peer relationships, exploration of the world, and the development of independence from the family are normal components of maturation, these factors may also contribute to the choice to engage in risk-taking behaviors, including drug use. Adolescence is also a period of development in which the opinion of peers becomes important, and peer influence is recognized as a factor motivating substance use among teens. If a teenager's peer group is using substances, he or she is likely to join in the behavior. The reverse is also true; if a teenager's peer group abstains from substance use, he or she is also likely to abstain. Low self-worth and status as an "outsider" (caused by any number of factors, including learning difficulties, academic challenges or failure, economic circumstances, and/or social awkwardness) can cause a person to gravitate toward acceptance in a group of risk takers, and check out of the mainstream, by using mind-altering substances. Substance use is also common among adolescents who have emotional or disciplinary problems and those who engage in outbursts or rebellious behavior. School avoidance, academic failure, and truancy are often seen in combination with substance use by teenagers. In contrast, in some cases, the search for perfection or the pressure to perform at elite standards may also contribute to the use of substances by youth.[5]

Teenagers and young adults are more vulnerable to the use of psychoactive drugs because the PFC of the brain remains in an active stage of development until the mid-twenties. Similarly, there is an increased risk that individuals who begin gambling in childhood or early adolescence will develop a gambling disorder.[6] Essentially, the immaturity of teenagers and the exploratory development phase of adolescence, combined with the physiological vulnerability of the adolescent brain, make adolescence itself a risk factor for the transition from experimental use to the development of a lifelong problem with addiction.

ENVIRONMENTAL FACTORS

There are numerous environmental factors that can present risks for the development of addictive disease. As demonstrated by the MTF survey results, there is an inverse relationship between perception of risk and use of a substance. Thus, children raised in homes or communities where the use of drugs is accepted and routine and in which drugs are readily available are more likely to abuse drugs in adolescence and adulthood. Similarly, where drug use is common among a person's friends, associates, and peers, he or she is more likely to participate in the use of drugs. The stress associated with growing up in poverty and living in communities where there is a sense of hopelessness, few support services, and insufficient social and recreational opportunities has also been identified with an increased risk for the development of addictive disease.

Across all communities and populations, the availability and ease of access to low-cost legal or illegal intoxicants is known to be a risk factor for substance use. Both legal and illicit drugs are widely available to minors. While we cannot alter this reality, there are some steps we can take, as individuals and communities, to help mitigate access. As individuals, we can be mindful of the risk presented by household products that can be inhaled or abused, as well as the contents of our medicine and liquor cabinets. The 2016 NSDUH indicates that of the estimated 11.5 million Americans who misused pain relievers in 2016, more than half (53 percent) obtained the misused drugs from a friend or relative.[7] Parents of adolescents may choose to secure prescription medicines and place alcohol in a locked cabinet. Pharmacists can provide advice on how to properly dispose of unused prescription medications, and local police departments may collect unused prescription pain relievers and other medications to prevent them from diversion for the purposes of abuse.

The role of knowledge and acceptance in taking personal actions to promote the recovery of our loved ones and support our own recovery is the subject of Part Three of this book. For those among us who wish to take organized action to combat addiction on a more global basis, issues related to access and perception of risk are subjects on which we can take a public stand. Significant public policy issues are presented regarding the enactment and enforcement of laws restricting the availability of and access to alcohol and other drugs by minors. Foremost among these issues is the question of whether the legalization of marijuana will increase its use by vulnerable populations by decreasing the perception of risk associated with its use and increasing its availability. We can contact our state and federal representatives to voice our opinions on such legislation and to support funding for treatment programs for SUDs and wider availability of medications that reverse opioid overdoses.

The misperception of risk and the effects of easy access to alcohol and other drugs also present opportunities for community education and activism. For example, community and neighborhood groups may choose to sponsor educational programs on topics ranging from the risks of drugs to the use of naloxone. Groups may also wish to combat abuse of prescription pain relievers by organizing efforts for the safe collection of unneeded prescription medications. Neighbors and activists may choose to band together to address issues impacting their individual communities such as efforts to promote the enforcement of current zoning laws and to oppose the issuance of liquor permits in areas where sales may increase access to intoxicants by minors.

EXPERIENTIAL FACTORS: NEGLECT, TRAUMA, GRIEF, AND LOSS

There is a significant relationship between the experience of trauma and the later development of an SUD. In studies of individuals seeking treatment for substance abuse, between 42 and 95 percent of clients reported past experiences involving trauma.[8] Other studies suggest that between 80 to 90 percent of clients (about nine out of every ten) reported a history of trauma.[9] In one study, 71 percent of adolescents in treatment for substance use reported a history of physical, emotional, or sexual victimization.[10]

More specifically, there is an exceptionally high correlation between the experience of neglect or abuse as a child, sexual assault or abuse, and partner violence with the later onset of addictive disease. For women in treatment for SUDs, a high percentage, 80 percent or more, have a history of sexual assault, abuse, or partner violence.[11] In her treatment of young women for substance use disorders, the clinician Janice E. Gabe finds that therapy uncovers the fact that most of the young women had a traumatic sexual experience in the six to twelve months before they started using, and that often they did not know what to say or do about the situation.[12]

While women often report sexual assaults and physical abuse, men are more likely to report incidents of physical violence, such as combat experiences, physical assaults, muggings, or being threatened with a weapon. Reports of past trauma by clients in treatment for SUDs include a wide variety of situations, such as being the victim of a crime, witnessing the death of another, witnessing violence, being involved in or witnessing a serious accident, and a history of being bullied. Trauma includes threats to personal health, safety, and property, as well as threats to emotional well-being such as injuries to self-esteem and self-respect. In one study of adults in treatment for SUDs, 53.1 percent reported that they had experienced damage to their self-esteem before their substance use began.[13]

A history of repeated traumas exacerbates the difficulty of recovery. Stress responses to trauma can be identified as a continuum of symptoms which, in their most severe form, are manifested in posttraumatic stress disorder (PTSD). Individuals who have experienced trauma may fall along that continuum and use substances to try to relieve their distress, whether or not they meet the criteria for diagnosis of PTSD. Generally, high relapse rates have been reported among substance use clients who were victims of interpersonal violence. Studies have also indicated that those clients who reported the highest numbers of traumatic experiences suffered significantly higher rates of relapse. In one study, 90 percent of relapse-prone substance use clients reported a history of sexual abuse.[14] The long-term impact of the experience of repeated sexual abuse is reflected in the relapsing behavior of such clients.

The experience of trauma in combat or military service is associated with high rates of substance abuse among veterans. Symptoms of PTSD or major depression were reported by one in five veterans returning from Iraq and Afghanistan.[15] There is a significant relationship between PTSD and alcohol use disorders.[16] Data for the period of 2004 to 2006 reflect that 7.1 percent of US military veterans satisfied the criteria for diagnosis of an SUD.[17] Recent studies have also shown that about half of the veterans diagnosed with PTSD also have an SUD.[18] While many veterans may not meet the diagnostic criteria for PTSD, their experiences of a variety of repeated traumatic events may contribute to an increased use of substances, presenting the risk for development of an SUD.

Unresolved grief and loss are common among individuals with addictive disease and can arise from many different situations. Children and adolescents may be profoundly impacted by the loss of a parent or someone close to them through death, divorce, separation, or abandonment. In addition to feelings of grief and loss, they may experience feelings of rejection, shame, and low self-worth. The significance of these experiences is not limited to losses that occurred in childhood. Adults in substance abuse treatment also report a variety of losses predating their use, such as divorces, the death of someone close to them, financial reversal, academic failure, job loss, career stagnation, and failed romantic relationships.

While young people may feel at fault for a parental divorce, these feelings are compounded when a parent abandons the family. Mark Sanders, a licensed clinical social worker and certified alcohol and drug counselor practicing in Chicago, has found that young women who have suffered the loss of their fathers are more prone to engage in risky behaviors, including substance use. Among the young women who experienced the loss of fathers, he found that those who lost a father due to his desertion or abandonment of the family are at greatest risk, followed by those who lost a father through divorce and, finally, those who suffered the loss due to the parent's death.[19]

While not all children who experience the divorce of their parents will turn to substance use, studies do show an increased risk of substance use among such children compared to their peers who have not experienced parental divorces. The risk has been found to be long-term and is not a temporary reaction to the divorce. The stress leading up to a divorce is reflected in the fact that a study of substance use by the children of divorced parents supports the conclusion that their substance use began two to four years prior to the actual divorce.[20]

Similar issues are presented by adoptees as they come to question why their birth parents placed them up for adoption. Even children who were adopted as infants and never knew their birth parents suffer loss and experience grief for the family they lost. These feelings can complicate the formation of their identity. The lack of information about their background and family history can make it harder for some adoptees to define themselves. While these issues often come to the fore in adolescence, which is the development phase when young people begin to form and define their own identities apart from their parents, an adoptee's struggle with identity is not a task that can be completed or mastered. Rather, the issue appears and is reevaluated at various stages of the life cycle. Adoptees, like children who feel abandoned by parents, may feel unworthy, unloved, and rejected. These feelings can manifest in anger, defiance, maladaptive and risk-taking behaviors, and substance use.[21]

Veterans also grapple with complex issues of grief and loss. They may suffer grief for the loss of comrades or feel guilt for acts taken in war, having left family members including young children during deployments, and for leaving comrades behind after completing a tour of duty. Some veterans may suffer from survivor's guilt, which is distinct from ordinary grief as it includes a component of guilt for surviving when others did not. These factors may contribute to substance use and the development of an SUD.

Individuals who have had traumatic experiences or suffered significant losses may turn to substance use to numb their pain, escape, and forget, for a time, their painful memories. While their experiences may, consciously or subconsciously, motivate their use, they may keep their history a secret. To allow these individuals to succeed in recovery, it is important that they bring the prior traumas and losses out into the open and verbalize them in the context of a therapeutic relationship so that they can begin to process the impact these events have had on their lives and their substance abuse. While what happened in the past cannot be mitigated, in addressing these issues directly the client may be able to find new coping skills and move forward in a healthy way. Understanding the role of past trauma and loss in a loved one's use of substances may also help us support him or her in finding the help he or she needs to address the underlying events.

CO-OCCURRING DISORDERS

It is common for a person with an SUD to have another co-occurring disorder. Persons with mental disorders are more likely to have an SUD than the general population, and people with SUDs are more likely to have a mental disorder than the general population. It is reported that 45 percent of persons seeking treatment for an SUD in the United States have also received a diagnosis of a mental disorder.[22] While the disorders that commonly co-occur with substance abuse vary depending on the drug of choice, they often include depressive disorders, bipolar disorders, anxiety disorders, attention deficit disorders, and stress-related disorders such as PTSD.

Because of the correlation between mental disorders and substance use, the diagnosis of certain conditions may be indicative of a risk for substance use. The *DSM-5* draws a correlation between impulsivity and the development of both substance- and gambling-related addictive disorders. Individuals with schizophrenia or bipolar disorder have been found to be highly vulnerable to development of an SUD. Gambling disorders are reported to be comorbid with SUDs, particularly alcohol use disorder. Gambling disorder has also been found to co-occur with antisocial personality disorder, as well as depressive and bipolar disorders.[23] There is also a high correlation between diagnosis of a tobacco use disorder and the diagnosis of another SUD.

The *DSM-5* states that the co-occurring disorders that commonly occur with a diagnosis of cannabis use disorder include depression, anxiety, and personality disorders. Sixty percent of adolescents with a cannabis use disorder are reported to have externalizing disorders, which are characterized by maladaptive behaviors directed toward the environment, including ADD and ADHD.[24] Thus, the existence of these disorders in adolescents could indicate that they have an increased risk for substance use.

Studies have shown that nicotine, a stimulant like that used to treat attention deficit disorders, may modulate the symptoms of ADHD.[25] Similarly, it appears that some users with ADHD and anxiety disorders may use alcohol and marijuana, which have relaxing effects, to ease the hyperactivity components of the disease. The theory that adolescents self-medicate with marijuana to lessen the effects of hyperactivity and mood disorders may be supported by research indicating that early detection and treatment of attention deficit disorder decreases the likelihood that a child may develop an SUD in adolescence.[26]

When dealing with adolescents, it is important to determine what came first—the attention disorder or the drug use. An adolescent who is using marijuana heavily and receives a late diagnosis of attention deficient disorder may, in fact, be exhibiting the symptoms of marijuana use and may not suffer from an attention disorder.[27] Chronic marijuana use is also associated with increased anxiety and depression. Thus, teenagers could be medicating preexisting symptoms of an anxiety or depressive disorder, or the symptoms could arise from drug use. These issues highlight the fact that a diagnosis should be informed by a full and complete history and that the physician diagnosing an adolescent should account for the possibility that he or she may be using drugs.

RECOMMENDED RESOURCES

- Veterans Crisis Line, US Department of Veterans Affairs, (800) 273-8255 (press 1), chat online, or send a text message to 838255, https://www.veteranscrisisline.net/.

- David M. Brodzinsky, Marshall D. Schecter, and Robin Marantz, *Being Adopted: The Lifelong Search for Self,* Anchor Books, 1993.

CHAPTER 5 NOTES

1   HHS, *Facing Addiction in America*, 1-15–1-16.

2   NIDA, "Genetics and Epigenetics of Addiction," in "Drug Facts," last modified February 2016, https://www.drugabuse.gov/publications/drugfacts/genetics-epigenetics-addiction.

3   HHS, *Facing Addiction in America*, 2-22.

4   APA, *DSM-5*, 494.

5   Mark Sanders, *"Gender Responsive Services: A Focus on the Unique Counseling Needs of Women and Men"* (Seminar, Haymarket Center, Chicago, IL, September 30, 2017).

6   APA, *DSM-5*, 588.

7   CBHSQ, "2016 NSDUH," 1.

8   Merith Cosden et al., "Trauma Symptoms for Men and Women in Substance Abuse Treatment: A Latent Transition Analysis," *Journal of Substance Abuse Treatment* 50 (2015): 18, doi.org/10.1016/j.jsat.2014.09.004.

9   Melissa Farley et al., "Trauma History and Relapse Probability among Patients Seeking Substance Abuse Treatment," *Journal of Substance Abuse Treatment* 27, no. 2 (2004): 164, doi: 10.1016/j.jsat.2004.06.006.

10   Rodney R. Funk et al., "Maltreatment Issues by Level of Adolescent Substance Abuse Treatment: The Extent of the Problem at Intake and Relationship to Early Outcomes," *Child Maltreatment* 8, no. 1 (2003): 38, doi: 10.1177/1077559502239607.

11   NIDA, "Women's Treatment for Trauma and Substance Use Disorders," in "Research Studies," https://www.drugabuse.gov/about-nida/organization/cctn/ctn/research-studies/womens-treatment-trauma-substance-use-disorders.

12   Gabe, "Marijuana Use in Teens."

13   Susan R. Furr, W. Derrick Johnson, and Carol Sloan Goodall, "Grief and Recovery: The Prevalence of Grief and Loss in Substance Abuse Treatment," *Journal of Addictions & Offender Counseling* 36, no. 1 (2015): 44, 49, doi: 10.1002/j.2161-1874.2015.00034.x.

14   Farley et al., "Trauma History and Relapse Probability," 164.

15   NIDA, "Addiction and Co-occurring Mental Disorders," in "NIDANotes" (2007), https://www.drugabuse.gov/news-events/nida-notes/2007/02/addiction-co-occurring-mental-disorders.

16   HHS, "Facing Addiction in America," 2-22–2-23.

17   SAMHSA, "Veterans and Military Families," last modified September 15, 2017, http://www.samhsa.gov/veterans-military-families.

18   NIDA, *Research Report on Comorbidity: Addiction and Other Mental Illnesses* (2010), www.drugabuse.gov/publications/research-reports/comorbidity-addiction-other-mental-illnesses/how-can-comorbidity-be-diagnosed.

19   Mark Sanders, "Gender Responsive Services."

20   Jeremy Arkes, "The Temporal Effects of Parental Divorce on Youth Substance Use," *Substance Use and Misuse* 48 (2013): 296.

21   David M. Brodzinsky, *Being Adopted: The Lifelong Search for Self* (New York: Anchor Books, 1993).

22 SAMHSA, "Behavioral Health Treatments and Services," last modified September 20, 2017, http://www.samhsa.gov/treatment#co-occurring.

23 APA, *DSM-5*, 484 and 587.

24 Ibid., 515.

25 Eugene M. Dunne, Jonathan J. Rose, and William W. Latimer, "ADHD as a Risk Factor for Early Onset and Heightened Adult Problem Severity of Illicit Substance Use: An Accelerated Gateway Model," *Addictive Behaviors* 39, no. 12 (2013): 1755–756, doi: 10.1016/j.addbeh.2014.07.009.

26 NIDA, *Addiction and Co-occurring Mental Disorders.*

27 Janice E. Gabe, "Marijuana Use in Teens."

6 TREATMENT: HOW AND WHY IT WORKS

Treatment does not necessarily bring recovery, but it always provides hope. For many of our loved ones, treatment offers them the chance for a future. It is often said, erroneously, "Treatment won't work unless the addict is ready." Many people also believe the fallacy that "Addicts have to hit bottom before treatment can help." These misconceptions are mired in the false view that addiction is a choice, not a disease, and that the addict needs to choose to want to get better. These untruths stand in the way of early intervention and are detrimental to the provision of effective treatment for those in need.

Since a "bottom" can only be identified in hindsight, it is an ineffective means by which to identify readiness for treatment. In his book *Now What? An Insider's Guide to Addiction and Recovery*, William Cope Moyers explains that when he is asked by family members whether they should wait until a loved one hits bottom, he responds by saying, "Don't wait for them to die." As he explains, with addiction, death is the final bottom and "[a]nything short of death is an opportunity."[1] In his advice to parents, Brad Reedy, PhD, acknowledges that individuals need to have a desire to change before meaningful change can occur, but emphasizes, "[P]art of our job as parents is creating motivation for that change."[2] This is sound advice for all of us who are coping with another's addiction, whether we are the parent, spouse, sibling, or friend of the person with the disease. Treatment can and does work even if the client enters treatment without the desire to change. It has been shown that involuntary treatment (e.g., when it is court mandated or when a minor is placed into care) can succeed even when the client has no intention of seeking recovery upon admission. The controlled sober environment of a treatment facility can allow an unwilling client to begin to think clearly outside the haze of drug use and may encourage reexamination of old behaviors, motivating a desire to change.

The therapeutic process supports identification of the underlying issues that contribute to patterns of use and helps clients to develop coping skills and practical tools to change their behavioral responses to stressors. Ideally, treatment should respond to individual needs, address the totality of the client's physical and mental health, and support recovery in all aspects of life, including health, housing, relationships and support systems (family, partners, friends, and sober peer support), purpose (work or school, volunteerism, caregiving, or creative pursuits), self-care, financial independence, community engagement, and social interaction.[3]

In the addiction field, treatment is said to be evidence-based if scientific research has shown that there is a positive correlation between the treatment and favorable outcomes for clients. While there are no uniform standards, generally, evidence-based treatment (EBT) is supported by controlled trials that are independent, peer-reviewed, and randomized. The term "well supported" is used to refer to research obtained from multiple controlled trials or studies involving many participants. The term "supported" refers to positive outcomes derived from fewer but no less rigorous trials, or those based on a smaller number of subjects. When evidence of a treatment's effectiveness comes from widely used and accepted clinical practice, it is said to be "promising."

Examination of the unique treatment needs of specific groups of people is intended to lay the foundation for identification of the type of EBT that may be most effective for a loved one. When considering treatment, it is important to remember that addictive disease encompasses a wide range of behaviors along a continuum between risky practices that may lead to the development of a problem and the existence of a severe SUD. Similarly, there is no single solution for all problems. Rather, there is a continuum of services and treatment options to respond to individual needs, ranging from the provision of information and education to long-term residential substance use treatment lasting for a year or more. Given its nature as a chronic, relapsing disease that impairs choice, a single, short-term treatment program will not generally result in lasting recovery. Rather, for many people suffering from the disorder, treatment is a long-term process that may involve multiple interventions and follow-up care.[4] Treatment may also include several phases along the continuum of care ranging from initial inpatient treatment followed by sober-living outpatient treatment, and finally, self-help. To understand the purpose of the various levels of care, it is helpful to examine the preventative role of routine screenings and to review the role of a clinical assessment in the diagnosis of mild, moderate, and severe SUDs.

SCREENING AND BRIEF INTERVENTION

Research has shown that early intervention to address an individual's substance abuse may prevent the behavior from progressing to an SUD.[5] For this reason, screening of clients for use of alcohol or other drugs has become a part of the provision of routine primary healthcare services for adults and adolescents. In taking a client's history, healthcare providers use screening questions to solicit information about the client's substance use to identify any potentially problematic patterns of behavior. For example, screening may reveal that a patient is taking more of a pain medication than prescribed or engages in occasional binge drinking. When the screening identifies issues of concern, the healthcare provider can immediately render advice and offer counseling to the patient. This process is known as screening and brief intervention (SBI). Brief intervention includes counseling with the purpose of informing the patient of the risks presented by his or her behavior in an effort to motivate change. When the problem is too serious to address in a brief consultation, the healthcare provider can engage in brief counseling to apprise the client of the risk presented and refer the client to an addiction professional for a clinical assessment. This is known as screening, brief intervention, and referral to treatment (SBIRT).

CLINICAL ASSESSMENT AND DIAGNOSIS

A clinical assessment is used to inform a recommendation as to whether treatment is warranted and, if so, the level of an appropriate intervention. An assessment of alcohol and other drug use is different from a routine screening. Rather, an assessment is a clinical interview by a trained and licensed drug and alcohol counselor or other addiction specialist. A physician referral is not necessary, and individuals can self-refer for a clinical assessment. Inquiries about the use of alcohol and other drugs are placed in the context of a holistic, biopsychosocial evaluation. For example, the assessment interview should include a full inquiry regarding the subject's health and medical history, current medications, family relationships, work history, housing, military service, criminal history, and prior experience of trauma. In this way, the evaluation should identify any special circumstances (such as a history of trauma or abuse) that may have contributed to the development of the disease, as well as any history of suicidality and/or any co-occurring disorders.

The assessment process is designed to gather information relevant to application of the diagnostic criteria for SUDs as set forth in the *DSM-5* and any special circumstances that will inform recommendations for care. The interview will elicit information, in the context of a discussion about the subject's life, to determine which, if any, of the eleven diagnostic criteria are satisfied. Under the *DSM-5*, the severity of an SUD is based on the number of problematic behaviors presented, and only the most severe form of the disorder is equated with addiction. The diagnostic criteria are used to objectively measure the scope and severity of a person's substance use as mild, moderate, or severe to inform the diagnosis and determine what type of treatment will be most appropriate for the individual.

THE CONTINUUM OF CARE

The recommended level of care for treatment of an SUD should be determined in relation to severity of the disease and be commensurate with the impact that substance use is having on the client's life. Typically, treatment should start with the least invasive intervention that is likely to succeed. A college student who finds that he often drinks more on weekends than he intended and has missed a few classes because of his Monday morning hangovers may satisfy two of the eleven diagnostic criteria and qualify for a diagnosis of a mild alcohol use disorder. In this context, however, the diagnosis does not support entry into a residential treatment program. Rather, a less invasive intervention, but one that is likely to modify the problematic behavior, is appropriate for the treatment of the student's mild alcohol use disorder.

Attendance at an educational session or one or more individual counseling sessions may represent an appropriate intervention for this hypothetical student. Research supports the effectiveness of brief interventions to treat mild alcohol use disorders, and there is some evidence of the effectiveness of brief interventions in the treatment of other mild SUDs (i.e., those involving the use of other drugs).[6] This finding is consistent with studies equating brief intervention at college health clinics with a reduction of alcohol use on campus.[7]

When the assessment results in a diagnosis of a mild or moderate SUD that is too serious to be addressed in a brief intervention, the client may be referred to outpatient treatment. Outpatient substance use treatment, sometimes referred to as basic outpatient (BOP) or outpatient level I.0, generally involves individual and group-based treatment for one and a half to eight hours a week. Intensive outpatient treatment (IOP), or outpatient Level II.1, typically involves group and individual counseling for nine to fifteen hours a week. The term *partial hospitalization* or *day treatment* is used to refer to substance use treatment programs of at least twenty hours a week where the client returns home at night. Inpatient treatment is residential treatment in a therapeutic sober environment for an initial period of between one and twenty-eight days.[8] Individuals diagnosed with severe SUDs will likely receive a recommendation that they receive inpatient treatment.

An initial intervention may be followed by further treatment. The intensity of the treatment is reduced over time, as the client progresses through levels of care, each affording greater freedoms to the client, while providing continued support for recovery before the client is discharged from all care. Inpatient treatment may be followed by partial hospitalization or residence in a group sober house or in a sober-living facility. Clients may attend IOP after an inpatient stay, but the frequency of the outpatient sessions may be reduced over time. Ultimately, in many cases, formal treatment is transitioned into other support programs, including twelve-step recovery programs such as AA or Narcotics Anonymous (NA). Such self-help programs are often integral to primary treatment and provide a link between treatment and a lifelong support network.

A DIFFERENCE IN PHILOSOPHY: ABSTINENCE-BASED AND HARM REDUCTION PROGRAMS

While there are numerous theories and methodologies of treatment, there is a major distinction between abstinence-based programs and those that are based on theories of harm reduction. Abstinence-based treatment rests on the principle that the best chance for long-term recovery is linked to the client's total abstinence from all mind-altering substances. Under this philosophy, a person in remission from opioid dependence is not sober or abstinent if he or she drinks a beer from time to time. The science supporting this approach is that abstinence from all psychoactive substances breaks the cycle of chemical reactions in the brain from binge and intoxication to withdrawal and cravings. Abstinence also breaks the pattern of the maladaptive behavior of using substances to control painful feelings and manage stress. The principle of complete abstinence is also consistent with the concept of a dependent user's lack of control over mind-altering substances.

Harm reduction principles are based on the theory that if, for any of a variety of reasons, abstinence cannot be achieved, the next-best intervention is one that reduces the harm. A classic example of harm reduction is a needle exchange program in which IV drug users can swap dirty needles for clean ones. The program does not address or impede the progress of the user's addictive disease, but it may lessen the risk of the contraction of HIV, hepatitis, or other diseases.

DETOXIFICATION

Detoxification is the process by which the body rids itself of drugs. During this process, the drug-dependent person will experience symptoms of withdrawal from the drug or drugs habitually used. While withdrawal symptoms vary based on the drugs involved, withdrawal is often painful or uncomfortable and, in some cases, can be life-threatening, particularly when the client is dependent on alcohol or sedatives. Detoxification in a medical facility is appropriate when withdrawal presents a potential health risk to the client.

Medication can be used to ease withdrawal symptoms and reduce cravings. Clonidine is used to manage the symptoms of withdrawal from opioids and alcohol. Phenobarbital may be used to prevent seizures and other symptoms of withdrawal from alcohol and sedative-hypnotics. In addition to its use for the management of opioid dependence, methadone may be used in managing opioid withdrawal symptoms. Similarly, buprenorphine (Subutex and Suboxone) is used in the treatment of opioid dependence and may also be used in detoxification from opioids. Certain antidepressants and antipsychotic medications may be used to manage withdrawal from cocaine, amphetamines, and other stimulants.[9] Detoxification is not treatment. Rather, it is a period of stabilization that begins the process by which the brain and the body attempt to return to a drug-free equilibrium. For most drugs, the period of initial or acute withdrawal lasts between three to five days.[10]

TIME IN TREATMENT: THE THERAPEUTIC BENEFITS OF ABSTINENCE

One way in which treatment leads to change and recovery is that it enforces abstinence and allows the brain and body to recover from the artificial stimulation of repeated drug use. This promotes clear thinking and cogent analysis of past behaviors. Abstinence is enforced in the secure environment of inpatient programs and in outpatient programs that use drug tests to monitor compliance with the expectation of continued sobriety. Continued abstinence due to ongoing treatment or monitoring is, therefore, of therapeutic value to the client's recovery.

While acute withdrawal is completed within days, it takes far longer for drugs to completely leave the system and far longer for the brain to return to equilibrium after the repeated overstimulation resulting from drug use. Cocaine does not completely leave the body for about a week, and it takes between one and ten months for the chemical reactions in the brain of the former user to become more normalized.[11] The THC in marijuana stays in the body of a chronic user for up to three months.[12] Similarly, it takes about thirty days of abstinence from alcohol for the vestiges of the drug's impact on the brain and body to subside.

Because it takes so long for drugs to leave the body, clients may only be starting to think more rationally at about the time that they are released from a twenty-eight-day inpatient program. Moreover, symptoms of post-acute withdrawal from drugs (PAWS) occur for months, even years, after the cessation of use. For these reasons, treatment takes time and the length of time in treatment is important. As reported by NIDA, "[R]esearch has shown unequivocally that good outcomes are contingent on adequate treatment length." NIDA further advises that where outpatient or inpatient treatment is warranted, treatment of less than ninety days is generally of "limited effectiveness," and that "treatment lasting significantly longer is recommended for maintaining positive outcomes."[13] In many cases, long-term inpatient care of a year or more is necessary. For drug-dependent adolescents in treatment, the time spent in a drug-free environment also promotes future health by protecting their developing brains from further bombardment by psychoactive drugs.

GETTING PAST DENIAL: THE STAGES OF CHANGE

One of the hallmarks of addictive disease is denial of a problem. Substances have more appeal to the dependent user than logic. It is an axiom of social work that the counselor needs to start where the client is. This means the counselor should understand the client's situation and the point of view from which the client perceives his or her environment. In the behavioral sciences, there are five recognized stages of change: (1) *pre-contemplation*, the stage before a person has begun to think about making a change; (2) *contemplation*, when a person begins to think about making a positive change; (3) *preparation*, when a person starts to make plans to change; (4) *action*, when specific plans to facilitate change are put into place; and (5) *maintenance*, when steps to support and continue the new patterns of behavior are acted upon. For treatment to facilitate change, it needs to break through the cycle of denial, cause the user to perceive the harm being done by addictive behaviors, and move the user along the continuum of the stages of change.

THE TREATMENT PLAN

After intake and admission, the primary counselor or care team develops a detailed treatment plan that is individual to the specific needs of the client. The treatment plan is designed to address the underlying causes of the person's substance use and any co-occurring disorders. Since the disease is defined by recurrent patterns of maladaptive behavior despite adverse consequences, clients need to learn new coping and problem-solving skills and develop healthy ways to respond to external stimuli. Since many clients cannot return to their old friends and social patterns, they also need to find ways to foster new sober and/or abstinent support systems and plan sober activities.

To meet these needs, treatment will typically include a combination of individual counseling, group counseling, skill building, the use of community recovery support services (RSS), and an introduction to twelve-step principles and programs. The plan may also include medication-assisted treatment. Effective programs also empower clients and help them to restore self-esteem and belief in their own abilities. Treatment programs for adults and adolescents should also provide information on the risk of IV use and sexually transmitted diseases and should test for HIV and hepatitis B and C.

The treatment plan, which is subject to review, refinement, revision, and expansion over the course of treatment, lays the foundation for the development of a comprehensive discharge plan. The discharge plan should not only support continued abstinence and recovery but also address all major areas of the client's life. For many, the disease has completely disrupted their life course and they need to plan and prepare for a life apart from drugs.

MEDICATION-ASSISTED TREATMENT

Certain medications are used in treatment to ease withdrawal symptoms and lessen craving for the user's drugs of choice. The use of medications in combination with behavioral therapies is called medication-assisted treatment (MAT). A common application of the use of a medication to assist recovery from a certain form of addiction is the use of nicotine patches by someone who is trying to quit smoking. The nicotine satisfies the user's cravings while allowing a controlled reduction in use of tobacco with the goal of complete cessation of the use of both tobacco and nicotine substitutes. Medications are currently in use for the treatment of tobacco, alcohol, and opioid use disorders, and research continues to identify pharmacological treatments for other SUDs. Medications to treat co-occurring disorders such as depression and anxiety may also be used as part of a comprehensive treatment plan.

Clients who begin abstinence-based treatment directly after detoxification from opioids have been shown to have high rates of relapse.[14] The cravings experienced during withdrawal from opioids often precipitate relapse and result in abandonment of treatment. Relapse presents a substantial risk of overdose to those dependent on opioids due to the reduced tolerance that follows a period of abstinence. Medications that moderate or control opioid withdrawal symptoms have been shown to reduce relapse and the deaths attributable to overdose following relapse and have been found to keep clients in treatment for longer periods of time. NIDA reports that, despite the effectiveness of MAT in the treatment of opioid addiction, pharmacological therapies remain highly underutilized in treatment of opioid dependence.[15]

While the ultimate treatment objective of MAT may be for the client to maintain abstinence without medication, it may take months or years before that can occur. Clients who have had severe and long-term dependence on opioids may need to remain on medication indefinitely. The decision of whether to cease medication should be made on a case-by-case basis and in consultation between the patient and the prescribing physician. If a decision to cease pharmacological support is made, the medication should be withdrawn gradually.[16]

There are three different medications approved for use in the treatment of opioid addiction: methadone, buprenorphine, and naltrexone. Methadone is a synthetic opiate that, when taken in therapeutic doses, prevents the symptoms of withdrawal from opioids, including heroin and prescription opioids such as oxycodone and hydrocodone. Methadone is an opioid agonist, which means that it binds with and stimulates opioid receptors in the brain. Methadone interacts with the brain's opioid receptors more gently than other opioids so that the opioid-dependent user does not experience euphoria from the administration of a therapeutic dose of methadone. Rather, it merely prevents the symptoms of withdrawal, including craving.

Methadone maintenance therapy (MMT) has been in use since 1947. It originated as a harm reduction program to medically manage the symptoms of withdrawal from heroin to combat the risks attendant to the use of street heroin for the benefit of those addicted to the drug and the community. MMT manages the symptoms of withdrawal, but the client remains dependent upon the ingestion of an opioid (methadone) to function. MMT alone does not represent treatment of the underlying causes of heroin addiction. Methadone maintenance is, however, often provided with therapeutic counseling and treatment to improve the individual's coping skills and may eventually lead to a plan to reduce the dose of methadone over time and ultimately eliminate the maintenance therapy. When it is used in the context of behavioral therapy, methadone can be used as part of MAT.

Methadone can only be distributed by an opioid treatment program (OTP) that is certified by SAMHSA and registered by the DEA. Methadone is produced in liquid, pill, and wafer form. Most OTPs providing methadone therapy do so on an outpatient basis. Typically, clients are required to present themselves in person at the OTP daily for supervised ingestion of the prescribed dose of methadone. Clients who have exhibited consistent compliance with program requirements may be permitted to take doses home for use as scheduled. Studies have shown that to be effective, MAT with methadone requires administration of the drug for a minimum of one year. Many clients continue methadone maintenance for a period of years or indefinitely.[17] Cessation of methadone use causes symptoms of opioid withdrawal and should be medically managed.

Buprenorphine (Subutex) is a synthetic opioid medication that has been approved for use in the treatment of opioid dependence. Buprenorphine is a partial agonist because, while it binds with opioid receptors, it is less strong than full agonists like other opioids, including methadone. Buprenorphine does not produce euphoria, nor does it have the sedative effects of other opioids. It is produced in tablets or films that are dissolved under the tongue. A six-month dose may also be administered by means of a subdermal buprenorphine implant. Federal law permits authorized physicians to prescribe buprenorphine or dispense it in their offices, which eases access for clients when compared to the necessity of a daily visit to an OTP. Physicians must obtain special waivers to prescribe buprenorphine and are limited in the number of clients they may treat with the drug.

Suboxone contains both buprenorphine and naloxone. Naloxone, which is the drug used for emergency reversal of opioid overdose, is an opioid antagonist, meaning that it binds with opioid receptors to block opioids from binding with those receptors. This formulation is intended to minimize diversion of the drug for abuse. When taken as directed, the drug is effective to block opioid withdrawal symptoms, but if the tablets are crushed and injected, the naloxone will control, blocking the opioid effects and negating an opioid high.[18] Since naloxone blocks the effects of opioids and reduces cravings, it may be used alone (without buprenorphine) as a deterrent for clients deemed to be at risk for relapse on opioids.[19] The medication cannot be used until the client is detoxified from opioids or the drug will obviate the effects of the opioids and send the client into opioid withdrawal.

Another opioid antagonist, naltrexone, is used in the MAT of opioid use disorders. Naltrexone can be taken orally, in pill form (ReVia, Depade), or by extended-release intramuscular injection (Vivitrol). A dose of the long-acting injectable lasts for thirty days and avoids issues of noncompliance with self-administration of pills. The drug produces no opioid effects and the user is not subject to withdrawal when the medication is stopped. Naltrexone is not a controlled substance. It can be prescribed by any healthcare provider who is licensed to write prescriptions, so it is more widely available than buprenorphine. Naltrexone may be prescribed for individuals who are reentering the community after periods in drug-free environments such as treatment facilities or jail and who wish to have some protection against relapse. Naltrexone may be prescribed for clients who do not wish to take a medication that produces opioid effects or who do not wish to remain dependent upon an opioid-replacement drug. It may also be appropriate for the treatment of opioid-dependent adolescents or young adults.[20]

Three medications—naltrexone, acamprosate, and disulfiram—are approved for MAT in the treatment of alcohol use disorders. Naltrexone, the opioid antagonist used in the treatment of opioid dependence, is also used in the treatment of alcohol use disorders. Like opioids, alcohol is a CNS depressant. By blocking opioid receptors in the brain, naltrexone also blocks some of the pleasurable aspects of drinking alcohol. Clients with acute hepatitis, renal failure, or liver failure should not be treated with naltrexone.[21] Acamprosate normalizes reactions to alcohol in the brain's glutamate systems to reduce craving as an aid to the treatment of severe alcohol use disorders. It may reduce long-lasting symptoms of post-acute withdrawal such as insomnia, anxiety, and lowered mood. If the client drinks alcohol while taking disulfiram (Antabuse and Antabus), the drug will interfere with the body's elimination of acetaldehyde as part of the metabolism of alcohol, resulting in an increased accumulation of acetaldehyde in the blood. The excess acetaldehyde causes discomfort to the user, such as a rapid heartbeat, nausea, vomiting, sweating, or dizziness, negatively reinforcing the use of alcohol.

THERAPY MODELS

A treatment plan typically includes group counseling and individual counseling sessions between the client and a primary counselor. Counseling can be based on a variety of different evidence-based clinical approaches. Cognitive behavioral therapy (CBT) is often used because it has been shown to be effective in the treatment of addictive disorders when used as part of a broader treatment plan. This therapy is part of a related group of behavioral therapies that also include cognitive therapy (CT) and dialectical behavior therapy (DBT). Behavioral therapies are based on the principle that learned behavior can be modified. The client is encouraged to examine the positive and negative consequences of prior behaviors, including drug use. Clients are taught coping skills and strategies to develop new responses to existing problems and replace old, ingrained behaviors with new, healthy alternatives. Clients are trained to recognize what activates their cravings and to develop strategies to avoid high-risk situations.

Motivational enhancement therapy (MET) is based on the use of motivational interviewing techniques. The techniques are intended as a nonjudgmental, empathetic method of communicating with clients to assist them in defining their own goals for the future and exploring their plan to reach those goals. Rather than telling the client that his or her substance use is preventing achievement, the technique is intended to allow the client to come to that conclusion independently, and to motivate and empower the client to effectuate change. Contingency management, which is based on a contractual agreement to take specific actions and offers tangible rewards to clients as incentives to achieve those goals, has also been found to be effective in treating SUDs.

Family therapy is also commonly used as part of an overall treatment plan. The engagement of family members, spouses, parents, or children in therapy sessions, jointly with the client, allows exploration of existing family dynamics and issues that may impact the client's long-term recovery. Therapy provides a supportive environment in which parents and adolescents can foster healthy communication skills and discuss needs, rights, privileges, rules, expectations, consequences, and boundaries. The principles of behavioral couples therapy (BCT) include a "daily sobriety contract" between the client and spouse in which the client affirms a choice not to use and the spouse affirms support for the client's efforts to stay abstinent.[22]

GROUP COUNSELING

Group counseling is so integral to substance use treatment that it is a thing, place, or event that needs no introductory prepositions, for example, "I have group" or "Something happened in group." Group provides social reinforcement of principles learned in treatment[23] and provides peer support for individuals who are processing life events and current challenges. Group can be a powerful place when members are engaged in and own the process; no one is judged or ostracized, and peers understand each other and are accountable to each other. It is, for example, far more impactful to a teen when a peer calls him out on plans to attend a concert because the use of drugs will be pervasive, than if his parent or counselor expresses a similar concern.

The mystery of what happens in group was explained by Irvin D. Yalom, MD, the existential psychiatrist who was one of the founders of group therapy. Dr. Yalom identified the following eleven primary therapeutic factors of group therapy:

1. Instillation of hope

2. Universality

3. Imparting information

4. Altruism

5. The corrective recapitalization of the primary family group

6. Development of socializing techniques

7. Imitative behavior

8. Interpersonal learning

9. Group cohesiveness

10. Catharsis

11. Existential factors[24]

Attendance at group counseling sessions can "instill hope" in clients. When entering treatment, clients meet others who may have been in the program longer and can explain the positive life changes they are experiencing. Group presents a feeling of "universality," in other words, the client is not alone, but rather among others who are experiencing the same problems. New group members will be immediately understood and welcomed. The therapist "imparts information" and provides advice to the group members. Group also presents the benefit of sharing information among peers and the altruistic value of helping others.

Dr. Yalom's reference to the "corrective recapitalization of the primary family group" refers to the value of reprocessing events and discussions that occurred within the family in a noncharged, objective, calm, and supportive environment. The benefit of the "development of socializing techniques" refers to the fact that clients who are in the process of changing old, maladaptive patterns of behavior relating to the use of drugs have a chance to practice social interaction. Group facilitates "imitative behavior," that is, in group the therapist and peers model how to approach problems and react to challenges. The "interpersonal learning" that happens in group is a reference to the fact that members learn from each other's successes and failures. When a member reports a relapse, it allows the group to consider their own vulnerability to relapse and how they will respond when their personal cues are activated. Group also fosters the development of social relationships, provides practice in handling emotions in an interpersonal context, and operates as a social microcosm of the larger external community.

The value of "cohesiveness" refers to the fact that the group becomes a unit. When group members feel ownership of their discussion, choose and direct what they will discuss, create their own rules, and support and challenge each other, they become a team. The "catharsis" that Dr. Yalom has identified arises from the ability to relieve one's self by speaking of horrible or traumatic events, and to confess to grievous harm done to others or past actions that make the speaker feel ashamed. Speaking publicly of these things is a way to process feelings and let go of past events. The existential factors identified by Dr. Yalom refer to the fact that there is no escape from problems and that individuals are ultimately responsible for the way they live their own lives.

SKILL TRAINING

Teenagers in treatment and adults who have been out of the job market for years due to their addiction typically need to learn or relearn basic skills and explore job training and vocational or educational opportunities. Some clients may need to develop a plan to complete a GED degree. Clients often need to learn basic job readiness skills (which include an understanding of how to dress, what is expected in a workplace, and basic computer skills) and job search techniques (such as résumé writing, researching job openings, obtaining references, explaining gaps in their résumé, and how to dress and conduct themselves in interviews). Other clients need training in basic life skills that they neglected while they were using. Many clients need to learn how to manage money, budget for expenses, maintain hygiene, access healthcare, navigate the justice system, apply for public benefits, take public transit, maintain a car, do the laundry, and shop and cook basic meals. Skill training that meets individual needs will increase client confidence and self-esteem, help clients plan for their future, and ease their reentry into the community.

Most clients face the issue of finding appropriate housing after treatment. Cravings may be activated by people, places, and things associated with prior use or that remind the client of prior behaviors. Many clients cannot go back to their former living arrangements and need to locate appropriate housing they can afford. Clients may need to consider how they will meet the financial qualifications to obtain a lease, how they will pay for housing, and whether they may be entitled to any benefits or subsidies. If the client is to return to a family home, family counseling sessions may assist in planning for the client's return. Other clients may need to locate a sober house or halfway house to ease their transition into the community.

The process of thinking through practical problems in a supportive environment and making specific plans for how they will meet their essential needs after treatment will lay the foundation for the client's success in recovery. In other words, when planning for discharge, clients are learning and practicing problem-solving skills.

These skills will foster self-efficacy and build confidence in their ability to find solutions to their own problems without returning to old behaviors.

RECOVERY SUPPORT SYSTEMS

Recovery support services (RSS) are community, faith-based, or governmental service programs that work with those seeking to recover from the use of substances by providing support for their basic needs, including health, housing, education, job training, and the management of preexisting legal issues. Referral may be made to service providers while a client is in treatment, and support from RSS can be built into the client's discharge plan.[25]

Twelve-step recovery programs are the best-known RSS. Clients in treatment programs who embrace the twelve-step model as a component of care are introduced to the twelve-step philosophy and attend meetings (both on-site and in the community) during treatment. Twelve-step facilitated (TSF) treatment is an EBT intervention based on the Twelve Steps. Orientation to the twelve-step support system provides a bridge to continued peer support after discharge. Attendance at twelve-step meetings and working a recovery program provide major support to millions of people in recovery. Attendance at twelve-step meetings is often an important component of a client's discharge plan.

TREATMENT IN THE CONTEXT OF CO-OCCURRING DISORDERS AND FOR SPECIFIC POPULATIONS

Individualized care should be sensitive and responsive to the client's specific needs. Some groups or populations with similar characteristics or histories have been found to respond favorably to specific treatment practices. Such populations include individuals with co-occurring disorders, those with a history of trauma, women, veterans, adolescents, the LGBTQ community, and older adults. Understanding a client's *culture*, a term that can be used broadly to include special populations as well as racial and ethnic groups, is essential to effective treatment. As explained by SAMHSA: "Culture is the lens through which reality is interpreted."[26] For this reason, distinct populations are best served by providers who are culturally competent to provide the most up-to-date evidence-based practices to address their needs.

Culturally competent care is based on respect for and knowledge of the language, cultural beliefs, needs, and traditions of individuals, and includes the development of policies and behaviors that allow staff to work effectively in cross-cultural situations. For example, the treatment environment should reflect sensitivity to the clients it treats. Treatment providers may wish to consider whether the composition of the staff is representative of the composition of the population served.

Co-occurring Disorders

SUDs often coexist with other mental health disorders. The best practice is for the concurrent treatment of both the mental health disorder and the SUD. This approach, which is referred to as integrated treatment, requires collaboration among providers and treatment planning that addresses each problem in the context of the others.[27]

Trauma-Informed Care (TIC)

Trauma-informed care (TIC) is important to the recovery of individuals with a history of trauma. Recovery can be impeded if a client's past traumas are not identified, and the treatment plan is not informed by an understanding of the client's full history. In some cases, clients may be retraumatized by the treatment process or environment. With full knowledge of a client's prior experiences, providers can be sensitive to individual needs and use their best efforts to provide an environment that does not resemble or remind the client of the past trauma.[28] It is also important to consider whether the client has any co-occurring disorders such a PTSD or depression and provide concurrent treatment.

Clients who have experienced trauma need to feel safe, both physically and emotionally, to succeed in treatment. The creation of a safe environment for these clients goes far beyond normal security measures. For example, clients who have felt trapped in a prior relationship or been restrained or confined as part of their history of trauma may be retraumatized and become extremely uncomfortable in small rooms or sitting in spaces where they cannot easily reach an exit. Any discipline, such as isolation or loss of privileges, may also remind the client of controls imposed by past perpetrators.

Care providers need to take affirmative steps to ensure the client is not retraumatized by external stimuli that may activate the feelings that arose during the trauma. For example, procedures can be put in place to minimize male intrusions into women's units, and provisions can be made for private changing areas and to afford privacy when giving urine samples. Clients may also be retraumatized by anger expressed during role play in groups or in confrontational group sessions. Informed counselors know how to control the tone of group sessions and protect the trauma victim from demeaning or bullying behavior by other clients.

Clients may also be intimidated and retraumatized by providers who they perceive to resemble or who remind them of individuals who abused, threatened, or injured them in the past. Thus, in a TIC environment, gender should be considered in the selection of the members of a client's care team. The assignment of a male counselor or the choice of a male physician to conduct a necessary physical exam may not be appropriate for a client who was the victim of abuse from a man. Similarly, female victims of trauma may feel more comfortable in groups composed only of women, particularly peers who have had similar experiences. The clients should be consulted as part of this process because not all clients have the same issues or preferences. For example, a male client who was victimized by a woman may feel judged as less masculine by a male counselor and may prefer to work with a female counselor.

TIC supports recovery by using a strengths-based approach to empower clients, increase their self-confidence, promote their resilience, and teach them to view themselves as strong survivors. Many clients who have experienced trauma have been controlled by others. To provide these clients with a sense of control and build their self-esteem, it is important to allow them to make choices and give them a role in decision making regarding their care plan. Clients can, for example, make decisions regarding not only the gender of the primary counselor, but the type and composition of therapy groups to which they are assigned, and can select the type of skills-training workshops that interest them.

Not all treatment providers have extensive training in the treatment of clients with a history of trauma. They may move too quickly to address the trauma without laying a foundation of rapport and trust, or discount the client's reports of trauma. While in treatment sessions, clients with a history of trauma may relive some of the feelings they experienced during the original trauma and act out. Trauma-informed providers recognize this conduct as a stress reaction to trauma rather than a behavioral problem, and respond to the client appropriately.

Structure and routine have also been found to help clients with a history of trauma because they can rely on the schedule and not be thrown off by sudden changes in routine. The use of opening and closing rituals as part of sessions may contribute to feelings of stability and safety. Consistent enforcement of rules and expectations is also important for treatment of this population because victims of trauma may feel controlled by arbitrary and inconsistent rules.[29]

Recovery from trauma is the primary goal of treatment for clients in this population. In other words, unless the client's reaction to trauma is addressed, progress toward recovery from substance use will be impeded. While many clients may not recognize that trauma continues to influence their use of substances, in a TIC setting counselors will help the client bridge the gap between the past trauma and his or her use of alcohol and other drugs.[30]

Women

Many women suffering from SUDs have a history of trauma and are best served by programs offering TIC. There are other issues unique to the treatment of women with addictive disorders. Women metabolize alcohol differently than men. Women also progress faster from the inception of drug use to the development of addictive disease and experience adverse medical consequences from use more quickly than men. Women seeking treatment are subject to a great deal of stigma, which often acts as a barrier to treatment. Many women in treatment have been devalued and have low self-esteem. They respond to supportive, strengths-based treatments, and benefit from a nurturing environment rather than a confrontational approach to their problems. For women, family history and relationships often play a pivotal role in the initiation and continuation of substance use. Women may begin use of substances with a partner, and use may remain integral to the maintenance of that relationship. Some women may be also dependent upon a using partner for financial support.[31]

Gender roles and the responsibilities of women as caregivers also impact the treatment of women for addictive disease. Women may feel shame and guilt over their perceived failure as a mother. Some clients need to resolve complex issues of grief and loss relating to children or others they cared for. Some women are grieving the death of a spouse, partner, or child or the failure of a relationship. While in treatment, some women may also be dealing with legal problems and the emotional issues attendant to loss of custody of their children. There are other practicalities involved in the treatment of women who are caregivers. Some residential programs house patients and their children and others provide childcare on-site while mothers are in outpatient treatment. Mothers who suffer from addictive disease may also require training in basic parenting skills and childcare techniques.

Pregnant women who are abusing drugs or are in treatment for SUDs present special concerns because drug use can cause significant long-term risks to the unborn child. When a mother uses alcohol during pregnancy, the child may be born with a fetal alcohol spectrum disorder. The most serious of this range of disorders is fetal alcohol syndrome (FAS). Symptoms of FAS include low birth weight, abnormal facial features, and long-term cognitive and behavioral problems. Drug use during pregnancy, particularly the use of opioids, may cause newborns to experience withdrawal. Neonatal abstinence syndrome (NAS) occurs when a child becomes dependent on drugs due to the mother's use during pregnancy. NAS places infants at higher risk of low birth weight, seizures, respiratory and feeding problems, and, potentially, death. Methadone maintenance therapy and MAT with buprenorphine, while they may cause withdrawal symptoms in infants, minimize risk to the infant when used in the context of medically managed treatment and monitoring of pregnant women.[32]

Veterans

To provide effective treatment to veterans, a care provider needs to understand what it means to serve. The military has its own code of honor, values, culture, hierarchy, and a vernacular that includes heavy use of acronyms. To adequately serve this population, counselors must possess the special knowledge and cultural competence to work with this population. To facilitate trust and build rapport with clients, the treatment provider, if not also a veteran, needs to demonstrate an understanding of military service and culture as well as the unique problems experienced by veterans after returning to their families, communities, and the workforce after extended deployment or discharge.

Many veterans have co-occurring PTSD or a history of traumatic experiences. Veterans often benefit from treatment in groups with other veterans. Studies support the conclusion that concurrent treatment of both PTSD and SUDs produces better outcomes. Reduction in substance use has been found to significantly reduce violence in clients with PTSD. Similarly, treatment of PTSD symptoms supports reduction of substance abuse. Studies have also shown that veterans experience improved outcomes from long-term, intensive programs, the use of psychiatric medication for co-occurring disorders, discharge planning that supports recovery, and participation in program reunions as a part of post-discharge care.[33]

CBT has been found to be effective in the treatment of PTSD. Other therapies for this population include narrative exposure therapy (NET), during which the client directly explores memories of trauma and the feelings those memories create. Eye movement desensitization and reprocessing (EMDR) is an evidenced-based practice that is widely used by certified professionals in the treatment of trauma and PTSD.[34] EMDR was developed in 1987 and uses eye movements like those typical to REM sleep to process traumatic memories. Mindfulness practices, when used in combination with other therapies, have also been found to be effective in the treatment of PTSD.

Adolescents

A treatment plan for adolescents that does not account for the adolescent stage of development (i.e., which treats them in the same way as adults) is unlikely to succeed.[35] According to NIDA, one important distinction between the treatment of adults and adolescents is the fact that adolescents may benefit from drug use intervention even if their use does not yet rise to the level of an SUD.[36] As minors, adolescents may be placed into treatment by their parents and may enter treatment without a readiness to change. Thus, an early goal of treatment for adolescents is often to facilitate the client's examination of the impact their use of substances is having on their lives and life goals. Motivational interview techniques may help teens explore those realities. Given the importance of peers in adolescent development, positive role models in group may gently confront reluctant peers and assist in breaking through their denial, thereby motivating change.

Any history of trauma, abuse, or suicidality should be explored during the assessment and/or intake interviews of adolescents. Co-occurring disorders, including anxiety, depression, and ADHD, are common among adolescents in treatment for substance use problems and should be identified and treated concurrently with the SUD. Gender-based differences should be considered in the development of a treatment plan for adolescents and explored in treatment. Male depression may be presented as anger, and young men may externalize their pain because they lack the capacity to feel. The absence of a father or a strained father-son relationship may also impact substance use.[37] Substance abuse by young women is often impacted by their relationships with peers and within the family.

Consideration of the family dynamic is important in the treatment of all adolescents. NIDA reports that adolescent treatment programs that "facilitate positive parental involvement, integrate other systems in which the adolescent participates (such as school and athletics), and recognize the importance of prosocial peer relationships are among the most effective."[38] Family dynamics, communication patterns, and conflicts can be examined in the context of family therapy sessions. Parents can also benefit from education sessions about the disease and from training in development of skills for improved communications with their teenagers. The discussion of expectations and the development of rules and boundaries should be considered in the context of planning for discharge and the potential return of the teen to the family home.

Adolescents benefit from the consistent enforcement of clearly stated rules and expectations. To build trust and rapport, providers need to find the proper amount of structure without becoming authoritarian. Adolescents will tune out or rebel against what they see as another rigid attempt to get them to conform.

Counselors can build trust and promote the safety and security of clients by protecting individuals from teasing or harassment by other clients. Effective treatment for adolescent clients may also include programming to increase their self-esteem. The foundation for fostering adolescents' belief in themselves is built by providing a safe, secure, and supportive environment in which to explore their problems. It is also empowering for adolescents to allow them to have a voice in planning choices for treatment, discharge planning, and identifying rights, responsibilities, and consequences within the family.[39]

Therapeutic wilderness programs are an alternative to inpatient treatment for adolescents. They provide adolescents and young adults with behavioral counseling (individual and group) while they are engaged in hiking and camping in remote areas. The clients are empowered by the experience of mastering the survival skills that are taught as part of the program curriculum. These skills include building fires from friction, constructing their own shelters, hiking with a pack, and cooking their own food over a fire. The programs provide a natural environment that totally separates clients from the distractions of modern society. The experience allows clients to see their own success and demonstrated competence, building confidence and self-esteem. In long-term programs for adolescents, provision needs to be made for their schooling while in treatment. Many inpatient programs coordinate with the client's school district to satisfy academic requirements. Some programs have the credentials to provide academic credit for an on-site curriculum.

Emotional growth and development is stymied when adolescents use drugs. Many teens with addictive disorders missed the chance to develop life skills. Older adolescents in treatment for SUDs are likely to have experienced academic failure and lack plans for post-high school training, education, or employment. Effective treatment programs take a holistic approach to the client's well-being and help him or her develop a plan and purpose for the future. For these reasons, basic training in life skills and the development of a plan for work, training, or education after discharge are important components of treatment for adolescents and young adults.

The LGBTQ Community

Members of the LGBTQ community may be dealing with issues of identity and may have experienced trauma, shame, denial, discrimination, or social ostracism that contributed to the development of their problem with alcohol or other drugs. Some clients may be experiencing the stress of coming out and some may not have the support of their families. These issues need to be addressed in the development of treatment plans for LGBTQ clients. Only a small percentage of treatment facilities offer specialized treatment programs for members of the LGBTQ community.[40] If specialized treatment programs are not available, other providers may be equipped to provide a supportive environment and culturally competent care to this population. Studies have shown that LGBTQ clients benefit from treatment in an environment that reflects an understanding of sexuality and sexual orientation, as well as socialization in the LGBTQ community. To ensure a culturally sensitive, safe, and supportive treatment environment for all clients, policies should be put into place to prevent, or respond to, indicia of transphobia, homophobia, isolation, discrimination, or harassment that may harm clients.[41]

Therapies that have been shown to be effective with gay or bisexual men in treatment for an SUD include motivational interviewing, CBT, and contingency management.[42] Individual treatment may help an LGBTQ client who is uncomfortable in a group primarily composed of heterosexual clients.[43] Since clients may be ostracized from some members of their families of origin, they may benefit from the engagement of friends rather than (or in addition to) family members in the treatment process.[44]

Older Adults

Older adults experiencing increased isolation, depression, ill health, grief, loss, or perception of diminished self-worth may develop SUDs for the first time in their lives. Substance abuse among this population may arise from feelings of grief and loss over the death of a spouse, the feelings of a lack of purpose following retirement, or the completion of duties as a caregiver. Because older adults may use alone and conceal their practices, substance abuse among seniors is referred to as a hidden disease.[45]

Among this population, the most commonly used substances of abuse are alcohol and prescription medication. Given their age and physical health, older adults may have lower tolerance for alcohol and other substances, magnifying their effects. Additional problems are created by the fact that alcohol may adversely react with prescription medications and because older adults may not be compliant with the recommended regime for taking their prescribed medications. At times, it may be difficult to identify symptoms of intoxication in older adults because forgetfulness, falls, and other symptoms of intoxication may be mistaken for the effects of aging.[46]

A treatment plan should be prepared in collaboration with the client's primary care doctor and address all medical and co-occurring conditions that impact the client's health. Treatments that have been found to be effective with older adults include brief interventions, CBT, group therapy with groups of their peers, family engagement, case management (to coordinate social services), and referral to self-help programs.

TREATMENT OF GAMBLING DISORDERS

Gambling is increasingly present in our society and the number of outlets for gambling, including internet-based gaming, continues to grow. Consistent with this increase in access, the number of individuals with gambling disorders is rising. Society has been slow to recognize problematic gambling as a disease. Compared to substance-based addictive disease, less research has been conducted on behavioral compulsions such as gambling, and there are far fewer treatment facilities for individuals with gambling disorders.

Screening tools such as the Problem Gambling Severity Index (PGSI), the Brief Biosocial Gambling Screen (BBGS), and the NORC Diagnostic Screen for Gambling Problems–Self Administered (NODS-SA) are available to individuals who wish to conduct self-administered screening to identify whether they should modify their gambling habits or seek help for gambling issues. Outpatient treatment is available for persons with gambling disorders, and while not common, residential treatment programs exist for treatment of the disease. Generally, insurance companies will not cover treatment for gambling disorders unless there is a co-occurring medical disorder, such as a mood disorder. Some states, notably Oregon and Connecticut, use state money, including a portion of gambling revenues, to provide treatment for the disorder.[47] Another barrier to treatment is denial, which is common among those with a gambling disorder. Many gamblers think that they can control the behavior and refuse to admit that a problem exists until they are confronted with serious legal or financial problems.

There is a significant correlation between gambling disorders and the co-occurrence of other psychiatric disorders, particularly SUDs. It has been reported that 73.2 percent of pathological gamblers also had an alcohol use disorder, 38.1 percent had a drug-related SUD, and 60.4 percent were dependent on nicotine.[48] It is recommended that both the gambling and the substance-based disorder be treated at the same time because one behavior activates a desire to engage in the other behavior. Gambling disorders also co-occur with other psychiatric disorders. Approximately 49.6 percent of pathological gamblers also had a mood disorder, 41.3 percent were found to suffer from an anxiety disorder, and 60.8 percent had a personality disorder.[49] There also appears to be a correlation between depression and compulsive gambling. There is a high rate of suicide among compulsive gamblers, and the evaluation and treatment of persons for compulsive gambling issues should include screening for past suicide attempts and suicidal thoughts or ideation, and an assessment of whether a risk for suicide is presented.

There are no drugs that are approved to treat gambling disorders. Naltrexone, which is approved for the treatment of opioid dependence and which can be prescribed by any professional who is authorized to prescribe medications, is used "off label" to treat compulsive gamblers. Studies have also shown promising results that another opioid antagonist, nalmefene (Revex), which is being developed for the treatment of nicotine and alcohol use disorders, may reduce compulsions in gamblers.[50] Clients with depression, anxiety, or other mood disorders may benefit from medication to treat those co-occurring disorders.

Individuals with a gambling disorder often think they can beat the odds. Many chase their losses, thinking they are due for a win. Players often harbor superstitions or illogical thoughts about their chances of winning that defy the laws of probability. For example, they may think that their odds improve the more they play even though the odds of a single play of every game of chance are always the same. In other words, with every roll of a single die, there is a one–in–six chance of rolling a five. Other gambling fallacies include the perception that, through skill, gamblers can control the outcome of a game that is purely a matter of chance or that a "near miss" is indicative of a prospective win.[51]

Cognitive therapy and CBT have been found to be effective in helping gamblers overcome irrational thinking about their chances of winning. Mindfulness training has shown promise as a support to recovery from gambling disorders. Individuals struggling with gambling are often referred to Gamblers Anonymous, a twelve-step support group for those with gambling problems. Tools such as self-help CBT workbooks are also used in the treatment of gambling disorders.

CHAPTER 6 NOTES

1   William Cope Moyers, *Now What? An Insider's Guide to Addiction and Recovery* (Center City, MN: Hazelden, 2012), 53.

2   Brad M. Reedy, *The Journey of the Heroic Parent* (New York: Regan Arts, 2016), 87.

3   SAMHSA, *Trauma-Informed Care in Behavioral Health Services, Treatment Improvement Protocol 57 (TIP 57)* (Rockville, MD: SAMHSA, 2014), xviii.

4   NIDA, "What Is Drug Addiction Treatment?" in "Frequently Asked Questions," in *Principles of Drug Addiction Treatment: A Research-Based Guide*, 3rd ed. (2012), https://www.drugabuse.gov/publications/principles-drug-addiction-treatment-research-based-guide-third-edition/principles-effective-treatment.

5   HHS, "Facing Addiction in America," 4-1.

6   Ibid., 4-2.

7   See, e.g., Michael F. Fleming et al., "Brief Physician Advice for Heavy Drinking College Students: A Randomized Controlled Trial in College Health Clinics," *Journal of Studies on Alcohol and Drugs*, January 2010, doi: 10.15288/jsad.2010.71.23.

8   Inaba and Cohen, *Uppers, Downers, All-Arounders*, 9.12–9.13.

9   Ibid., 9.38.

10   HHS, "Facing Addiction in America," 4-12.

11   Ibid.

12   Inaba and Cohen, *Uppers, Downers, All-Arounders*, 6.39.

13   NIDA, "How Long Does Drug Addiction Treatment Usually Last?" in "Frequently Asked Questions," in *Principles of Drug Addiction Treatment*.

14   NIDA, "How Do Medications to Treat Opioid Addiction Work?" in *Research Report on Medications to Treat Opioid Addiction* (2017), https://www.drugabuse.gov/publications/research-reports/medications-to-treat-opioid-addiction/how-do-medications-to-treat-opioid-addiction-work.

15   Ibid., "Overview."

16   Ibid., "Misconceptions about Maintenance Treatment."

17   NIDA, "How Long Does Drug Addiction Treatment Usually Last?" in "Frequently Asked Questions," in *Principles of Drug Addiction Treatment*.

18   SAMHSA, "Buprenorphine," last modified May 31, 2016, https://www.samhsa.gov/medication-assisted-treatment/treatment/buprenorphine.

19   SAMHSA, "Naloxone," last modified March 3, 2016, https://www.samhsa.gov/medication-assisted-treatment/treatment/naloxone.

20   HHS, "Facing Addiction in America," 4-24.

21   Cynthia L. Vuittonet et al., "Pharmacotherapy for Alcoholic Patients with Alcoholic Liver Disease," *American Journal of Health-System Pharmacy* 71 (2014): 1273, doi: 10.2146/ajhp140028.

22   Ibid., 4-30.

23   NIDA, "What Is Drug Addiction Treatment?" in "Frequently Asked Questions," in *Principles of Drug Addiction Treatment*.

24   Irving Yalom and Molyn Leszcz, *The Theory and Practice of Group Psychotherapy*, 5th ed. (New York: Basic Books, 1995), 1–2.

25 SAMHSA, "Recovery and Recovery Support," last modified September 20, 2017, https://www.samhsa.gov/recovery.

26 SAMHSA, *Trauma Informed Care, TIP 57*, 131.

27 SAMHSA, "Co-occurring Disorders," last modified March 8, 2016, https://www.samhsa.gov/disorders/co-occurring.

28 SAMHSA, *Trauma Informed Care, TIP 57*, 18, 45–46.

29 Ibid., 19–20, 113.

30 Ibid., 20–21.

31 SAMHSA, *Substance Abuse Treatment: Addressing the Specifc Needs of Women, Treatment Improvement Protocol 51 (TIP 51)* (Rockville, MD: SAMHSA, 2009), xix, 9.

32 NIDA, "What Are the Unique Needs of Pregnant Women with Substance Use Disorders?" in "Frequently Asked Questions," in *Principles of Drug Addiction Treatment*.

33 Kendell L. Coker, Elina Stefanovics, and Robert Rosenheck, "Correlates of Improvement in Substance Abuse Among Dually Diagnosed Veterans with Post-Traumatic Stress Disorder in Specialized Intensive VA Treatment," *Psychological Trauma: Theory, Research, Practice, and Policy*, June 2015, 6, doi: 10.1037/tra0000061.

34 SAMHSA, *Trauma Informed Care, TIP 57*, 144–45.

35 SAMHSA, *Treatment of Adolescents with Substance Abuse Disorders, Treatment Improvement Protocol 32 (TIP 32)* (Rockville, MD: SAMHSA, 1999), Chapter 3.

36 NIDA, "Principles of Adolescent Substance Use Disorder Treatment," in *Principles of Adolescent Substance Use Disorder Treatment: A Research-Based Guide* (2014), https://www.drugabuse.gov/publications/principles-adolescent-substance-use-disorder-treatment-research-based-guide/principles-adolescent-substance-use-disorder-treatment.

37 Sanders, "Gender Responsive Services."

38 NIDA, "What Are the Unique Needs of Adolescents with Substance Use Disorders?" in "Frequently Asked Questions," in *Principles of Drug Addiction Treatment*.

39 SAMHSA, *Treatment of Adolescents, TIP 32*, Chapter 3.

40 Bryan N. Cochran, K. Michelle Peavy, and Jennifer S. Robohm, "Do Specialized Services Exist for LGBT Individuals Seeking Treatment for Substance Misuse? A Study of Available Treatment Programs," *Substance Use & Misuse* 42 (2007), 168, doi: 10.1080/10826080601094207.

41 HHS, "Facing Addiction in America," 4-38.

42 Kelly E. Green and Brian A. Feinstein, "Substance Use in Lesbian, Gay, and Bisexual Populations: An Update on Empirical Research and Implications for Treatment," *Psychology of Addictive Behaviors* 26, no. 2 (June 2012), 276, doi: 10.1037/a0025424.

43 SAMHSA, *Trauma Informed Care, TIP 57*, 135.

44 SAMHSA, *Addressing the Needs of Women, TIP 51*, 125.

45 SAMHSA, *Substance Abuse among Older Adults, Treatment Improvement Protocol 26 (TIP 26)* (Rockville, MD: SAMHSA, 1998), 127.

46 Ibid.

47 Inaba and Cohen, *Uppers, Downers, All-Arounders*, 9.49.

48 Nancy M. Petry, Frederick S. Stinson, and Bridget F. Grant, "Comorbidity of *DSM-IV* Pathological Gambling and Other Psychiatric Disorders: Results from the National Epidemiologic Survey on Alcohol and Related Conditions," *Journal of Clinical Psychiatry* 66, no. 5 (2005): 564–74.

49 Inaba and Cohen, *Uppers, Downers, All-Arounders*, 9.49.

50 Ibid.

51 Luke Clark et al., "Pathological Choice: The Neuroscience of Gambling and Gambling Addiction," *Journal of Neuroscience* 33, no. 45 (November 2013): 17619, doi: 10.1523/JNEUROSCI.3231-13.2013.

7 WHAT RECOVERY MEANS AND HOW IT CAN BE SUSTAINED

What we hope for family members and friends with severe SUDs is long-term remission and recovery. There is no cure for addiction, and no one recovers from the disease. The diagnostic qualifiers for SUDs, as identified in the *DSM-5*, include "in early remission" (the criteria for an SUD have not been met for at least three but not more than twelve months) and "in sustained remission" (the criteria for an SUD have not been met for a period of twelve months or more). Similar specifiers are used for diagnosis of gambling disorders. Thus, even with long-term abstinence from substances or addictive behaviors, the disease remains present but in remission. Treatment that reduces problematic patterns of use and brings about remission of symptoms for individuals diagnosed with mild or moderate SUDs is considered to be successful despite the fact that the clients are not abstinent.[1] For example, a brief intervention with a woman who was diagnosed with a mild or moderate alcohol use disorder that brings about a change in her behavior, reducing her drinking to levels below the diagnostic threshold, places her in remission from the SUD. She is not, however, in recovery.

RECOVERY GOES FAR BEYOND ABSTINENCE

While remission is not recovery, recovery includes remission of clinical symptoms. Recovery is far more than mere abstinence. Recovery represents a holistic change in an individual's approach to living. It requires that a person accept his or her disease and change his or her lifestyle with the intention of maintaining lifelong sobriety. Such individuals are said to be "in recovery" from addictive disease. The psychologist Abraham Maslow developed a theory of human behavior explaining that motivation is dictated by a hierarchy of needs, and the most basic needs, those essential to survival, take precedence. Under Maslow's theory, there are five categories of human need: (1) *physiological needs,* the elements necessary to survival, such as air, food, water, warmth, and reproduction; (2) *safety needs,* personal safety and financial security; (3) *social needs*, belonging to a unit or community; (4) *self-esteem*, dignity and respect from others; and finally, (5) *self-actualization*, personal growth and fulfilling one's potential. Maslow theorized that the lower levels of need must be satisfied before humans can move on to address higher and more complex functions. Thus, those in recovery cannot master the complex tasks of fostering their self-esteem and striving for their full potential unless their basic needs have been satisfied.

SAMHSA defines recovery as "a process of change through which individuals improve their health and wellness, live self-directed lives, and strive to reach their full potential."[2] Four major components are central to recovery, according to SAMHSA: (1) health, (2) home, (3) purpose, and (4) community. This description of recovery recognizes the importance of maintaining health by remaining abstinent from the use of substances and making other choices to support physical and emotional health. Consistent with Maslow's explanation that basic needs, such as food and shelter, must be met before individuals can strive to achieve more advanced goals, SAMHSA recognizes that the existence of a safe home is central to recovery. The SAMHSA principles also recognize the importance of having a daily purpose (whether it be school, work, caregiving, volunteerism, or engaging in creative pursuits), and having the income or resources necessary to achieve financial independence. Finally, SAMHSA identifies the importance of a supportive social network or community to recovery.[3]

Sobriety does not instantly solve problems or create a direct path to well-being and the achievement of planned goals. To the contrary, the journey to recovery is fraught with difficulty. Our loved ones may feel that everything needs to be relearned as ingrained patterns of behavior are replaced with totally new ways of thinking and acting. At first, simply maintaining sobriety is the primary task, and those new to recovery should not try to take on too much at once. Mastery of integral tasks and incremental progress toward ultimate goals are sufficient.

PLANNING FOR SUPPORTED RECOVERY AFTER DISCHARGE

All clients should leave treatment with a written discharge plan that specifically relates to their individual needs and addresses each of the four dimensions that are critical to recovery. A holistic discharge plan supports and facilitates the transition from the shelter of a drug-free treatment facility or the monitored accountability of an outpatient program to the absolute freedom of the outside world. It takes time to make such transformative changes and rebuild a life without the use of substances. In this context, there is growing recognition of the need for a chronic care management model for the treatment of severe SUDs, as well as the coordination of treatment and post-treatment support systems for management of the disease. This model is known as a recovery-oriented system of care (ROSC).

Clients in an ROSC may have periodic face-to-face meetings with their prior care team after discharge, to allow staff to follow up on clients' continued abstinence and progress toward goals. These meetings are called recovery management check-ups (RMCs) and may be conducted on a quarterly basis for several years as a follow-up to initial treatment. Studies have shown that RMCs are effective in the early identification of relapse, allowing intervention and referral for further treatment. An ROSC may also use periodic telephone or electronic communications to maintain a connection with the client, monitor the client's progress, and offer assistance when clients exhibit at-risk behaviors.[4]

Many individuals cannot return to their former housing after treatment because of the need to avoid exposure to drug use, due to ongoing family conflicts or to facilitate their self-growth and independence. Their recovery may be best supported by residence in recovery-supportive housing where abstinence is mandated as a condition of occupancy. This type of housing also provides a supportive peer community and is generally more cost-effective than traditional housing options. Many sober residences are peer managed, while other sites employ an individual to oversee the site.

Adolescents and young adults face challenges in returning to school after treatment. While few in number, recovery high schools provide a sober educational environment and supportive recovery services. Private, therapeutic boarding schools also provide an opportunity for continued care and education. Some collegiate programs offer separate, sober dormitories and a range of additional services for students (such as counseling and on-campus twelve-step or other mutual-aid meetings). While further research regarding the effectiveness of recovery-based education is needed, preliminary findings are promising.[5]

THE TWELVE-STEP RECOVERY FELLOWSHIPS

Twelve-step recovery fellowships represent the most utilized and successful support system for those in recovery, having helped countless millions of people achieve and maintain sobriety. Discharge plans often call for active participation in a twelve-step recovery program such as AA or one of the other programs that have adapted its principles to individuals suffering from other addictive diseases, such as Narcotics Anonymous (NA), Cocaine Anonymous (CA), and Gamblers Anonymous (GA). These twelve-step fellowships will be referred to herein as "recovery fellowships" to distinguish them from fellowships for the family members of those with addictive disease. Recovery fellowships are groups of men and women who share their experiences, strength, and hope in an effort to solve their common problem and help themselves and others recover from addiction based on the principles of the Twelve Steps. There is well-supported scientific research that participation in AA supports recovery. While most of the research has been conducted with regard to AA, there is also promising evidence regarding the benefit of participation in other recovery fellowships.[6]

For the person leaving treatment, these fellowships provide continuity and reinforce what was learned in treatment. They provide a welcoming, safe, familiar, consistent, reliable, and easily accessible sober support system for those in recovery. Thus, recovery fellowships address several of the key dimensions of recovery. They help individuals maintain health and abstinence, provide a purpose, and supply a supportive community for those entering recovery. While they offer a bridge from treatment to community living, treatment is in no way a prerequisite for participation in twelve-step groups. Many people have achieved recovery by choosing to participate in a twelve-step program to address their problems with alcohol, other drugs, or behaviors such as gambling. Millions of people use twelve-step principles and participate in twelve-step programs as an integral part of ongoing recovery throughout their lifetime.

Recovery fellowships are not religious organizations and, while they are spiritual in nature, religious belief is not required for participation. When the word *God* is used in the context of the Twelve Steps, it means a higher power, as understood by the individual member. The identification of a higher power is an individual, private choice. For example, nonreligious participants may choose to consider the consensus of the group as their higher power. No fees or dues are required for attendance at meetings, although a basket is passed to collect donations to defer costs such as rent, literature, and refreshments. Local groups also contribute a portion of donations to the administrative offices of the fellowship.

Participation is wholly anonymous, and members identify themselves by first name or by first name and last initial only. The fellowships are based on a foundation of absolute confidentiality. Nothing that is seen, said, or happens at meetings is to be discussed or repeated outside of the meeting. The fact of a person's attendance at a meeting is also wholly confidential. In other words, attendees who recognize someone at a meeting are not to reveal to anyone else that the person was in attendance.

AA was founded in 1935. It is an easily accessible, nonprofessional, self-supporting, apolitical fellowship of men and women who wish to do something about their drinking problem.[7] AA is founded on the Twelve Steps, which define a path to serenity based on acceptance of members' inability to control their use of alcohol, the decision to make changes in their behavior and outlook, a willingness to make amends for past actions, and a commitment to provide service to others:

The Twelve Steps of Alcoholics Anonymous

1. We admitted we were powerless over alcohol—that our lives had become unmanageable.

2. Came to believe that a Power greater than ourselves could restore us to sanity.

3. Made a decision to turn our will and our lives over to the care of God *as we understood Him*.

4. Made a searching and fearless moral inventory of ourselves.

5. Admitted to God, to ourselves, and to another human being the exact nature of our wrongs.

6. Were entirely ready to have God remove all these defects of character.

7. Humbly asked Him to remove our shortcomings.

8. Made a list of all persons we had harmed, and became willing to make amends to them all.

9. Made direct amends to such people wherever possible, except when to do so would injure them or others.

10. Continued to take personal inventory and when we were wrong promptly admitted it.

11. Sought through prayer and meditation to improve our conscious contact with God *as we understood Him*, praying only for knowledge of His will for us and the power to carry that out.

12. Having had a spiritual awakening as the result of these steps, we tried to carry this message to alcoholics, and to practice these principles in all our affairs.[8*]

Other recovery fellowships have adapted the Twelve Steps to reflect their specific purposes. The first step of CA denotes acceptance of powerlessness "over cocaine and all other mind-altering substances." Similarly, the first step of NA is the recognition of powerlessness over "our addiction," and in their first step GA members admit they are powerless over gambling.

The fellowships are not therapeutic groups because they are not led by a therapist or other mental health professional. Rather, they are self-led by peers. As self-help or mutual aid groups, however, recovery fellowships share the benefits that Dr. Yalom attributed to group therapy, particularly those of hope, universality, catharsis, interpersonal learning, cohesion, and imitative behavior. Regardless of the stability of other support systems in their lives, the fellowships provide a place where those in recovery will be understood and supported in their struggle.

---

* The Twelve Steps are reprinted with permission of Alcoholics Anonymous World Services, Inc. ("A.A.W.S."). Permission to reprint the Twelve Steps does not mean that A.A.W.S. has reviewed or approved the contents of this publication, or that A.A.W.S. necessarily agrees with the views expressed herein. A.A. is a program of recovery from alcoholism only—use of the Twelve Steps in connection with programs and activities which are patterned after A.A., but which address other problems, or in any other non-A.A. context, does not imply otherwise.

It is not difficult to begin participation in a recovery-step fellowship. A search by location or zip code on program websites will identify a link to the regional intergroup office of the fellowship. Typically, the regional websites provide detailed online directories of local meetings. The directories are searchable by proximity, date, time, and type of meeting. There are significant differences in meeting types. The most important distinction is whether the meeting is open or closed. The directories identify whether each meeting is open (anyone with an interest in the subject is welcome to attend) or closed (attendance at the meeting is limited solely to individuals who are members or potential members). According to the fellowship, "Attendance at an open AA meeting is the best way to learn what AA is, what it does, and what it does not do."[9] Further, as defined by AA under its concept and "singleness of purpose," "non-alcoholics may attend open AA meetings as observers, but only those with a drinking problem may attend closed AA meetings."[10] Many individuals who are in recovery from polysubstance abuse will satisfy this definition.

Procedurally, particularly in areas where there may be fewer meeting resources available to those addicted to drugs other than alcohol, attendees at closed meeting may, by consensus, agree to participation by those who wish to attend and have a problem with a substance other than alcohol. NA is more inclusive in its recognition that alcohol is a drug, welcoming attendance at closed meetings by all who are powerless over the use of drugs (including alcohol). CA also welcomes individuals who want to stop the use of cocaine and all other mind-altering substances, including alcohol and other drugs.

Meetings also have various formats. At speaker meetings, one or more individual members give a talk about their personal experiences and how AA has changed their lives. Open speaker meetings provide a good introduction to the workings of the program. During discussion meetings, which can be open or closed, a member briefly recounts his or her personal experience and provides a reading or a topic of discussion for the group. Step meetings are generally closed and involve a detailed discussion of one of the Twelve Steps, often in sequence from week to week or once a month.

The fellowship websites also allow individuals to locate a meeting by the language spoken or for specific populations, such as LGBTQ, women, or Native Americans only. The websites provide a telephone number for general assistance, and there is often a phone number or email address listed to facilitate inquiries about specific meetings. The websites of the recovery fellowships also contain links to online meetings. Meetings are available and accessible nationally and internationally. Individuals can easily locate meetings while traveling for business or on vacation. Meetings are often held on cruise ships, where they can usually be identified on the message board or on the activity list as gatherings for Friends of Bill (FOB), a reference to Bill W., one of the founders of AA.

The concept of working a program in one of the fellowships includes more than maintaining sobriety and attending meetings. Recovery fellowships are based on the concept of sponsorship, actively working the steps, reflection, self-growth, and service. To obtain a sponsor, members seek out a more experienced member whom they relate to and ask if the person will act as their sponsor. As defined by AA, sponsorship is "person-to-person service" to another alcoholic.[11] While sponsors are available to those they sponsor in times of crisis, the sponsor also directs the member in how to understand and work the steps of the program. It is also typical for the member and sponsor to develop their own plan of sponsorship. They may meet regularly, one-on-one, and the newer member may receive assignments from their sponsor. Traditionally, members and their sponsors are of the same sex to avoid complication of the relationship.

While consistent in mission, content, and format, groups have their own personalities based on their core membership. It is suggested that a person new to a fellowship try different meeting types and locations to identify those meetings where he or she is most comfortable and that provide the best fit for his or her circumstances. Adolescents and young adults, for example, often state their preference for meetings that are attended by members of their own age group. Some people prefer gender-specific meetings. After investigating a number of different meetings, members often find a group they wish to attend regularly, which they will call their home group. They may, however, find further benefit and support from attendance at meetings in addition to those of their home group. Many new to the fellowships make a plan to attend ninety meetings in their first ninety days in the program (completing a 90/90).

It may be helpful for those of us who are concerned about another's use of mind-altering substances to learn how the fellowships support recovery. A good way to start is by a review of the material available on the websites of the various fellowships. These sites provide general information, answer commonly asked questions, and provide links to program literature. However, attendance at an open speaker meeting is perhaps the best way to see how the program works and, by listening to the individual stories relayed by the speakers, gain an understanding of why it offers hope to family members with addictive disease. Attendance at open meetings with your loved one not only provides insight into the workings of the fellowship, but it demonstrates your support for his or her recovery. Remember, however, that you are welcome to attend open meetings for informational purposes, as long as you respect the traditions of the particular recovery fellowship for attendance and participation and are willing to abide by the requirement of complete confidentiality about what you see and what you hear at the meeting.

You may feel hesitant to be seen walking into an open meeting in your community and feel as if you are exposing your secrets publicly. You may need to resist the urge to tell everyone that you are attending not for your own problem, but for that of someone else. These feelings may give you a small taste of the fortitude and strength that it takes to publicly admit one's powerlessness over alcohol, other drugs, or gambling. Speaker meetings are often large, well-attended gatherings (picture a packed high school cafeteria), and you do not have to identify yourself or your purpose in attending.

If you choose to raise your hand when a speaker asks for a show of hands of those who are attending their first meeting, be prepared to receive a large round of applause. You may also be greeted by members who wish to welcome you to the fellowship. If you are so engaged, you can simply and anonymously explain that you are attending because you are worried about another person's drinking or drug-taking behaviors and want to learn more about the program. You may wish to so introduce yourself if you are attending a smaller open meeting. If you choose, you can approach the meeting leader before the meeting begins to express your interest in the fellowship. As long as you are genuine and have a reason to attend an open meeting, you will be welcomed and supported.

THERE ARE MANY DIFFERENT PATHS TO WELLNESS

In the words of the Surgeon General, there are many paths to recovery. Individuals find their own path to wellness based on their beliefs, values, support systems, specific needs, the nature of their SUD, and their financial abilities.[12] In referring to the need to devise a personal system of support, Benneth R. Lee, CADA, MISA I, and cofounder and CEO of the National Alliance for the Empowerment of the Formerly Incarcerated, has said that each person in recovery needs to "find their own guardian."[13] While participation in twelve-step programs is a tried-and-true method of supporting recovery, there are many other ways to design an individual support system that will guard personal recovery.

There are mutual aid programs that are not based on the Twelve Steps. While there is a great deal of research regarding the effectiveness of twelve-step recovery fellowships, there is little research on the benefits afforded by other mutual aid programs. Given the diversity and preferences among individuals struggling with addictive disease, recovery professionals have come to recognize the need for alternatives to twelve-step programs. Non-twelve-step groups may provide a better fit for some individuals. Others may choose to participate in both twelve-step and non-twelve-step support groups to obtain additional and complementary tools to work their own personal program of recovery. Many mutual aid programs offer online meetings, blogs, worksheets, newsletters, and information, which increase the range of accessible recovery tools to individuals. This may be of particular benefit in areas where there are few meeting options. Generally, there are no costs or fees for participation in mutual aid programs, although free-will offerings are typically collected at meetings to support the programs.

The SMART recovery program emphasizes self-empowerment as a means for individuals to overcome addiction to substances and behaviors, including gambling. The acronym SMART stands for self-management and recovery training. The program includes in-person and online meetings that are led by a trained SMART facilitator and provide tools and techniques in four areas: (1) building and maintaining motivation; (2) coping with urges; (3) managing thoughts, feelings, and behaviors; and (4) living a balanced life.[14] The SMART program professes the use of the type of evidence-based approaches that are used in clinical treatment as adapted for use by trained facilitators. For example, many of the approaches are based on CBT and include worksheets and self-assessment tools that help individuals explore their behaviors and motivation to change.

The group emphasizes empowerment and action rather than acceptance of one's powerlessness over substances. The SMART program does not use the labels "addict" or "alcoholic," nor does it require a belief in a higher power or acceptance of addiction as a disease, and it is not based on a concept of lifetime attendance. It has been suggested that SMART programs may be helpful to individuals who are internally motivated versus those who look outside themselves, such as to a higher power, for strength.[15]

Women for Sobriety, Inc. (WFS), describes itself as a self-help recovery program for women that encourages them to embrace an abstinent "new life" defined by positive life choices.[16] The program was founded to affirm the value and worth of women and to provide women with the opportunity to increase their self-confidence and strength by sharing experiences in groups apart from men and the role expectations of gender.[17] The program is based on thirteen affirmations that are intended to encourage emotional and spiritual growth. The nurturing, supportive, safe, empowering, gender-specific, and noncontrolling nature of WFS may meet the particular needs of many women in recovery. WFS has been primarily associated with recovery from alcohol use disorders, but it embraces participation by women suffering from other substance use issues. In-person meetings are led by a facilitator, and the organization maintains an online blog.

There are a number of other mutual aid groups that may provide support and tools for those in recovery. These include Secular Organization for Sobriety, which is based on self-empowerment principles in a non-religious context. LifeRing for Secular Recovery is another nonreligious support group that is based on behavioral change and positive psychology. Celebration Recovery is an openly Christian support group for those in recovery from substance use or who are dealing with other problematic behaviors.[18]

Some individuals use a recovery coach as an aid to maintaining sobriety and promoting personal growth. Recovery coaches may be volunteers or they may hold a paid position with governmental organizations or a nonprofit group. Some treatment programs use peer mentors or recovery coaches to support clients. Coaches are generally not certified addiction professionals, and they may or may not be in recovery themselves. The purpose of a recovery coach is to monitor and assist the client in planning for and maintaining abstinence, connecting the client with other social services and supports and assisting the client in the development of skills necessary to stay in recovery, solve the basic problems of living, and obtain financial independence.[19]

Many individuals utilize individual, couples, or family counseling. Others may become active in a church, temple, or other religious organization and may seek counseling with a member of the clergy. Similarly, the practice of mindfulness, meditation, or yoga complements a recovery plan. Individuals may also find solace in nature, in the creative arts, building projects, or gardening. Our loved ones may also engage in practices that foster resilience, that is, the ability to bounce back from trauma or adversity. Strategies for developing and fostering resilience include avoiding isolation and becoming part of a community, setting interim goals to achieve a larger objective, acting with purpose, maintaining a positive outlook, and expressing one's feelings.

RECOMMENDED RESOURCES

- Alcoholics Anonymous, https://www.aa.org/.

- Alcoholics Anonymous World Services, Inc., *Alcoholics Anonymous Big Book,* 4th ed. (New York: Alcoholics Anonymous World Services, Inc., 2001).

- Alcoholics Anonymous World Services, Inc., *Twelve Steps and Twelve Traditions* (New York: Alcoholics Anonymous World Services, Inc., 1953, 2006).

- Association of Recovery Schools, https://recoveryschools.org/.

- Cocaine Anonymous World Services, https://ca.org/.

- Gamblers Anonymous, http://www.gamblersanonymous.org/ga/.

- Narcotics Anonymous World Services, https://na.org/.

- Narcotics Anonymous World Services, Inc., *Narcotics Anonymous*, 6th ed., (Chatsworth, CA: 2008).

CHAPTER 7 NOTES

1   HHS, "Facing Addiction in America," 5-3.

2   SAMHSA, "Recovery and Recovery Support," last modified September 20, 2017, https://www.samhsa.gov/recovery.

3   Ibid.

4   HHS, "Facing Addiction in America," 5-6–5-7, 5-13–5-14.

5   Ibid., 5-15.

6   Ibid., 5-2, 5-9.

7   Alcoholics Anonymous, "What Is AA?" https://www.aa.org/pages/en_US/what-is-aa.

8   Alcoholics Anonymous World Services, Inc., "The Twelve Steps of Alcoholics Anonymous" (Alcoholics Anonymous Publishing, k/n/a Alcoholics Anonymous World Services, Inc., 1952, 1953, 1981), https://www.aa.org/assets/en_US/smf-121_en.pdf.

9   Ibid.

10   Alcoholics Anonymous, "Information on Alcoholics Anonymous," https://www.aa.org/pages/en_US/information-on-alcoholics-anonymous.

11   Ibid.

12   HHS, "Facing Addiction in America," 5-2.

13   Benneth R. Lee, "Adolescents and Criminal Behavior: Rethinking the Problems and Answers," Seminar, Haymarket Center, Chicago, November 7, 2015. As detailed on the NAEFI website, Mr. Lee is a recovering addict, former Insane Vice Lords gang leader, and death row inmate who has become an addiction counselor, social service counselor, trainer, and administrator. See http://www.naefi.com/about.html.

14   SMART Recovery: Self-Management and Recovery Training, http://www.smartrecovery.org/facldtrain/JointheFacilitatorTeam.htm.

15   A. Tom Horvath and Julie Yeterian, "SMART Recovery: Self-Empowering, Science-Based Addiction Recovery Support," *Journal of Groups in Addiction & Recovery* 7 (2012): 108–109, doi: I:10.1080/1556035X.2012.705651.

16   Women for Sobriety, https://womenforsobriety.org/

17   John F. Kelly and William L. White, "Broadening the Base of Addiction Mutual-Help Organizations," *Journal of Groups in Addiction & Recovery* 7 (2012): 91, doi: 10.1080/1556035X.2012.705646.

18   Ibid., 88–93.

19   HHS, "Facing Addiction in America," 5-10–5-11.

8 OBSTACLES TO RECOVERY, AND RELAPSE

While the promise of recovery fills us with light and hope, the potential for relapse frightens us. We fret over whether our loved ones will pick up again and lead us back to the abyss. While worry is not productive and we cannot fully live if we are tiptoeing around a loved one or cowering over what might happen, the risk of relapse is profoundly real. Knowledge can help us to understand the challenges faced by those in recovery and accept that their journey is often a winding road.

THE REALITY OF RELAPSE

Addiction is, by its nature, a chronic, progressive, relapsing disease. Relapse is commonly identified as any use of a mind-altering substance after a period of abstinence. Even after completing treatment and making a commitment to sobriety, some individuals may continue to cycle in and out of use for years. Studies indicate that up to one-half of patients who receive treatment for SUDs relapse within the first six months after discharge.[1] Other studies support the conclusion that between 40 and 60 percent of clients treated for alcohol and substance use disorders resume active use within a year after completion of treatment.[2] Even for individuals who have been in remission for one or two years, the risk of relapse does not fall to below 15 percent (the risk of developing an SUD in the general population) until after a total of five to seven years in remission from the disease.[3] While these statistics are disheartening, as summarized by NIDA, the fact that a relapse occurs does not mean that treatment has failed. Rather, a relapse signifies that adjustments need to be made in an individual's recovery plan or that further treatment may be warranted.[4]

RISK FACTORS FOR RELAPSE

One of the foremost predictors of relapse is craving. The root of the difficulty lies in the brain's response to drug use, and the fact that the use of drugs conditions the brain to seek more drugs. The cycle of use begins with craving. Cravings are activated by cues that are associated with prior use. In treatment, clients are strongly cautioned against returning to the same "people, places, and things" because if a person goes back to the same environment and routine where they will come into contact with the influences that contributed to the prior drug abuse, they are highly likely to return to their old patterns. In these situations, relapse does not represent a lack of willpower, but is prompted by biology. In other words, without a decided change in environment and lifestyle, the patient is doomed to failure and a return to the use of substances.

PAWS are emotional and physical symptoms that begin after the symptoms of initial withdrawal subside (within seven to fourteen days after abstinence begins) and peak after about two or three months of abstinence. These withdrawal symptoms activate cravings and the desire to use drugs, presenting a significant challenge to recovery. PAWS may last from six to eighteen months or longer (as much as a decade in some cases). The stress of living without drugs after having relied on substances for many years, combined with the changes in the brain that resulted from the prior pattern of use, are thought to influence PAWS. Symptoms include sleep problems, memory impairment, difficulty concentrating, impaired reasoning, hypersensitivity to stress, inappropriate emotional reactions, and mood swings. Symptoms may occur periodically without outside stimulus; they may be activated by cues or occur on or near dates with special meaning, such as holidays, or near the anniversary of a sober date.[5] Research indicates that a sudden spike in cravings can precipitate relapse. Individuals who experience lower-than-average cravings are particularly susceptible to a sudden increase in cravings. Older individuals are more vulnerable to an abrupt increase in cravings compared to younger people, and women were found to be about three times more likely than men to succumb to relapse when experiencing a spike in cravings.[6]

It is important to remember that the cues that induce cravings can be both external (environmental) and internal (thoughts, feelings, and emotions). Feelings and emotions that contributed to past drug use can, like people, places, and things, activate cravings. For this reason, an individual's mood (affect) has a significant relationship to relapse. Negative affect is considered to be a robust precursor to relapse.[7] The symptoms of PAWS can generate overwhelming negative emotions, such as hopelessness, inadequacy, shame, and lack of self-worth.[8] The acronym HALT is used in treatment and in self-help programs to remind those struggling to remain sober that they are at risk when they are hungry, angry, lonely, or tired. Symptoms of depression and other internal factors, such as feelings of sadness, anger, shame, guilt, and self-doubt, may activate the desire to use and contribute to relapse. The Chicago clinician Benneth R. Lee has said that a negative perception of self is the first stage of relapse.[9]

Relationships may have a positive or a negative impact on recovery. Many women began substance use in the context of a relationship, either in the family or with a partner. If they remain in relationships with individuals who continue to use drugs, their recovery is greatly at risk. While conflicts with intimate partners may contribute to negative emotions and relapse, the choice to abandon old relationships may cause feelings of grief or loss that complicate recovery. Individuals in early recovery, particularly women who have had to cut ties with loved ones, may find it difficult to identify new sources of support because they feel shame and lack trust and self-confidence.[10]

Family can be either a positive or a negative influence on recovery. Control issues and preexisting family conflicts, including those between parents and their teenagers or between intimate partners, may activate cravings. Similarly, a lack of understanding of the nature of the disease by family and friends and their failure to accept the concept of total abstinence may undermine recovery. If an individual has been able to manipulate family members in the past and is allowed to return to that behavior, it can precipitate his or her relapse. Similarly, honesty in relationships and within the family can promote recovery.[11]

Multiple relapses are common among those who are diagnosed with an SUD in adolescence. Many different factors contribute to patterns of relapse for this population. The influence of peers and social pressure to use is a major factor in relapse among adolescents. The desire to get high to escape their problems, conflicts with family and friends, negative emotions such as sadness and anger, and the lack of well-developed coping skills also contribute to relapse in the adolescent population.[12]

RELAPSE PREVENTION STRATEGIES

Traditionally, CBT and the development of coping skills have been used in treatment to teach clients how to avoid high-risk situations, modify behavioral patterns, increase self-efficacy in the refusal of substances, choose sober environments, develop sober support networks, and make plans for dealing with cravings. Research has indicated, however, that skills-based interventions alone are of limited effectiveness in preventing relapse.[13] The lack of effectiveness of skills training to thwart the powerful impetus of biological cravings highlights the importance of MAT as a tool in supporting recovery. In this regard, MAT reduces cravings and has become integral to relapse prevention in the treatment of opioid addiction.

While no single strategy can protect against relapse, a comprehensive aftercare and relapse prevention program both supports recovery and operates as a deterrent to relapse. Adherence to a relapse prevention plan with its regime of routines, practices, and measures of accountability can help sustain recovery. As is said in NA, "We keep what we have only with vigilance."[14] Without vigilance, denial and rationalization can creep back in and begin to undermine recovery. Sometimes people start to tell themselves they don't need to attend meetings or work a program, and they go on to take shortcuts and make exceptions. Soon some of these people have convinced themselves that they don't really have a problem and return to substance abuse.

Development of a sober network is a supportive factor in recovery. Recovery is also fostered by managing relationships and by setting and enforcing boundaries and limits for interaction with those who may compromise recovery. Clients who have a history of dysfunctional intimate relationships can strive to avoid the same type of relationships. Mothers are often motivated to maintain sobriety in order to develop a relationship with their children. Positivity, such as that found in recovery fellowships, has also been found to support recovery.[15] Although limited, research studies indicate that the use of social media and recovery-oriented online networks positively support recovery, particularly for adolescents and young adults.[16]

Research has also shown that individuals who accept the reality of their cravings as a manifestation of their disease are more successful in maintaining sobriety than those who try to distract or disengage themselves from their cravings.[17] The practice of mindfulness arises from Buddhist practices in which individuals acknowledge what they hear, feel, and see, and then accept those feelings and emotions in a nonjudgmental and nonreactive way. Mindfulness-based intervention therapy (MBIT), as used in the treatment of SUDs, combines CBT with the practice of mindfulness. MBIT therapy teaches clients to accept and acknowledge cravings and their feelings and emotions. Well-supported evidence indicates that MBIT supports recovery by reducing the impact of affect (emotion and mood) on cravings and substance use.[18] Other studies have found that MBIT results in the reduction of craving as self-reported by study participants.[19] While MBIT may not be accessible to all, there are innumerable books and online resources available to allow individuals to learn how to practice mindfulness.

RESPONSE TO RELAPSE

Some people refer to an initial relapse as a "slip." Arguably, this euphemism minimizes the significant relationship between abstinence and recovery, lacks the honesty essential to personal growth, and provides an excuse for the action. In fact, for those in remission, any use of a mind-altering substance is a relapse. It is proposed that the words *initial relapse*, rather than the word *slip*, be used to describe the first use following abstinence. This word choice highlights that the response to a relapse should be commensurate with the situation, and that what matters most is how the individual responds to the initial relapse.

For some, an initial relapse can demonstrate the importance of using the tools learned in treatment. It can help individuals understand the circumstances and feelings that activated their desire to use. A brief relapse can also cause a person to seek support to arrest a slide back into the depths of the disease, learn from the situation, and recommit to recovery. An extended binge and the inability to stop, however, may indicate the need for additional treatment. Left unabated, the resumption of the use of substances will likely return an individual to the same level of use that preceded abstinence. In other words, the disease can easily take off where it left off and continue to progress. For these reasons, early detection of relapse and prompt, appropriate intervention are believed to improve long-term outcomes.[20]

CHAPTER 8 NOTES

1   Todd Moore et al., "Ecological Momentary Assessment of the Effects of Craving and Affect on Risk for Relapse During Substance Abuse Treatment," *Psychology of Addictive Behaviors* 18, no. 2 (2014): 619, doi: 10.1037/a0034127.

2   A. Thomas McLellan et al., "Drug Dependence: A Chronic Medical Illness, Implications for Treatment, Insurance and Outcomes," *JAMA* 284, no. 13 (2000): 1689.

3   HHS, "Facing Addiction in America," 5–7.

4   NIDA, "Treatment and Recovery," *Drugs, Brains, and Behavior: The Science of Addiction* (2014), https://www.drugabuse.gov/publications/drugs-brains-behavior-science-addiction/treatment-recovery.

5   Inaba and Cohen, *Uppers, Downers, All-Arounders,* 9.23.

6   Moore et al., "Ecological Momentary Assessment," 619.

7   Ibid., 622.

8   Inaba and Cohen, *Uppers, Downers, All-Arounders,* 9.23.

9   Benneth R. Lee, "Adolescents and Criminal Behavior."

10 Suzanne Brown et al., "Personal Network Recovery Enablers and Relapse Risks for Women with Substance Dependence," *Qualitative Health Research* 25, no. 3 (2015): 381–82, doi: 10.1177/1049732314551055.

11 Ibid., 376.

12 Danielle E. Ramo et al., "Variation in Substance Use Relapse Episodes among Adolescents: A Longitudinal Investigation," *Journal of Substance Abuse Treatment* 43 (2012): 45, doi: 10.1016/j.jsat.2011.10.003.

13 Kurt L. Olsson et al., "Addressing Negative Affect in Substance Abuse Relapse Prevention," *Journal of Human Behavior in the Social Environment* 26, no. 1 (2016): 2, doi: 10.1080/10911359.2015.1058138.

14 NA, "Preamble to the Twelve Traditions," https://www.na.org/admin/include/spaw2/uploads/pdf/litfiles/us_english/misc/Twelve%20Traditions.pdf.

15 Brown et al., "Personal Network Recovery Enablers," 372, 375, 377–78.

16 HHS, "Facing Addiction in America," 5–16.

17 Moore et al., "Ecological Momentary Assessment," 622.

18 Olsson et al., "Addressing Negative Affect," 11.

19 Katie Witkiewitz et al., "Mindfulness-Based Relapse Prevention for Substance Craving," *Addictive Behaviors* 38 (2013): 1569, doi: 10.1016/j.addbeh.2012.04.001.

20 HHS, "Facing Addiction in America," 5–13.

PART TWO

ACCEPTANCE

Understanding the Impact That Another's Disease Has on You and the Need for Your Own Recovery

My happiness grows in direct proportion to my acceptance, and in inverse proportion to my expectations.

— MICHAEL J. FOX —

"We Aren't the Problem, They Are."

9 THE PARALLEL ROADS TO RECOVERY FOR THE ADDICTED AND THOSE WHO LOVE THEM

In Part One, we learned that the lives of those suffering from addiction become unmanageable because of their powerlessness over their habit. As family members of the chemically dependent and the problem gambler, we observed just how, in so many ways, their lives became utterly unmanageable. We, too, became desperate and obsessed with what was happening to our loved ones. We lost focus on other aspects of our lives. We thought constantly about another's problems. We couldn't sleep and startled easily. We hovered over our loved one and obsessed over whether he or she was staying clean and working a recovery program. In so many ways, another's use of drugs or his or her gambling problems caused our own lives to become unmanageable.

Some family members deny they have a problem and insist the fault lies solely with those abusing drugs or gambling. "We are not the problem, they are." This fallacy must be recognized and overcome before we can gain acceptance of our own need for recovery. Indeed, the crisis brought about by the addictive disease of someone close to us is so disruptive to familial relationships and so shakes the family to its core that addiction is often referred to as a family disease.

The first step of recovery for family members is the acceptance that we are "powerless" over another's use of drugs or gambling and that our lives have become unmanageable. No amount of love for another person will cure his or her disease. No one can control another person's addictive behaviors, and the attempt to do so wreaks havoc on the lives of those who try. Rather, the only things we can control are our own actions, including our reactions to another's destructive habits. Acceptance is the first step toward normalcy and provides the foundation upon which healing is built. Without an acceptance of our powerlessness, we cannot move forward to the final act when we bring together everything we have learned, take informed action to support recovery for our loved ones, and move forward with our own lives, regardless of whether those we love choose and sustain recovery.

As is true of those in recovery, acceptance of powerlessness over the disease is the hard first step. Recovery fellowships have adopted a definition of insanity often attributed to Einstein, stating that the definition of insanity is to keep doing the same things over and over again while expecting a different result. As said by some in family recovery, the definition of insanity is driving all the way across town in your pajamas to see if she is at a meeting. To regain our own sanity, we need to do the hard work of accepting the fact of our powerlessness over another's addiction and focusing on our own lives. It is all summarized in the Serenity Prayer.

SERENITY PRAYER

God, grant me the serenity
To accept the things I cannot change,
Courage to change the things I can, and
Wisdom to know the difference.

There are many strategies that help us put one foot in front of the other and move us from ineffective action to living fully and, eventually, thriving. While we may not describe ourselves as happy, we will obtain peace with what has occurred and find serenity. One of the best means of coping and moving forward is found in working the Twelve Steps of Al-Anon, Families Anonymous (FA), Nar-Anon, Gam-Anon, or one of the other family support groups. Given the number of different fellowships for the recovery of family and friends of addicts, alcoholics, and gamblers, and to distinguish them from recovery fellowships, they will be referred to herein as the "family fellowships." The difference between family fellowships and recovery fellowships is that members of family fellowships are powerless over someone else's substance use or gambling and not their own.

Like the recovery fellowships, all of the family fellowships are fully anonymous. No last names are exchanged. While no fees are required to attend meetings, a collection is taken to defer administrative costs. Similarly, like AA, the family fellowship programs are nonreligious, and belief in God is not a requirement for participation. The family programs require acceptance and a willingness to change. As those with addictive disease seek to abstain from the use of alcohol and other drugs or gambling, the family member seeks acceptance, peace, and serenity.

Al-Anon was founded in 1951, sixteen years after the founding of Alcoholics Anonymous. It was established by Anne B. and by Lois W., the wife of Bill W., the cofounder of AA. Al-Anon is a twelve-step recovery and support program for the family and friends of alcoholics. The Preamble to the Twelve Steps explains the purpose of Al-Anon:

PREAMBLE

The Al-Anon Family Groups are a fellowship of relatives and friends of alcoholics who share their experience, strength, and hope in order to solve their common problems. We believe alcoholism is a family illness and that changed attitudes can aid recovery.

Al-Anon is not allied with any sect, denomination, political entity, organization, or institution; does not engage in any controversy; neither endorses nor opposes any cause. There are no dues for membership. Al-Anon is self-supporting through its own voluntary contributions.

Al-Anon has but one purpose: to help families of alcoholics. We do this by practicing the Twelve Steps, by welcoming and giving comfort to families of alcoholics, and by giving understanding and encouragement to the alcoholic.[1]**

While the primary focus in Al-Anon is on the recovery of those who suffer due to another's use of alcohol, the fellowship welcomes attendance by individuals impacted by a loved one's use of drugs to allow them to see if they can relate to the discussion and determine whether they may be able to benefit from the program.[2] If you wish to attend a meeting, you can mentally substitute your loved one's drug of choice for every reference to alcohol. The Al-Anon fellowship website notes that, based on its 2015 Membership Survey, about 40 percent of Al-Anon members first came to the program because of a relative or friend's drug problem, but that "85 percent of these members eventually realized that someone['s] drinking also negatively affected their lives."[3] This is consistent with the recognition that the problematic use of multiple substances, including alcohol, is a qualifier for an individual's attendance at AA

**From *How Al-Anon Works for Families & Friends of Alcoholics,* copyright 1995, 2008, by Al-Anon Family Group Headquarters, Inc., and reprinted with permission of Al-Anon Family Group Headquarters, Inc. Permission to reprint does not mean that Al-Anon Family Group Headquarters, Inc., has reviewed or approved the contents of this publication, or that Al-Anon Family Group Headquarters, Inc., necessarily agrees with the views expressed herein. Al-Anon is a program of recovery for families and friends of alcoholics—use of this excerpt in any non-Al-Anon context does not imply endorsement or affiliation by Al-Anon.

meetings. This concept effectively broadens the applicability of AA and Al-Anon despite their primary focus on alcohol.

Families Anonymous (FA), which was founded in 1971 by a group of parents concerned about substance abuse and addiction, is a twelve-step fellowship for all "who have known a feeling of desperation concerning the destructive behavior of someone very near to them." FA encourages participation by those who are concerned about another's use of drugs, alcohol, or related behaviors, even if a problem is only suspected. Nar-Anon also provides support to those who have known the desperation caused by another's use of drugs, and welcomes attendance by anyone who is experiencing "a problem of addiction in a relative or friend."[4] Nar-Anon can also be described as the companion program to NA. While AA focuses on recovery from alcohol, NA provides support to those seeking recovery from their use of drugs, including but not limited to alcohol. Similarly, Nar-Anon supports those who are powerless over another's use of any and all drugs, including alcohol.

Both Al-Anon and Nar-Anon have programs for teenagers impacted by another's disease. Alateen is a recovery program for the teenagers impacted by the alcoholism of another. Alateen meetings are facilitated and monitored by adult members of Al-Anon who have been certified as Al-Anon Members Involved in Alateen Service (AMIAS). The local meeting directories identify the age range served at specific meetings. Al-Anon also invites teenagers to attend regular Al-Anon meetings when no teen program is available. Teens between thirteen and eighteen may register to participate in Alateen Chat meetings.[5] Alateen states that maintaining a safe environment for teens is their "primary concern." Safety and behavioral standards for events are determined by area offices of Al-Anon.[6]

Narateen programs are designed for teenagers who have someone close to them who is an addict.[7] Narateen meetings are facilitated by adult members of Nar-Anon who have passed a background check and have been certified by the fellowship to act in that capacity. Narateen meetings are closed, that is, attendance is limited to teenagers who are coping with the addiction problems of a family member or friend.[8]

Gam-Anon is a family self-help group that offers support for a person's concerns about another's gambling problem. As explained on the program's website,

> Gam-Anon is a 12 Step self-help fellowship of men and women who have been affected by the gambling problem of another. We understand as perhaps few can. We are familiar with worry and sleepless nights and promises made only to be broken.
>
> We may have become fearful and uncertain as to how to cope with the deterioration in our lives and our relationships, the financial problems, and the debts caused by the gambling. We know that living with the effects of another's gambling can often be too devastating to bear without help.
>
> With the help of Gam-Anon, we find our way back to a normal way of thinking and living, whether or not our loved ones continue to gamble. We believe that a change in our attitudes is of boundless [help] . . . to us as well as to our gamblers.[9]

In the family fellowships, the twelve-step journey to recovery is based on and mirrors that of individuals in recovery fellowships. The parallel nature of the programs is best explained by a comparison of the Twelve Steps of AA and the Twelve Steps of the family fellowships. There is only a one-word difference between the Twelve Steps of AA and the Twelve Steps of Al-Anon. Specifically, the Twelfth Step of AA states that "having had a spiritual awakening as a result of the steps," members will try to carry the "message to alcoholics," while the Twelfth Step of Al-Anon references action to carry the message to "others" rather than to alcoholics as a result of the same awakening.

The Twelve Steps of FA are also virtually identical to those of AA:

FAMILIES ANONYMOUS TWELVE STEPS

We have found that our success in this program is determined by how well we accept and apply the following suggested Steps:

1. We admitted we were powerless over drugs and other people's lives—that **our** lives had become unmanageable.

2. Came to believe that a power greater than ourselves could restore us to sanity.

3. Made a decision to turn our will and our lives over to the care of God **as we understood Him.**

4. Made a searching and fearless moral inventory of ourselves.

5. Admitted to God, to ourselves, and to another human being the exact nature of our wrongs.

6. Were entirely ready to have God remove all of these defects of character.

7. Humbly asked Him to remove our shortcomings.

8. Made a list of all persons we had had harmed, and became willing to make amends to them all.

9. Made direct amends to such people, whenever possible, except when to do so would injure them or others.

10. Continued to take personal inventory, and when we were wrong, promptly admitted it.

11. Sought through prayer and meditation to improve our conscious contact with God as we understood Him, praying only for knowledge of His will for us and the power to carry that out.

12. Having had a spiritual awakening as a result of these Steps, we tried to carry this message to others and to practice these principles in all of our affairs.[10]***

Step One of FA is written more broadly than Step One of AA to (1) reference all drugs, not just alcohol; (2) emphasize that we are powerless over the use of drugs by others, not ourselves; and (3) emphasize, with italics, that it is *our* lives that have become unmanageable. Further, the Twelfth Step of FA, like that of Al-Anon, also calls for action to carry the message to others rather than just to alcoholics.

The parallel wording is not merely a matter of semantics. It is significant for several reasons. First, members of family fellowships and their loved ones who participate in a recovery fellowship share a common language and vocabulary. They can communicate with each other about the steps and principles of working a program in recovery and be understood. This shared knowledge helps to rebuild healthy communications and relationships with our family members. Second, the commonality aids our understanding and respect for the value of recovery fellowships to those who are battling addictive disease. Third, the universality of the programs levels the playing field, and brings us together with our loved ones as individuals seeking to improve ourselves. In other words, we all need to make changes, and in the context of addiction, recovery is not just for those who have abused alcohol or other drugs.

While participation in twelve-step programs of the family fellowship may bring us closer to our loved one, it is important to remember that the purpose of a family group is to help us accept the situation and our powerlessness to change it, and to achieve

---

*** Reprinted with permission of the Board of Directors of Families Anonymous, Inc. Excerpts from Families Anonymous World Service Board Approved literature may be reprinted only with such permission. Permission to reprint these excerpts does not imply that Families Anonymous, Inc., has reviewed or approved the contents of this publication or that Families Anonymous, Inc., agrees with the views expressed herein. Families Anonymous is a program of recovery for the families and friends of persons with a substance abuse problem or related behavioral problem; use of these excerpts in any non-Families Anonymous context does not imply endorsement by or affiliation with Families Anonymous, Inc.

our own serenity. These programs are not intended to promote the recovery of those suffering from addictive disease and do not help participants find out how to cure another's disease or solve a loved one's problems. Some people come to a family group meeting, leave frustrated because no one could tell them how to cure their loved one, and never return. Not only is it beyond the purpose of the family fellowships to help the person with addictive disease; solving the addict's problems is an objective that is outside of the family's control. The family fellowships are about our recovery, not theirs.

The process of recovery for family and friends is long and challenging, but it is easy to get started. First, you may wish to review the websites for Al-Anon, FA, Nar-Anon, and/or Gam-Anon. The family program websites have information explaining how and why the programs work. The individual sites identify the Twelve Steps as modified by the fellowship, explain what meetings are like, and describe the program's philosophy. The websites generally have links to the key readings that set forth the basic principles of the fellowship and are read aloud at each meeting. The websites also contain links to local directories that identify meetings by location and provide phone numbers to call for more specific information about meetings. After you have reviewed the information on the websites of the family fellowships, it is suggested that you attend some meetings. You will be welcomed and put at ease.

Differences in culture between family fellowships are, in part, attributable to the experiential background of the attendees. In family fellowships, the loved one who has brought you to the program is referred to as your qualifier. In many groups, regular attendees have the same familial relationship with their qualifiers, that is, the child, spouse, or parent of the qualifiers. This shared experience heightens the cohesion of the group. While the composition of each group varies, in my experience many Al-Anon members self-identify as adult children of alcoholics. Members may also be the spouse or partner of their qualifier. In FA, perhaps because it was established by parents of drug abusers and addicts, the typical meeting is often attended mostly by parents of those abusing or addicted to alcohol and other drugs. The experience of growing up in an alcoholic home is distinct from an initial experience of the disease as it impacts a teenaged child. For this reason, while you will be welcomed into any of the family fellowships, you may feel most understood and supported in a room of individuals whose point of view is based on similar experiences. Location may also drive your choice. There are, for example, more Al-Anon meetings than FA meetings. Similarly, if a Gam-Anon meeting is not available, FA might provide support for a person trying to cope with another's compulsive gambling.

In addition to the differences among fellowships, each individual group has its own personality, culture, and character. Often the culture of a meeting is driven by the personalities and experiences of its most active members. Philosophically, there is no group leader and the programs are based on the rotation of leadership. In other words, members take turns leading the meeting. Very often, however, one or more regular members set the tone of the meeting. It is suggested that you try different meetings to find not only the fellowship that suits your needs, but also the specific group that is the best fit for your situation and where you feel the most comfortable.

When attending a meeting for the first time, you may find it helpful to introduce yourself to the leader of the meeting (by first name only) and explain the reason you wish to attend. For example, you may simply say, "I am worried about my wife's drinking," or "I am concerned about my daughter's gambling." It will help to put you at ease and allow the members in attendance to reach out to you.

Initially, it may be awkward and difficult to attend meetings. Even though it is anonymous, it is hard to publicly admit the reality that your qualifier has a problem and that your life is unmanageable. Just try it. You have nothing to lose and a lot to gain. FA has words of welcome for newcomers that address this difficulty and demonstrate the welcome that will be made evident the first time that you step into a meeting of any of the fellowships:

TO THE NEWCOMER

Welcome to Families Anonymous. We know how you're hurting, because we too were once new in this fellowship. We were confused and in pain, but we found hope in our FA meetings.

We can't tell you what to do. We can only share our experiences with you and tell you how we found the strength to deal with our problems. Some of us have loved ones who are recovering from addictive disease. Others of us have loved ones who choose not to recover, at least for the present.

We've learned that we can lead fuller, richer lives by studying and practicing the Twelve Steps of Families Anonymous. The despair that brought us to this program no longer dominates our lives. We have learned that we have rights and deserve to be happy, but it's up to us to create that happiness.

These changes did not come about overnight. They happened because we attended our FA meetings, found sponsors, studied the Steps, made phone calls to other members, and turned to a Power greater than ourselves.

You are no longer alone. Welcome to Families Anonymous.[11]****

As we say in the program, "Keep coming back; it works if you work it and you're worth it." It is suggested you try at least six meetings before you give up on the concept or select your primary

---

**** Reprinted with permission of the Board of Directors of Families Anonymous, Inc. Excerpts from Families Anonymous World Service Board Approved literature may be reprinted only with such permission. Permission to reprint these excerpts does not imply that Families Anonymous, Inc., has reviewed or approved the contents of this publication or that Families Anonymous, Inc., agrees with the views expressed herein. Families Anonymous is a program of recovery for the families and friends of persons with a substance abuse problem or related behavioral problem; use of these excerpts in any non-Families Anonymous context does not imply endorsement by or affiliation with Families Anonymous, Inc.

"home" meeting. Remain open to new approaches and groups. A meeting that serves you well at the beginning may become less meaningful to you as you advance in your understanding of the program. Over time, you may come to prefer a more serious group that actively works the steps and embraces sponsorship.

Another way to get started is to use a daily meditation book and the other introductory literature published by the fellowships. The book *How Al-Anon Works for Families and Friends of Alcoholics*, published by Al-Anon, is an excellent guide to understanding the program and how it works. Al-Anon also publishes *One Day at a Time in Al-Anon* and *Courage to Change: One Day at a Time in Al-Anon II*. Both books have a reading for each day of the year and include a subject index to locate readings topically. FA also publishes a daily meditation book, *Today a Better Way*. These books are available at meetings and can be found on the fellowships' websites. The family fellowships also publish numerous other books, pamphlets, and materials to help individuals understand and practice the principles of the program, begin their own recovery, and cope with specific issues. The materials are generally available to view, download, or purchase on the websites of the fellowships.

The family fellowships use many slogans such as "One Day at a Time," "Let Go and Let God," "Take Care of Yourself," and "Keep It Simple." These slogans help newcomers understand the basics and help members cope with crises. It is important to note that the programs go far beyond these slogans and have far greater philosophical depth for those interested and willing to engage in further study and reflection.

To fully work a recovery program, you will need to do more than attend meetings. While the way you work your program will be individual to your needs and preferences, working a program in Al-Anon, FA, or any of the other family fellowships generally entails a study of the Twelve Steps and application of them to your own life. As set forth in Step Twelve, members learn to "practice these principles in all of our affairs." This does not happen instantly. Rather, it develops over time with study, reflection, and practice.

There are many ways to undertake a deeper study of the Twelve Steps. For example, the family fellowships publish pamphlets on the Twelve Steps and twelve-step workbooks to help members actively "work the steps." There is also an abundance of recovery information available to you. The family fellowships each publish a variety of literature. In addition, given the parallels between working the Twelve Steps of AA and those of the family fellowships, you can access the well-developed body of AA literature to work your own program. If an AA publication is discussing strategies for coping with loss, letting go of anger and resentment, or practicing mindfulness in recovery, you can consider the same strategies for maintaining your serenity. When reading from these sources, substitute the word "serenity" for "sobriety."

The meeting format allows time for the person leading the meeting to share their personal experiences and suggest a theme or issue for general discussion. It is strongly recommended that you volunteer to take the lead for a meeting. It is not necessary that you have significant experience before taking the lead, and it is suggested that you volunteer to do so after you have attended enough meetings to understand the basic concepts and meeting format. Generally, members sign up to do the lead in advance, allowing them time to prepare the lead. Many people find that preparing and presenting a lead gives them a significant opportunity to reflect on and process their own experiences. It often acts as catharsis to help the leader's growth in recovery and gives them an opportunity to receive additional support from the group.

You may also wish to seek a sponsor to guide you as you work the program and apply the steps to the specific challenges you face. As in AA, you can approach a member of your fellowship that you respect and ask him or her to sponsor you in the program. A sponsor works with the member, one-on-one, to facilitate the member's understanding and progress. Working with a sponsor also provides you with someone you can talk to about your individual situation and how to apply the twelve-step principles to your own life.

In addition to study, reflection, step work, and sponsorship, service to the group may be part of your recovery program. While acting as the lead for a meeting is one way to provide service, there are many other ways to do so. Members can provide service by helping to set up the room for meetings, managing the group's inventory of literature, reaching out to newcomers, or serving as the group's secretary or treasurer.

Many of the benefits of therapeutic groups identified by Dr. Irvin Yalom explain why attendance at self-help recovery meetings is so helpful for family members. Family members receive the same benefits as those received by individuals who participate in twelve-step recovery fellowships. There is an overwhelming feeling of relief when we walk into a room where everyone else understands the magnitude of the pain of seeing someone you love destroy his or her life with alcohol, drugs, or gambling. In other areas of our lives, most people do not understand the dysfunction brought into the family by addiction; however, in the rooms of Al-Anon, Nar-Anon, FA, and Gam-Anon, the new member will be immediately understood and welcomed. Meetings offer a safe place to share feelings, struggles, and frustrations in a nonjudgmental atmosphere under the protection of confidentiality.

One of the benefits of participation is the ability to learn new ways of approaching problems and coping with their situation. As a caution, however, it should be noted that family group members should not give advice. Members are not professionals, and their advice should not be taken as such. Caution is suggested when members present themselves as experts or seem certain of their view of what you should do. When attending meetings, it is suggested that you absorb the experiences of others, reflect on the views expressed, and then decide what is best for your own situation. As it is said in the closing statements that are part of the format for FA meetings, members "should take what you will, and leave the rest."

It has been said that individuals new to a twelve-step group should look for a sponsor or role model who has what they want. For those in family groups, what we truly want the most is recovery for our loved one. What we truly need, however, is serenity. Like those suffering from addictive disease, we should differentiate what we want from what we need. When you attend a meeting of a family fellowship, it might be tempting to give credence to the views of someone whose qualifier is in early recovery. The recovery of their loved one is not, however, a measure of the member's wisdom. Rather, when you attend meetings, listen carefully to identify those members who exhibit calm in the face of continued adversity and focus on what they say about how they were able to obtain and maintain their serenity. They are the ones who have what you need to survive.

The people in the rooms of the family fellowships who model serenity despite unsolved problems are often long-term members, but they are typically not the most vocal, nor do they impart advice. They will share their experiences and explain how they came to accept the situation and their powerlessness over it so that they could move on with their own lives despite the path chosen by their loved one. Remember, you are participating in the fellowship to change the things that you can. You can't change anyone else. You can change your reactions to what someone else does, and you can change your own actions.

The rewards that come with working the Twelve Steps of the family fellowships are set forth in the Promises. These Promises, like the journey itself, are adapted from and directly parallel to the twelve promises of AA:

THE TWELVE PROMISES OF FAMILIES ANONYMOUS
(Adapted from A.A. with permission)

These Promises will come true—sometimes quickly, sometimes gradually—as we study and work the Twelve Steps and practice making them a fundamental part of our lives.

1. We are going to know a freedom from worry and a new happiness.

2. We will not regret the past nor wish to shut the door on it.

3. We will comprehend the word *serenity*.

4. We will know peace.

5. No matter what we've been through, we will see how our experiences can benefit others.

6. Those feelings of resentment and self-pity will disappear.

7. We will lose interest in trying to change others, and gain an appreciation for those special people in our lives.

8. Self-righteousness will slip away.

9. Our attitudes and outlook on life will change.

10. Our insecurities and our fear of other people's opinions will leave us.

11. We will intuitively know how to handle situations which used to baffle us.

12. We will come to realize that God is doing for us what we could not do for ourselves.[12]*****

While the journey is difficult, the rewards of achieving serenity are profound.

***** Reprinted with permission of the Board of Directors of Families Anonymous, Inc. Excerpts from Families Anonymous World Service Board Approved literature may be reprinted only with such permission. Permission to reprint these excerpts does not imply that Families Anonymous, Inc., has reviewed or approved the contents of this publication or that Families Anonymous, Inc., agrees with the views expressed herein. Families Anonymous is a program of recovery for the families and friends of persons with a substance abuse problem or related behavioral problem; use of these excerpts in any non-Families Anonymous context does not imply endorsement by or affiliation with Families Anonymous, Inc.

RECOMMENDED RESOURCES

- Al-Anon Family Groups, http://www.al-anon.org/.

- Al-Anon Family Group, *How Al-Anon Works for Families and Friends of Alcoholics* (Virginia Beach, VA: Al-Anon Family Group Headquarters, Inc., 1995, 2008).

- Al-Anon Family Group, *One Day at a Time in Al-Anon* (Virginia Beach, VA: Al-Anon Family Group Headquarters, Inc., 1988).

- Al-Anon Family Group, *Courage to Change: One Day at a Time in Al-Anon-II* (Virginia Beach, VA: Al-Anon Family Group Headquarters, Inc., 1992).

- Families Anonymous Recovery Fellowship, http://www.familiesanonymous.org/.

- Families Anonymous, Inc., *Today a Better Way* (Des Plaines, IL: Families Anonymous, Inc., 1991, 2011, 2017).

- Gam-Anon International Service Office, Inc., http://www.gam-anon.org/.

- Gam-Anon International Service Office, Inc., *The Gam-Anon Way of Life: A Gam-Anon Manual* (Massapequa Park, NY: Gam-Anon International Service Office, Inc.).

- Nar-Anon Family Groups, http://www.nar-anon.org/.

CHAPTER 9 NOTES

1   Al-Anon Family Group, *How Al-Anon Works for Families and Friends of Alcoholics* (Virginia Beach, VA: Al-Anon Family Group Headquarters, Inc., 1995, 2008), iii.

2   Al-Anon, "My friend/loved one is a drug addict. Can I go to an Al-Anon meeting?" in "Frequently Asked Questions," https://al-anon.org/newcomers/faq/.

3   Ibid., "If I am concerned about someone's drug use, should I attend Al-Anon?"

4   Nar-Anon Family Groups (Nar-Anon), "Frequently Asked Questions," http://www.nar-anon.org/faq.

5   Al-Anon, "Find an Alateen Meeting," https://al-anon.org/al-anon-meetings/find-an-alateen-meeting/.

6   Al-Anon, "Alateen Participation in Events," https://al-anon.org/for-members/group-resources/alateen/alateen-participations-events/.

7   Al-Anon, "Narateen," http://www.nar-anon.org/narateen/.

8   Al-Anon, "Frequently Asked Questions—Narateen," https://static1.squarespace.com/static/53714efae4b0db8de8cdfaf8/t/55ef2628e4b0350add7 8c473/1441736232560/narateen-faq-revised.pdf.

9   Gam-Anon International Service Office, Inc., "Welcome, Gam-Anon," https://www.gam-anon.org/.

10 Families Anonymous, Inc., "The Twelve Steps of Families Anonymous," (Des Plaines, IL: Families Anonymous, Inc., 1977, 1981, rev. 9/2013), https://www.familiesanonymous.org/image/data/5003%204%20Twelve%20Steps%2009%20 2013.pdf.

11 Families Anonymous, Inc., *Today a Better Way* (Des Plaines, IL: Families Anonymous, Inc., 1991, 2011, 2017), 1.

12 Families Anonymous, Inc., "The Twelve Promises of Families Anonymous" (Des Plaines, IL: Families Anonymous, Inc., 1998, 2010, 2016, rev. 5/2017), https://familiesanonymous.org/image/data/The%20Twelve%20Promises%20of%20 FA%20-%202017_05.pdf.

10 HOW TO FACILITATE YOUR OWN RECOVERY

Recovery is a process for those battling the disease and for those around them. At the outset, all of us focus on the basics—finding support and coping strategies to get us through the immediate crisis and return to equilibrium. Over time, as our recovery progresses, we become less enmeshed with our loved ones and start to work toward personal growth as well as achievement of our own goals. A plan for recovery is self-designed and highly individual. It addresses personal needs and draws on individual strengths to foster healing, resilience, growth, and recovery. The immediate goal is not to achieve happiness, but rather to provide the means for us to accept the situation, obtain peace with what has occurred, and find joy in the moments of life.

DEFENSE MECHANISMS

Before defining a path to serenity, it may be helpful to clear away some of the defense mechanisms that we may unconsciously use to protect ourselves when coping with another's addiction. The subconscious employs various defenses to protect individuals from painful realities and unwanted thoughts and feelings. Many of these defenses are harmful. Foremost among these is denial. Individuals with addictive disease rationalize and minimize their problems to avoid awareness and acceptance of the fact that they have a problem. Similarly, denial of a loved one's problems with alcohol, other drugs, or behaviors may block us from recognizing a reality that is painful to us and can cause us to unconsciously resist any awareness of the problem. This is one reason why family members may deny clear evidence, or minimize or rationalize their loved one's behavior.

The response of family members to a loved one's disease may provoke the use of other unconscious defense mechanisms and maladaptive coping skills. These include projection, which occurs when one disavows his or her unwanted feelings and attributes or projects those feelings onto another. This defense may involve a shifting of blame. For example, a family member may deny his or her anger and attribute it to someone else in the family, saying, "I'm not angry, you are." Parents may project their feelings of powerlessness onto their teenage children. The parents may then perceive their teens as needy and dependent and attempt to control everything for them. Our anger at our loved one may also be displaced and directed toward someone else, either within the family, at work, or in the community. The stress of dealing with the crisis of another's addiction may also manifest itself in passive-aggressive behavior or escape through our own use of alcohol and other drugs. Self-reflection and awareness can help us to recognize our unhealthy responses to stress so we can consciously work on the development of more productive and healthy coping strategies.

STRESS MANAGEMENT IN CRISIS

When the problem of a loved one's use of substances or gambling is first identified, he or she is often in crisis and faces serious legal, health, financial, and social problems. We too are caught up in the crisis and experience trauma. We are consumed by worry when our loved one doesn't come home at night and avoids our calls and texts.

The phone rings in the middle of the night, jolting us awake and causing us to fear the worst. We dread calls from his or her school, landlord, supervisor, coworkers, and friends to report problems and concerns. One crisis follows another, and we experience repeated trauma. We physically react to that trauma: our heart rate increases, our blood pressure goes up, our fears for the future rise up, we feel nauseous, and we can't concentrate or sleep. Even when our loved ones are in recovery, we are retraumatized by the events and experiences that remind us of the prior trauma. Over time, we can develop practices that draw on our personal strengths and support a full life in long-term recovery from the trauma of addiction in the family. But first, we need to survive the crisis. There are many strategies for managing short-term chaos.

When in the midst of a crisis, take time to breathe. Sit quietly and try to relax your body, close your eyes and take in a deep breath, feel it all the way into your core, and exhale slowly. Repeat for a number of breaths until you feel restored. When managing a crisis, try to take care of your own health. While you don't want to let sleep give you an excuse to hide and avoid what needs to be done, try to get enough sleep. If you can't sleep at night, give yourself a break and take a nap during the daytime. Do your best to eat nutritionally and get some exercise. Exercise causes the release of life-affirming feel-good chemicals, including dopamine. It will help in a crisis. You may also wish to get a massage to ease some of your stress.

Getting out in nature and walking or sitting quietly can also help to restore you so that you can respond to the ongoing crisis. You can make a practice of setting aside some quiet time for yourself on a daily basis. The time can be used for simple reflection, focusing on your breath, or reading from a daily meditation book such as those published by the family fellowships. Whether you walk or set aside some personal time, turn off your phone or leave it behind. In most situations, you do not need to be constantly available. Take a break from all of it by setting a boundary and protecting yourself from interruption. You will feel a release by virtue of the fact that you know you will have at least a few minutes when you will not be called upon to respond to additional drama.

You may also wish to take a moratorium from the discussion of your qualifier within the family. It can be healing for a couple who has a son or daughter with addictive disease or the siblings or children of a person battling addiction to take a night or a weekend off when the qualifier and his or her problems are not to be mentioned. It provides an opportunity to take the focus off the addict and let the rest of the family reconnect. When dealing with a family member in crisis, it is also suggested that you try to prevent other members of the family from feeling neglected. For example, parents who are focused on the life-or-death struggle of an adolescent child may wish to make time to engage with the teen's siblings and attend to their interests and needs.

Research has shown that peer support is a major factor in helping people manage stress and recover from trauma. When you are in crisis, seek out a meeting of a family fellowship, get phone numbers of members whom you can call between meetings, and reach out to others who understand what you are going through. Online meeting and chat forums are another resource that is always available to you. You can also contact friends and family who you think will be supportive to you in the crisis. You may be surprised when individuals whom you did not expect to be supportive open up and share stories of addiction and recovery in their own families. Others with no experience of the disease will step up to support you, without question or judgment, in ways you did not imagine. There will, however, be some in your circle of family and friends who will disappoint you, even ostracize you. You will quickly be able to identify those individuals within your current network who will be supportive to you, and those who, from their own ignorance, will be nosy or judgmental. Narrow your current circle to those who will stand by you during this crisis and expand it to include others from your family fellowship. You owe no explanations to others, and you won't have the time or the energy to deal with friends or family who don't get it or who want to tell you what to do.

Similarly, while mindfulness is a better long-term strategy for achieving serenity in the face of another's addiction, mindless distraction does serve a function in crisis management. Online computer games, such as solitaire, can be repeated over and over to fill time, don't require long-term focus, and are distracting enough to provide a brief respite. Fantasy or futuristic fiction can also be absorbing and provide a break from reality. Humor is a defense mechanism that, when used appropriately, can be productive. Give yourself a break and watch a comedy. Laughter is therapeutic and, while it may surprise many, it is something that can be heard in meetings of the family fellowships.

Given our powerlessness over addiction, it is therapeutic to engage in an activity over which some control can be exercised. I learned to enjoy gardening when I realized that, unlike just about everything else in life, if it doesn't go well you can rip it out and start all over again. You may wish to tackle a project you can control and complete. If you choose to clean the clutter out of a drawer or closet, organize the basement or garage, paint a room, plant or weed a portion of your garden, build something, cook a favorite recipe, or wash and wax your car, you have at least the semblance of control over the outcome and you are rewarded with the immediate gratification of both finishing a task and exercising mastery over a problem.

HEALTH, FAMILY, PURPOSE, AND COMMUNITY

While quick fixes for dealing with crises are useful, more substance is required for the long haul. Over time, we can add depth to our toolbox by developing and working a recovery plan of our own. In this context, it is appropriate to revisit the meaning of recovery. SAMHSA defines recovery from addictive disease as "a process of change through which individuals improve their health and wellness, live self-directed lives, and strive to reach their full potential" in all aspects of their life: health, home, purpose, and community.[1] In the same way our loved ones put together an individualized, holistic plan to support a new lifestyle and enhance their personal growth, those of us whose lives have been totally disrupted by another's addiction may need to restructure our own lives to achieve *our* full potential. Our recovery plans, like theirs, should promote growth in all aspects of our lives. For our purposes, we can broaden the SAMHSA principles to replace the basic need for shelter with the need to stabilize and strengthen our family and personal relationships. Thus, for family members, personal recovery plans should address our own mental and physical health, relationships, purpose, and engagement in a broader community.

PROCESSING THE PAST TO CLEAR THE WAY FOR THE FUTURE

Health, for everyone in recovery as defined by SAMHSA, includes "making informed, healthy choices that support physical and emotional well-being."[2] To foster our own health, we may first need to process the past and clear the decks for new growth. To rebuild our lives, we need to let go of our guilt, anger, and resentments. In so doing, we will not only improve our health, but strengthen our family and personal relationships.

Armed with the knowledge that there is no single cause for the development of addictive disease and the fact that we did not cause our loved one's problem, we can try to release our guilt and forgive ourselves for making mistakes. We can accept our own failings, leave them in the past, focus on the here and now, and try to support our loved ones in the present with the hope of a healthy future. We may also be angry with our qualifiers for all of the harm their behavior has done to us. Anger is a normal human emotion, and we can acknowledge and accept those feelings in ourselves. The failure to do so can turn anger into resentment. Anger arising from a perceived injury turns into a resentment when it is allowed to fester, and the harm is relived over and over again, resulting in a feeling of permanent ill will. The keys to getting rid of anger and resentments lie in acceptance, empathy, and forgiveness. Understanding the disease model of addiction can allow us to change the narrative, see the situation differently, let go of the past, and forgive our loved ones.

The family members of those in treatment are sometimes asked to write a letter to their loved one to express how they feel and how the disease has impacted them. Professionals may use the letter as part of the therapeutic process to facilitate change by providing the client with a greater awareness of how his or her disease has affected others. The feelings of family members can also be addressed in therapeutic sessions involving the person in treatment and his or her family members. Some family members may find it beneficial to write a letter to their loved one even if their loved one is not in treatment or they have not been asked to do so by a therapist. Outside of the treatment process and in the absence of professional guidance, the letter should be written without the intention or purpose of delivery to their loved one. After the catharsis of getting his or her feelings on paper, the writer should destroy the letter. It may also help to let go of anger against a loved one by directing the power of one's emotions against the disease rather than the person. In other words, you may choose to write a letter to the disease. Others find it helpful to journal their thoughts and feelings.

When someone we love has addictive disease, we suffer the loss of our hopes and dreams for that person. We had envisioned a future that did not include the sad realities of substance dependence or problematic gambling. In our dreams, our loved ones took a traditional path with academic success, a good job, financial security, and a happy family life. Addiction destroyed those dreams, and life, at least as we expected it to unfold, will be forever changed. It is important for us to acknowledge the pain, recognize our sadness over the course of events, and grieve those losses. It is even more important that we prepare to embrace a new vision of the future where we can achieve our full potential, avoid expectations for our loved ones, and accept them for who they are. In other words, while things will be different than we planned, we can choose to embrace those differences.

In her book *Codependent No More*, Melody Beattie defines a codependent person as "one who has let another person's behavior affect him or her, and who is obsessed with controlling that person's behavior."[3] She also explains that codependent people may "care so deeply, and often destructively, about other people" that they forget "how to care for themselves."[4] To break this cycle, codependents need to accept that they are powerless to control another person's actions and detach from efforts to control that person's life. As is said in family fellowships, we need to detach with love.

Detachment is not disciplinary action, and it is different from "tough love." Detachment does not mean a lack of caring or resistance to action. To be detached does not mean we give up trying to facilitate needed treatment for our loved ones. Rather, detachment relates to our attitude. Detachment is rooted in acceptance of our powerlessness over the result of our intentional action. Detachment results from the decision to accept that, ultimately, our loved ones are responsible for their own lives, health, and happiness, as we are responsible for ours.

FOSTERING RESILIENCE

Resilience is the attribute that helps some people to recover quickly from difficult situations and allows them to remain focused and attentive and to complete tasks and achieve goals under difficult circumstances. Many of the traits that make some people better able to adapt following adversity can be practiced and learned. We can improve our mental health and strengthen our well-being by practicing habits that support resilience.

One of the major traits that promotes resilience is positivity. Positivity can be embraced by maintaining hope, trying to keep things in perspective, and taking a long-term, optimistic view of the future. Resilient people accept the reality of change and remain open to it. One way to increase positivity is to maintain a gratitude list, that is, a list of things you appreciate and are grateful for. Belief in yourself and confidence in your ability to handle situations also promotes personal strength and positivity. Efforts to keep your sense of humor may help you with a positive outlook.

Resilient people are often self-aware and acknowledge their emotions and feelings. They make plans and carry them out. If tasks seem overwhelming, it helps to break them down into smaller steps.

The practices of setting achievable goals, using problem-solving skills, considering alternative solutions, and taking decisive action all foster resilience and help individuals gain confidence as goals are accomplished.

Developing a community of positive peer support has been found to reinforce resilience. The need for a supportive network is a common thread in all aspects of this discussion. Peer support not only helps in crisis management and the development of resilience, it is one of the four factors that should be addressed in a recovery plan as defined by SAMHSA. Community, according to the SAMHSA definition of recovery, means "having relationships and social networks that provide support, friendship, love, and hope."[5] The importance of community engagement and peer support underscores the value of participation in twelve-step family groups or finding some other way to become part of a community or group, as well as the necessity of building your own individual support network.

MINDFULNESS AND MEDITATION

Mindfulness is a practice that originated as part of the Buddhist tradition. In this context, Buddhism is not a religion, but a spiritual practice and way of life. The Buddha, who lived in the sixth century BC, developed a path to enlightenment and defined the practices and principles that form the basis of Buddhist practices. The Buddha taught that there always will be suffering in life and what matters is the way that we, as humans, respond to suffering. The Buddha also taught that everything in life is impermanent and suffering is the result of selfish desires and a thirst for impermanent things.

Buddhist meditation incorporates mindfulness. Mindfulness is the practice of living in the moment and not reflecting on the past or speculating about the future. Mindfulness is not, however, based on a conscious focus on what is happening. Rather, mindfulness occurs when you lose yourself in what you are doing.[6] This simple principle is a powerful tool for those of us in recovery from another's addiction. Find something you can lose yourself in. The solution will be different for every individual. Some find mindfulness in the creative arts, painting, drawing, sewing, knitting, or making pottery. Others find they lose themselves in building and maintenance projects, such as woodworking, renovation, remodeling, interior or exterior painting, or in gardening or cooking. The principle is the same as managing a crisis—find a manageable project that absorbs your attention. Whether you renew an existing passion or seek out a new one, activities that engage you in the task at hand will provide a break from your worries and restore you. You may also advance your recovery and growth by finding a new passion or purpose.

Meditation is a practice in which you acknowledge your thoughts and feelings, accept them nonjudgmentally, and let them go. In his classic book on Buddhism, *What the Buddha Taught*, Walpola Sri Rahula explains a simple form of meditation that is based on an awareness of the breath. It builds on the simple concept of taking a moment to pause and breathe deeply when in crisis. To practice a breathing meditation, sit in a chair and hold yourself upright, let your hands rest comfortably in your lap, and relax your shoulders. You may close your eyes or gaze downward. Focus on your breath; try to note only an awareness of your breath, while excluding other thoughts. At first your mind will wander repeatedly. Sri Rahula predicts that if you practice this exercise twice a day for about five or ten minutes each time, you will become better able to concentrate only on your breath and will lose yourself "completely in the mindfulness of breathing" and your will feel at peace, calm, and tranquil.[7] There are many resources available if you wish to try meditation. Many community centers offer wellness courses on meditation, numerous books have been written on how to begin a practice, and videos providing guided meditations are available online.

Mindfulness and meditation not only support personal health and recovery, but these practices may also help us strengthen our relationships by increasing our compassionate connection with others. Ethical conduct, which is an essential component of Buddhism, includes the concept of love and compassion for all living beings. A Buddhist teacher, Narayan Helen Liebenson, explains that compassion is a caring response to another's suffering that includes openness, vulnerability, and strength. She describes an approach to the suffering of others in which tenderness is "balanced with a sense of confidence" to allow a wise and skillful response to others. The teacher further explains that rather than "becoming paralyzed and frozen," we can "hold the distress of others in such a way as to be effective in our efforts to help."[8]

Buddhist practices also include the concept of "metta meditation," in which phrases and thoughts are used to cultivate positive feelings toward ourselves and others. While sitting comfortably, you can repeat metta phrases to yourself and channel your thoughts and emotions to yourself and to your loved ones:

> May I be happy. May I be well. May I be safe. May I be peaceful and at ease.

> May you be happy. May you be well. May you be safe. May you be peaceful and at ease.[9]

In much the same way as a silent recitation of the Serenity Prayer, you can use metta phrases to calm and focus yourself in difficult times. There are numerous metta phrases that can be used in this fashion.

FINDING PURPOSE

In recovery, we take care of our health, foster our family relationships, and develop a support network. Finding purpose is the final component of recovery as defined by SAMHSA. Purpose in this context means "conducting meaningful daily activities, such as a job, school volunteerism, family caretaking, or creative endeavors, and the independence, income, and resources to participate in society."[10] Having been consumed by another's disease and, perhaps, having neglected our work, plans, goals, or dreams, in recovery we have a chance to reexamine our mission and our purpose. Recovery provides an opportunity to redefine ourselves, try something new, or return to what we gave up. Now is the time to reach our full potential in whatever capacity we choose.

BUILDING YOUR PERSONAL RECOVERY PROGRAM

There is no single route to wellness for family members seeking peace and serenity. An individual recovery plan may include many separate components. Some will choose to work the Twelve Steps of a family fellowship to support their mental health and well-being, while others may choose to receive individual therapy, seek couples or family counseling jointly with their qualifier, or seek counseling with a religious or spiritual adviser. Choose your tools and define a program that meets your needs, builds on your strengths, and serves your interests and preferences while supporting personal growth in each of the dimensions of recovery: health, relationships, purpose, and community.

A CHECKLIST: 50 RECOVERY TOOLS

☐ Work a twelve-step program.

☐ Define a personal or peer support network.

☐ Engage in individual, couples, or family counseling.

☐ Try an online meeting.

☐ Just breathe.

☐ Call someone from family group.

☐ Consult your spiritual or religious advisor.

☐ Plan regular exercise.

☐ Embrace nature.

☐ Maintain a gratitude list.

☐ Make time for yourself.

☐ Practice mindfulness.

☐ Find activities that engage your focus in the here and now.

☐ Practice breathing meditation.

☐ Study the art of mediation and develop a meditation practice.

- ☐ Practice yoga or tai chi.
- ☐ Make time for daily reflection.
- ☐ Seek adequate sleep and strive for good nutrition.
- ☐ Let go of maladaptive behaviors.
- ☐ Get regular checkups to maintain your health.
- ☐ Process guilt.
- ☐ Let go of anger and resentments.
- ☐ Forgive yourself and others.
- ☐ Grieve your losses.
- ☐ Recognize and accept your feelings and emotions.
- ☐ Foster positivity.
- ☐ Exercise compassion.
- ☐ Empathize with others.
- ☐ Believe in yourself and your abilities.
- ☐ Take a walk.
- ☐ Set realistic goals and achieve them.
- ☐ Be decisive.
- ☐ Laugh and keep a sense of humor.
- ☐ Accept what you cannot change.
- ☐ Find and develop your purpose.
- ☐ Attend an open AA meeting.
- ☐ Strengthen family relationships.
- ☐ Improve communication style in the family.
- ☐ Set appropriate boundaries.
- ☐ Set a temporary moratorium on family discussion of your qualifier.
- ☐ Devote time to family members other than your qualifier.
- ☐ Be hopeful.
- ☐ Learn a new skill.
- ☐ Return to past activities that gave you pleasure but that you gave up.
- ☐ Detach from your loved one's problems.
- ☐ Be flexible.
- ☐ Recite the Serenity Prayer to yourself.
- ☐ Silently reflect on a metta meditation for your loved one.
- ☐ Educate yourself about recovery.
- ☐ Let go of feelings by writing them down.

RECOMMENDED RESOURCES

- Jack Kornfield, "Meditations," https://jackkornfield. com/meditations/.

- Sharon Salzberg, *Real Happiness: The Power of Meditation, a 28-Day Program* (New York: Workman Publishing, 2011).

- Walpola Sri Rahula, *What the Buddha Taught*, 2nd ed. (New York: Grove Press, 1974).

CHAPTER 10 NOTES

1   SAMHSA, "Recovery and Recovery Support."

2   Ibid.

3   Melody Beattie, *Codependent No More*, 2nd ed. (Center City, MN: Hazelden, 1986, 1992), 34.

4   Ibid., 5.

5   SAMHSA, "Recovery and Recovery Support."

6   Walpola Sri Rahula, *What the Buddha Taught*, 2nd ed. (New York: Grove Press, 1974), 71.

7   Ibid., 69–71.

8   Lion's Roar Staff, "Ask the Teachers: How Can I Accept the Suffering of Others?" *Lion's Roar, Buddhist Wisdom for Our Time*, July 21, 2017, https://www.lionsroar. com/ask-the-teachers-35/.

9   Metta Institute, "Metta Meditation," http://www.mettainstitute.org/ mettameditation.html.

10 SAMHSA, "Recovery and Recovery Support."

PART THREE

INFORMED
ACTION

Bringing It All Together to Support
Recovery for Yourself and Your Loved One

*Knowledge is of no value unless
you put it into practice.*

— ANTON CHEKHOV —

11

MAKING REASONED DECISIONS TO FACILITATE TREATMENT

Armed with knowledge about the disease, treatment, and recovery and having come to truly accept that we are powerless over the result, we can take informed action to support the recovery of our loved ones and ourselves. Thus, in the final part of this book, the discussion shifts from the academic to the practical and examines how we can support another's recovery from addictive disease while protecting our own serenity.

ACTION WITHOUT ENABLING; LETTING GO WITHOUT GIVING UP

The family fellowships caution us not to enable our loved ones. Enabling is doing things for others that they can do for themselves and protecting them from the consequences of their choices. Enabling includes a variety of behaviors, such as making excuses for loved ones, denying or minimizing their issues, fixing their legal problems, and giving them money or shelter, effectively providing the means for them to continue their habit. While, as it is said in the family fellowships, we need to "let go" of those we care about, stop trying to control their behavior, and "turn our lives over to the care of" our higher power, that does not mean we have an excuse for inaction in the face of a life-threatening illness. Taking informed action to facilitate treatment for someone with a medical disease is not enabling.

Effective action is rooted in acceptance of the fact that it is not in our power to bring about change in another person. The family members of cancer patients know they cannot control the outcome of evidence-based cancer treatment, but they do not hesitate to help their loved ones to find quality care and do everything they can to support their battle against the disease. No one says they are enabling the cancer. In the same way, we can support our loved ones in their fight against addictive disease, even though we have detached from the result and accept that we are powerless over whether or not they survive the disease.

THE INITIAL INVESTIGATION

Faced with evidence that another's addictive behaviors have become problematic, the initial challenge is identification of the nature of the problem presented and, if warranted, finding and securing his or her admission to an appropriate treatment program. The investigative process is influenced by whether the person you are concerned about is a minor who can be placed into treatment by a parent or legal guardian without his or her consent, or an adult who, short of a court order, must consent to treatment.

Adolescents

If a problem is suspected, it is suggested that you conduct an investigation, talk to your teen, and take your loved one to a physician or addiction professional for a consultation and drug testing. One way to obtain more information before talking to your child is to partner with a trusted teacher, counselor, or social worker at your child's school to see if school personnel have identified any patterns of behavior that may help you to evaluate the situation. They will be able to provide objective facts that you can put into the context of what you have observed at home.

NIDA does not recommend a confrontational approach or intervention with adolescents. Rather, NIDA suggests that parents seek to create "incentives" to encourage teens to go to the doctor because they may be more responsive to a professional's recommendations than those of their parents. NIDA specifically cautions that "if your teen has a driver's license and you suspect drug use, you should take away your child's driving privileges" to avoid the potential for tragedy. At the same time, however, NIDA notes that driving privileges may present an incentive to gain your child's agreement to be evaluated for substance use by a professional.[1] In other words, when cause for concern exists, you may choose to tell your teen that driving privileges are off the table unless the concerns are resolved by a drug test and evaluation.

In facing this disease, it is often advisable to start with the most simple, straightforward approach and work your way up to more specialized interventions. Thus, unless you are presented with a medical emergency, your teen's primary care provider (PCP) is a good initial point person to facilitate an evaluation of the issues presented. The PCP can screen your child and arrange for drug tests. In a screening, a physician asks questions privately, one-on-one, to elicit detailed information about the teen's use of substances and risky behaviors such as driving under the influence. The physician can discuss the risks of substance use with your child and provide brief counseling, intervention, and referrals, if appropriate. It is suggested that you advise the PCP of the circumstances that have given rise to your concern in advance of the appointment so the doctor has sufficient information on which to base a thorough inquiry. It is helpful, according to NIDA, to ask your child's doctor in advance if he or she is comfortable screening for drugs and making any necessary referrals, and if not, to seek a referral to a doctor or counselor familiar with addiction.[2]

Most doctors are not experts in SUDs, and parents may wish to consult with experts in the addiction field in lieu of consulting with the child's PCP or after a preliminary investigation or drug test confirms the existence of a problem. NIDA recommends use of the SAMHSA Behavioral Health Treatment Locator to identify potential providers. The online tool can be used to search for adolescent programs by geographic location. While the tool does not identify individual doctors, it will identify programs that treat adolescents and provide links to their websites. Program websites typically provide information on how to proceed when a drug problem is suspected and provide a number to call for additional information on how to arrange for a preliminary evaluation or consultation and drug testing. See the SAMHSA Behavioral Health Treatment Services Locator, https:// findtreatment.samhsa.gov/, to search for specific programs. SAMHSA also maintains a twenty-four-hour toll-free treatment referral helpline: 1-800-662-HELP (4357). Your teen's PCP or counselors at your child's school may also be able to provide you with referrals to addiction professionals.

While some teens may open up to a professional, given the attributes of the disease, others continue to deny, falsify, and hide their use from everyone, including their parents and their doctors. For this reason, a preliminary investigation of suspected substance use will likely include urine or blood tests. When you have a reason for concern, ask your teen's PCP or another treatment provider to order lab tests to screen for indications of drug use. A basic ten-panel urine test screens for the presence of different classes of drugs, including marijuana. Many drugs pass through the system quickly and, depending on timing, may not show up on the results of a urine test. THC is more easily detectable because it remains in the system for a longer period of time, often up to a month. In chronic users, THC builds up over time and may be identified in urine as long as sixty days after the cessation of chronic use.[3] A separate test is necessary to detect the presence of synthetic cannabinoids. An alcohol EtG test of urine detects alcohol use for about eighty hours after ingestion. The test is generally used to monitor sobriety in clinical settings and in connection with criminal proceedings.

It may be best not to alert your adolescent to the reason for a medical visit so that no attempts will be made to influence the result of a urine test. You may also wish to schedule a test after the weekend or following a party or special event to obtain a more accurate picture of what, if anything, is being ingested. The physician or counselor can also assist you in arranging for a series of tests at random intervals. While over-the-counter test kits are available at the drugstore, it is much easier for you to let medical professionals or lab personnel supervise the provision of a urine sample, rather than try to oversee the process at home.

Not only is THC detectable in urine for a long time after use, routine tests also measure the concentration of THC in the sample. This makes it possible to quantify changes (decreases or increases) in marijuana usage. If your child receives a drug test that is positive for cannabis, request that the lab provide the specific level of THC detected. This number will indicate whether the exposure was likely to have built up over time from repeated use. The Mayo Clinic states that a urine test with a concentration of tetrahydrocannabinol carboxylic acid (THC-COOH) less than 3.0 ng/mL is negative, while a concentration of more than 100.0 ng/mL "indicates relatively recent use, probably within the past 7 days," and levels of THC-COOH greater than 500.0 ng/mL "suggest chronic and recent use."[4] If the potency is high, you will have confirmation of regular, continuing use. The first test result will also provide you with a baseline. Later tests will reveal a pattern that may be indicative of declining, continued, or increased use. It is suggested that you keep a record of the date of each test and the potency of THC detected to help you to track patterns of use over time.

Because the concentration of THC in urine can be easily detected, routine annual drug tests for all adolescents would permit the early detection of chronic cannabis use. The results of the 2016 NSDUH indicate that 6.5 percent of adolescents between twelve and seventeen were current users of marijuana in 2016.[5] Similarly, the 2016 MTF survey supports the finding that 6 percent of twelfth graders reported current daily use of marijuana (defined as use of marijuana on at least twenty days during the prior thirty-day period). The MTF survey results indicate that 14 percent of 2016 twelfth graders reported that they had met the criteria of daily use for at least one month at some time in the past, even if they were not current daily users.[6] Given this prevalence, routine annual testing of the entire adolescent population would provide an opportunity for identification of the six to fourteen out of every 100 teenagers who are at risk for the serious health consequences arising from the regular use of marijuana beginning in adolescence. It is not, however, current pediatric practice to routinely test all adolescents for drugs.

Adults

Ideally, adults will be involved in the decision to seek treatment. If you are worried about an adult's substance use, NIDA suggests that you try to talk to him or her about your concerns and refer the individual to a self-assessment tool on the NIDA website.[7] Similarly, the website of the National Council on Problem Gambling includes the ten-question NORC Diagnostic Screen for Gambling Problems–Self Administered (NODS-SA). The NODS-SA was developed as a self-assessment tool based on the criteria of the *DSM-IV* for diagnosis of pathological gambling, to assist individuals in determining whether to modify or seek help for their gambling behaviors.[8]

Television programs and media reports refer to the staging of interventions to confront individuals who are in need of treatment. NIDA cautions that "there is no evidence that confrontational 'interventions' are effective at convincing people they have a problem or motivating them to change." NIDA continues, stating that it is "possible for such confrontational encounters to escalate into violence or backfire in other ways."[9] In lieu of confrontational approaches, and consistent with its advice for adolescents, NIDA suggests trying to create incentives to motivate adults to consult a doctor. In this regard, NIDA notes that adults may be more willing to listen to the objective recommendations of a medical professional than the often emotionally charged opinions of family and friends. Medical visits provide the opportunity for a screening and brief intervention with referrals, if warranted.

It is appropriate for an adult to consult with his or her PCP about substance use. Should your loved one wish to consult an addiction specialist, NIDA suggests use of the directory of the Academy Board of Addiction Medicine (ABAM), which certifies physicians in various disciplines who have knowledge of addiction medicine. The directory can be searched by geographic location to identify member physicians. See ABAM, https://www.abam.net/about/. Similarly, the website of the American Board of Addiction Psychiatry also provides a list of providers by state under the link for patient resources. See https://www.aaap.org/patient-resources/find-a-specialist/.[10] The SAMHSA treatment locator can also be used to identify knowledgeable providers as a stepping-stone to identification of an individual counselor.

Your adult qualifier may often be unwilling to discuss the issue or consider talking to a professional. In that event, it is suggested that you remain opportunistic and use circumstances as leverage to facilitate his or her willingness to take the next step. With adults, the consequences of the person's abuse of drugs or problematic gambling may narrow his or her choices to the extent that he or she may consent to an assessment and treatment even if he or she denies a problem and has no desire to change. You may also be able to foster motivation in adults by setting appropriate boundaries. For example, things may be so untenable that, to protect your own safety and security, you advise the person you are worried about that he or she cannot live with you unless he or she stops using. You may also give someone a choice to go into treatment or leave home. It may be appropriate to tell your adult child that you refuse to support their habit and that as a result you cannot give them any money or pay their rent, but that you will pay for them to enter a treatment program. Keep in mind, however, that when you give a choice, you are also providing an ultimatum. You don't want to do it unless you are willing to follow through. If the boundary is crossed, you need to enforce the consequence, or you will teach your qualifier that your boundaries mean nothing and that you can be taken advantage of.

NIDA suggests you do research ahead of time to identify programs that might be appropriate for your loved one, in the hope that what you find might appeal to him or her and help motivate entry into treatment.[11] Individuals under the influence of alcohol and other drugs are unpredictable, and your loved one may cycle through different emotions and, at his or her most vulnerable, may express willingness for treatment. You want to take advantage of any short-term opportunity presented by a fleeting acceptance of the need for treatment. You often need to act quickly before your loved one cycles back into use and avoidance. If you have done advance research, you will have a platform from which to move forward when an opportunity presents itself.

HOW TO CHOOSE APPROPRIATE TREATMENT PROVIDERS

As you begin to investigate your options, it is helpful to remember you will maximize insurance coverage for services if you use providers who are in the insurer's preferred network. Most insurers have an online directory of preferred providers, which is a good place to start a search for appropriate care. If an initial investigation, evaluation, or drug test indicates that a substance use problem may be present, the next step is to obtain a clinical assessment. The

SAMHSA behavioral treatment locator does not have a search filter for assessments, but it is nevertheless an excellent tool to identify providers who offer assessments. Most treatment programs provide a telephone number you can call to talk to someone about your situation, find out how the program handles the assessment process, the fees and costs involved, and whether any applicable insurance coverage is accepted. Calling for a consultation does not commit you to using the facility. You have nothing to lose by investigating multiple options and gathering information to assist you in making an informed choice.

Remember, a clinical assessment is a preliminary, diagnostic step and assessments can be conducted by any certified professional. By seeking an assessment, you are not committing to treatment at the same facility. Rather, your goal is to obtain a clinical diagnosis and recommendations for the appropriate level of care and placement. Some providers will conduct an assessment over the phone. If possible, however, an in-person assessment is preferable because it will permit the counselor or physician to observe your loved one's demeanor during the interview.

A clinical assessment may result in a diagnosis of a mild, moderate, or severe SUD or gambling disorder and recommendations for treatment at an appropriate level of care. Based on an understanding of the diagnostic criteria for identification of an addictive disorder and the levels of care and types of treatment, you have the knowledge to consider whether the care recommendations are commensurate with your loved one's needs and specific diagnosis. In other words, you have the tools to ask informed questions about the recommendations. For example, you can ask why IOP is recommended for a severe SUD and whether inpatient treatment should be considered.

You can't control the disease, but you can conduct a diligent and rigorous investigation of treatment options. Generally, professionals working in the addiction field are passionate about what they do and want to help those in need of services. Despite their mission, expertise, and commitment, not every program represents the best choice for the specific needs of an individual. Thus, even if the counselor who conducted the assessment recommends treatment at the facility where it was performed, you should gather as much information as possible about a variety of treatment options. Whether you are looking for a program for adolescents or adults, it is suggested that you investigate the full range of options identified from all of the available sources, that is, the insurer's network, the SAMHSA treatment locator, recommendations received from the PCP, a teenager's school, an addiction specialist, and others. You do not need to confine your search to your geographic location and may wish to consider programs in other states. In some cases, it may be advisable for your loved one to be distant from the people, places, and things associated with use. Most providers will arrange to have someone meet clients at the airport.

The SAMHSA treatment locator is a valuable tool for locating programs for both adolescents and adults. The general results for a geographic area can be narrowed to meet many different specifications, including type of treatment, populations served, and financial considerations such as types of insurance, benefits accepted, and financing options. Based on your knowledge of the disease and the treatment options available, you can tailor a search to the specific type of treatment that will provide the best fit for your loved one. The process illustrates how an understanding of the drugs of abuse, the criteria for diagnosis of an addictive disease, the underlying causes, the levels of care, and the types and modalities of treatment supports informed decision making in identifying a provider to meet the specific needs presented.

Some providers reduce the cost of services on a sliding scale based on income. You can discuss these options with the provider in advance of treatment. NIDA also suggests using the SAMHSA hotline (1-800-662-4357) to inquire about low-cost and zero-cost treatment options in your area. Further, according to NIDA, you can contact your state substance abuse agency to explore the availability of affordable treatment options. A SAMHSA tool identifies the appropriate agency in each state. See State Agency Locator, https://findtreatment.samhsa.gov/locator/stateagencies.[12]

SAMHSA has two other search tools to identify programs and physicians offering MAT treatment for opioid disorders. SAMHSA's Buprenorphine Treatment Practitioner Locator allows a search by zip code or city and state to identify practitioners who are authorized to prescribe buprenorphine in the treatment of opioid use disorders. See www.samhsa.gov/medication-assisted-treatment/physician-program-data/treatment-physician-locator. SAMHSA also maintains an Opioid Treatment Program Directory. See dpt2.samhsa.gov/treatment/. The US Department of Veterans Affairs provides an online tool to search for SUD treatment for veterans. See https://www.va.gov/directory/guide/SUD.asp.

Notably, the SAMHSA treatment locator contains a filter that allows a specific search for providers that treat gambling disorders. Numerous resources are also available on the website of NCPG to assist individuals to locate providers that treat gambling disorders. The site contains links to a directory of certified gambling counselors, links to state affiliates of NCPG, a list of treatment facilities, and tips for choosing a treatment provider.[13] NCPG operates a National Problem Gambling Helpline Network (1-800-522-4700) as well as text, chat, and an online forum for "those seeking help for a gambling problem."[14]

Ideally, it is best to involve your loved one in treatment decisions. At the outset, when your qualifier remains resistant to treatment, it may not be practical or productive to leave the choice up to him or her. Your loved one may choose a program because of its location in a warm climate, or a perception of which program is the shortest and least intrusive, or which gives clients the most freedom. As they progress through levels of care, however, those in treatment are empowered by making their own decisions. This is part of our work, as family members, to let go of control and cede responsibility to our loved ones as they manage their own health, well-being, and recovery. In the complex world of modern healthcare, however, those facing a serious illness need a strong advocate until they are healthy enough to navigate the system on their own behalf.

After you have identified a universe of potential options, it is suggested that you conduct a detailed review of each program to compare the services offered with the needs presented. You may find it helpful to create a spreadsheet to compare the features and costs as well as the pros and cons of different programs. A good place to start a comparative evaluation is with a review of the websites of the potential providers, which should provide a general description of the programs offered, the projected length of treatment, the philosophy of care, and cost. After a preliminary overview of a range of options, you will be positioned to obtain a better understanding about the depth of services offered when you speak with a program representative.

As part of your inquiry, you will want to understand fees, financing options, and whether the program bills insurance and advocates for you with the insurer. Under law, insurance coverage must afford coverage for treatment of SUDs on par with the treatment of other medical conditions; however, the need for the service must be demonstrated and care must usually be precertified. While your coverage may provide treatment for what appears to be a generous number of days, treatment for the maximum number of covered days for treatment of an SUD is not guaranteed by the insurer. Rather, only those days that are authorized as necessary by the insurer will be covered. Insurers may dole out authorization for care in periods of days, rather than providing authorization for a full treatment program of twenty-eight days or more. Typically, insurers are more optimistic than providers about the outcome following a short period of treatment and can deny authorization for additional days of service before the treatment provider believes that discharge is warranted. Generally, the provider is responsible to obtain precertification and continued documentation of the need for care.

It is suggested that you ask potential providers how they measure the success of their programs and view their answers in the context of your understanding that the success rate for treatment is between 40 and 60 percent. Some may use the percentage of clients who complete treatment as a measure of success. You are far more interested in whether clients sustain their recovery after treatment. Some providers may report that they reach out to graduates at periodic intervals over a period of years to check in and ask if they continue to work a program in recovery. A program that uses a questionable method of measuring its success or that claims a success rate far over the average may lack credibility, and any claim that a program cures addiction should end the discussion.

It is suggested that you investigate and research all potential options and identify the best fit for your loved one's needs and financial means. Don't be afraid to ask questions. Treatment is expensive, and you don't always get multiple chances to facilitate another's care, so you want to get it right. While your understanding of treatment options and the underlying needs of your loved one will drive your specific inquiries, the following checklist is offered to aid you in gathering information for the purpose of comparing options:

1. What is the program's philosophy of care? Is it evidence-based, abstinence-based, or based on harm reduction principles?

2. Does treatment incorporate a twelve-step approach to recovery, and if so, how are the Twelve Steps integrated into the program? Do clients attend meetings on-site and/or off-site?

3. What types of therapy are used, for example, CBT, group, motivational interviewing, or MAT?

4. How are co-occurring disorders treated?

5. How does the program provide TIC?

6. How does the program address the needs of a specific population to which your loved one belongs (e.g., veterans, women, trauma survivors, LGBTQ community, or older adults)?

7. How and with what frequency do clients receive individual therapy and group therapy? What are the credentials of those who provide therapy and lead the groups?

8. What, if any, skills training is provided for clients?

9. What connections are made with RSS to support recovery after discharge?

10. What is the projected length of treatment?

11. Is there an educational program for family members?

12. Will couples therapy or family sessions be scheduled?

13. Is the family involved in discharge planning?

14. Are there financing options; are applicable benefits or insurance accepted?

15. Does the program obtain insurance precertifications and advocate for the client with the insurer?

16. How is the success of the program measured, and what do the results of those measurements indicate?

A number of additional considerations are presented in connection with the review of long-term residential programs, halfway houses, sober-living facilities, therapeutic boarding schools, and nontraditional treatment programs. Notably, the SAMHSA treatment locator includes filters for long-term residential and sober-living programs. While many wilderness and other nontraditional programs offer exceptional care and meaningful therapeutic experiences, you will want to dig deep and get as much information as possible about any nontraditional programs that you are considering, particularly those for adolescents.

Generally, staff biographies detail the credentials and qualifications of the individuals who are running the program. Certifications, which may be represented by abbreviations, vary by state. If you do an internet search of the letters contained in the abbreviation and the state of licensure, you will gain an understanding of the credentials of the staff. It is suggested you identify who among the staff is credentialed in the addiction field and those who hold other complementary professional credentials. It is also advisable to understand how often clients receive individual counseling and who provides the counseling. You will want to know if there is a physician who provides medical oversight and, if applicable, how care is provided for co-occurring disorders.

Many programs, particularly those providing treatment to adolescents, use peer coaches or mentors to support programming for clients. A coach may be an individual who does not have any training as a drug counselor, but who is roughly the same age as program participants or slightly older and is in recovery from an SUD. Coaches can model behavior for clients and support their struggles in the program. Peer mentors or coaches can be a valuable asset to those in treatment because they have credibility with clients. In other words, those in treatment feel they can relate to and trust a more experienced peer. It is suggested, however, that you ask the provider about the basic qualifications for hiring nonprofessional staff. For example, a program that hires coaches who have lived independently in the community and have sustained recovery for a period of years will likely provide far stronger support than recent graduates of the same program who have "stayed on" to act as coaches in the program without having lived outside of the controlled environment of the treatment center.

For long-term care, many providers charge fees for the whole program rather than per day of service. It is advisable to understand the program rules for penalties and whether there is a refund of any prepaid fees if your loved one leaves treatment voluntarily or is dismissed from the program. You will want to ask how the program handles rule enforcement, how violations are disciplined, and what behavior constitutes grounds for dismissal from the program. In that same vein, you would like to know what percentage of patients leave voluntarily before completion of treatment and what percentage are expelled. Some programs may offer references. While privacy needs may explain the absence of references, some programs serving adolescents have lists of parents who placed their teens in the program and who have volunteered to discuss their experiences.

It is also easy to conduct an internet search on treatment facilities. You may be surprised to find press reports in local media about a program you are considering. Press reports may demonstrate good relations between the facility and the community. For example, the program may have received accolades or awards, its directors may serve on local boards, or its participants may have provided community service. You may also find reports about accidents or injuries at the site, lawsuits, settlements, or reports of former program participants who have caused problems in the community after leaving treatment. You simply want to exercise due diligence to see if the program has made the local news.

Since your loved ones, particularly young adults, may develop a community of support in the area where they receive treatment, they may want to remain there after discharge. For this reason, you may wish to consider whether the community in which the program is located is supportive of recovery. A simple way to do so is to search the directories of AA and NA to identify whether there are a lot of twelve-step meetings in the area.

The following is a supplemental checklist of questions to ask when considering a long-term or nontraditional treatment program for adolescents:

1. Who is the clinical director and what credentials does the director have?

2. How long has the program been in operation, and how long has the current clinical director been with the organization?

3. Is there a physician available to meet general health needs of clients?

4. If the program is conducted in a remote area, what safety precautions are taken, and how does the team remain in contact with an administrative office?

5. What are the qualifications required of nonprofessional staff?

6. What percentage of clients drop out voluntarily?

7. What constitutes grounds for termination from participation in the program, and what percentage of clients are asked to leave the program?

8. Are any prepaid amounts refunded if the client leaves treatment or is asked to leave treatment?

9. How are rules enforced, and how are infractions disciplined?

10. Is a list of volunteer references available (past patients, family members of patients, or community members familiar with the program)?

11. What support services are offered to family members, such as progress updates, educational services, family therapy sessions, and involvement in discharge planning?

12. If treatment is provided to adolescents, what provisions are made to allow them to continue schooling, and do they receive academic credit for work done while in treatment?

13. How are prescription medicines secured, controlled, and administered (i.e., are medications taken under supervision to ensure that medications are not crushed and snorted or otherwise abused)?

RESISTANCE TO ENTERING TREATMENT

All of your investigation and research will be in vain if you cannot facilitate your loved one's admission to a treatment program. To support entry into treatment, NIDA recommends that parents reassure their adolescents that they will be safe and cared for in a treatment facility, and that, as parents, they will provide loving support to them during and beyond treatment.[15] NIDA offers suggestions for talking to an adult family member or friend about his or her use of substances, which are equally applicable to parents who want to talk to their teens about the same issue. In this regard,

NIDA recommends emphasis on the fact that you recognize "it takes a lot of courage to seek help for a drug problem because there is a lot of hard work ahead," but that treatment can, and does, work and that the disease can be managed. It is also important, according to NIDA, that you advise your family member or friend that you "will be supportive in his or her courageous effort."[16]

If your adult qualifier refuses help, it is suggested that you watch and wait. Events have consequences that may present the opportunity for intervention. Just because your qualifier is in trouble with the police does not mean you need to step in and fix it. Whether the offender is an adolescent or an adult, it is his or her problem, and he or she is responsible for the consequences of his or her actions. In some cases, the justice system may work in your favor. Evaluation, education, drug tests, a clinical assessment, or treatment may be ordered as part of a legal proceeding. In fact, criminal court judges may be the only individuals who are not completely powerless over another's use of alcohol and other drugs. They can apply a whole range of significant consequences that can motivate an individual's desire to change. Timing may be everything, and the families of those with addictive disease need to be opportunistic and use openings provided by changes in circumstances to facilitate evaluation and appropriate treatment, if warranted.

The fact that adolescents are minors and can be placed into treatment by their parents or legal guardians is a valuable tool that can be used to promote recovery. Parents of adolescents have an obligation to care for their minor children and to obtain medical treatment for them when needed. It is a window of opportunity that closes when a child reaches the age of eighteen. When an adolescent is in a secure, sober environment, he or she receives the added benefit of a break in the exposure of his or her developing brain to drug use.

While it is not suggested that any parent rush to judgment, once there is evidence of a problem, take steps to fully evaluate the issue. When intervention is warranted, take commensurate action, as soon as possible, to break the cycle of addiction. If your child needs treatment and remains adamant in a refusal to undergo evaluation or treatment, it is suggested that you discuss the specifics of the situation with a counselor or other specialist at a chosen treatment facility, and then obtain their advice and assistance in arranging for a professional to safely escort your teen to treatment.

RECOMMEND RESOURCES

- Academy Board of Addiction Medicine (ABOM) (directory), https://www.abam.net/about/.

- American Board of Addiction Psychiatry (patient resources, find a specialist), https://www.aaap.org/patient-resources/find-a-specialist/.

- Association of Recovery Schools, https://recoveryschools.org/.

- Gary Ferguson, *Shouting at the Sky: Troubled Teens and the Promise of the Wild* (New York: St. Martin's Press, 1999).

- National Alliance of Recovery Residences, http://narronline.org/. (The website provides links to regional affiliates, and their websites identify recovery housing within their service areas.)

- National Council on Problem Gambling (NCPG), https://www.ncpgambling.org/.

- NCPG helpline: call or text: 1-800-522-4700; chat: www.ncpgambling.org/chat; online peer support forum: www.gamtalk.org.

- SAMHSA Behavioral Health Treatment Services Locator, https://findtreatment.samhsa.gov/; toll-free treatment referral helpline: 1-800-662-HELP (4357).

- SAMHSA, Buprenorphine Treatment Practitioner Locator, www.samhsa.gov/medication-assisted-treatment/physician-program-data/treatment-physician-locator.

- SAMHSA, Opioid Treatment Program Directory, http://dpt2.samhsa.gov/treatment/directory.aspx.

- US Department of Veterans Affairs, Substance Use Disorder (SUD) Program Locator, https://www.va.gov/directory/guide/SUD.asp.

CHAPTER 11 NOTES

1   NIDA, "What to Do if Your Teen or Young Adult Has a Problem with Drugs," last modified January 2016, https://www.drugabuse.gov/related-topics/treatment/what-to-do-if-your-teen-or-young-adult-has-problem-drugs.

2   Ibid.

3   The Mayo Clinic, Mayo Medical Laboratories, Test ID: THCU, Carboxy-Tetrahydrocannabinol (THC) Confirmation, Urine, https://www.mayomedicallaboratories.com/test-catalog/Clinical+and+Interpretive/8898.

4   Ibid.

5   CBHSQ, 2016 NSDUH, 15.

6   Miech et al., *2016 MTF, Vol. I,* 515.

7   NIDA, "How Do I Know if I Am Addicted?" in "What to Do if You Have a Problem with Drugs: For Adults," https://www.drugabuse.gov/related-topics/treatment/what-to-do-if-you-have-problem-drugs-adults.

8   National Council on Problem Gambling (NCPG), "Screening Tools," in "Help & Treatment," https://www.ncpgambling.org/help-treatment/screening-tools/.

9   NIDA, "What to Do if Your Adult Friend or Loved One Has a Problem with Drugs," last modified January 2016, https://www.drugabuse.gov/related-topics/treatment/what-to-do-if-your-adult-friend-or-loved-one-has-problem-drugs.

10   Ibid.

11   NIDA, "What to Do if Your Adult Friend or Loved One Has a Problem with Drugs."

12   Ibid.

13   NCPG, "Help & Treatment," https://www.ncpgambling.org/help-treatment/.

14   NCPG, "National Problem Gambling Helpline," https://www.ncpgambling.org/help-treatment/national-helpline-1-800-522-4700/.

15   NIDA, "What to Do if Your Teen or Young Adult Has a Problem with Drugs."

16   NIDA, "What to Do if Your Adult Friend or Loved One Has a Problem with Drugs."

"We're Walking on Eggshells."

12 TAKING ACTION TO LIVE COMFORTABLY WITH THE RECOVERING ADDICT

When our loved ones are in treatment, we have time to take a breath, get a sound night's sleep, and take care of ourselves. But all too soon, our loved ones are outside of a controlled environment and back in our lives, if not our homes. In many ways, the time after treatment is the most difficult because we have already done our best by facilitating treatment, and afterward we need to step back, let go, and take care of our own recovery.

PREPARATION: WHAT TO DO WHILE YOUR LOVED ONE IS IN TREATMENT

We do get a respite while a loved one is safe in the controlled environment of a treatment center and should do our best to take care of ourselves during that time. Patience is required during another's treatment. If the person in treatment is an adult, you must respect the rules protecting patient privacy and confidentiality. The program staff cannot discuss an adult's care with anyone unless the client has consented to the disclosure. If your loved one affords such consent, it will allow you to work more closely with staff to support treatment and recovery. Further patience is needed when your loved one does not appear to be making progress, seems to deny the need for change, is making demands, and exhibits a poor attitude. Your knowledge of the impact of withdrawal, the role of cravings, and the need for the brain and body to return to a state of equilibrium after stopping the use of drugs will aid your understanding of what may appear to be a very slow change in your loved one's attitude. Progress may be more apparent after a longer period of abstinence, when the brain has begun to restore itself from the stimulus of alcohol and other drugs and after your loved one has completed more treatment.

The counselor may ask for information or give you assignments to complete as part of the treatment plan. Remain open to change and a new way of approaching problems, seek meaningful dialogue with the primary counselor and staff, and do your best to honor their recommendations and requests. It is suggested that you follow the lead of the counselor in setting your expectations, as well as the tone of your communications with your loved one. It is also recommended that you avail yourself of all of the resources offered to family members. Take full advantage of educational programs for family members and request as many sessions of couples or family counseling as can be accommodated, to allow yourself to work through issues with your loved one.

In treatment and early recovery, many people feel guilt, shame, and remorse. They may not apologize to family and friends because they are struggling with the need to accept and forgive themselves. You may be able to promote self-acceptance and facilitate healing by expressing love and support for the person in treatment, acknowledging the value of the treatment program, and demonstrating belief in your loved one's ability to change. You can do this by visiting your loved one and by sending letters, cards, and photographs of family members and supportive friends.

You may also wish to rebuild healthy connections by facilitating communications from those individuals in your extended family or in your loved one's group of friends who you think will provide positive support for recovery and encouragement to your loved one while in treatment.

It is particularly important to work with program staff in connection with discharge planning. The counselor may provide recommendations and referrals for further treatment or for postdischarge services. Joint sessions with your loved one and the counselor will provide transparency and an open, nonconfrontational, safe environment for exploration of potential problems and issues that may arise after discharge. The counselor can assist the parties in managing their expectations, setting rules, and defining healthy boundaries as an aid to the development of a fully informed postdischarge plan to support recovery.

TRAVERSING THE MINEFIELD OF EARLY RECOVERY

Regardless of the degree of preparation and thought given to a discharge plan, a loved one's return from treatment will be awkward. This is true whether or not he or she comes back home or lives independently. Hope is tempered by uncertainty. The buffer of treatment is gone, and we are left without a safety net. The fear of relapse pervades the atmosphere. Despite everyone's best efforts, trust, so severely broken by addiction, is lacking. Recovery does not usually progress in a straight line, and there will often be as many setbacks as advances. A new phase is beginning, and there are many adjustments to be made. This time, however, we have knowledge to understand the disease and the tools to inform our response to it.

Work Your Own Program

Family members in recovery from the impact of another's disease are vulnerable to relapses of their own. Like those recovering from addictive disease, external stimuli, or cues, can activate old feelings in family members and threaten a return to prior behaviors. When a qualifier is late, doesn't pick up the phone, or appears angry, frustrated, or depressed, our fears for him or her return. We may also tiptoe around issues in an effort to avoid saying or doing the wrong thing and bringing about a relapse. To prevent or respond to our own relapses, we need to go back to basics and remember that we don't have power over what happens. By placing our focus on working our own recovery program, we avoid trying to manage and control the recovery of another. We are also better able to maintain our own serenity despite uncertainty.

Maintaining Healthy Boundaries

Boundaries are personal limits. They represent clearly defined ground rules for interaction with others and provide protections against a return to old patterns of behavior. While basic boundaries were established, ideally with the help of a counselor, in the development of a discharge plan, they can also be self-defined and can be adapted as circumstances change. Boundaries may include the basic premise that your loved one can live with you only so long as abstinence is maintained and will need to leave if he or she returns to using. A teenager or young adult may be welcomed back home with the understanding that he or she will work his or her recovery program, attend school or look for a job, and help with family chores.

Managing your availability is one way you can set healthy boundaries. You are not on call twenty-four/seven, and you can turn off your phone at night or when you want to focus on something else. You do not have to respond immediately to a call or request from your loved one. If you are asked about something, it is okay to say that you need to think about it. You can also tell your loved one that you are not available on certain nights because you have another commitment or other plans, such as attendance at meetings of your family fellowship.

When welcoming back a family member from treatment, it is suggested that you commit to maintaining a sober environment.

While you may enjoy an alcoholic drink when you are not in the presence of your loved one, there is no reason to present cues that may activate another's cravings. Boundaries are a two-way street, and those in recovery may ask that you afford them certain rights and respect their needs, including, for example, expectations of privacy. Some people find it useful to establish a contract with a teenager or young adult. While in some cases a written contract may clearly define mutual rights and obligations, it can set a confrontational tone. Its effectiveness may well depend on the family dynamic and the personalities involved. Most teens will agree to just about anything if they see the value in the rights afforded them under the contract, but will contest the imposition of consequences. If they return to their old behaviors, many adolescents would tear up or set fire to the contract rather than accept its adverse consequences.

Boundaries define the fact that your family member has your love and support in recovery, but that you will not go back to enabling their addictive behaviors. Your enforcement of boundaries will, however, be informed by your understanding of the nature of recovery and relapse. An initial relapse may not warrant the immediate banishment of your loved one, as you may choose to watch and wait to see how he or she will respond to the relapse and whether it will reinforce a recommitment to sobriety and recovery.

The Money Chase

Consistent with Abraham Maslow's hierarchy of human needs and SAMHSA's explanation of the components necessary to support recovery, those in recovery cannot master the complex tasks of fostering their self-esteem and striving for their full potential unless their basic needs have been satisfied. Many individuals in early recovery, particularly young adults, are starting from scratch and are without any resources to support themselves. They may lack the ability to pay for food, housing, healthcare, and transportation. While you wish to foster self-sufficiency and growth in your loved one, they may need some help to make it to the long term. Family members may choose to provide financial support to meet basic needs so that their loved one can focus on recovery and personal growth. In this context, provision of a financial lifeline is not enabling. Rather, in some circumstances, it may represent a healthy way to support recovery. Basic support may, for example, be on par with parental support for other family members who are in college or pursuing post-high school training or education. When provided, however, short-term financial support should be part of a larger plan in which your qualifier is taking steps to move toward financial independence.

It is also important that monetary support be conditioned on the understanding that the recipient will keep up his or her end of the bargain and work his or her program in recovery. If we provide support, we want to make sure that we are not duped into supporting a drug habit. For this reason, financial assistance should be balanced by accountability. If your loved one is in another city or state, it can be difficult to confirm that the conditions of financial support are being met. While in the past we may have attempted to micromanage behavior, we know that it is not helpful to relapse into our old behaviors in an effort to check up on our loved one's sobriety. Thus, the difficulty with providing financial support lies in oversight, which can beget the very control we are trying to avoid and begin the dance that I call the "money chase."

If you wish to provide financial support to a loved one in recovery and avoid getting caught up in the money chase, it is suggested that you work with your loved one and a counselor, if possible, to develop a plan that is reasonable, meets basic needs to support recovery, empowers self-sufficiency, and includes accountability measures. As a show of good faith, a young adult may, for example, agree to submit to periodic drug tests and disclosure of the test results to his or her parents. Arrangements could also be made for the young adult to check in periodically with the counselor at a prior treatment program and authorize the counselor to provide continued updates to the family members. Similarly, families may choose to arrange for in-person or telephonic family therapy sessions to provide some transparency regarding progress toward goals and discussion of issues as they arise.

If you choose to make a financial gift to your loved one in recovery, you are doing it as an informed choice. You define your own limits and boundaries, with full acceptance of the risks and with your eyes wide open. The gift is on your terms, and it is not open-ended. You may decide to fund basic needs or provide tuition for further education but refuse to give in to your quantifier's wants and desires. For example, a young adult does not need a car if he or she can get to work, school, and/or twelve-step meetings by taking public transit, walking, or getting rides. Rather than giving money directly to your qualifier, you may agree to pay certain bills or buy groceries on occasion. You don't need to step in and provide funds to fix problems; rather, let your loved one experience the natural consequences of his or her actions and figure out how to solve the problems that arise.

There are some additional steps you can take to protect your interests if you choose to provide financial support to a loved one in early recovery. An article in *AARP The Magazine* provides some general tips on personal lending and loan guarantees that are appropriate in this context. AARP points out that by providing a larger down payment for the purchase of a car you may avoid the need to cosign a car loan. The article also notes that a letter from the borrower's employer may satisfy the lender and alleviate the need for a cosigner. Further, AARP advises that if you choose to cosign a loan for a car, your name should appear on the title along with that of the buyer.[1]

In some cases, your loved one may not be able to obtain a lease without a cosigner. Companies such as Insurent, LeaseLock, and Co-Signing.com that are in the business of cosigning leases for a fee of about 10 percent of the cost of the lease may provide a means for your qualifier to obtain a lease without a personal cosigner.[2] Should you choose to cosign a lease for your loved one, assume that you may very well pay the entirety of the rent for the duration of the lease and accept the fact that you may be liable to the landlord for any damages incurred in addition to surrender of the security deposit. If you choose to pay rent for your qualifier, it is suggested that you make payment directly to the landlord, rather than giving money to your loved one to cover the rent.

You may choose to help a loved one with rent in a shared apartment with friends from rehab or whom they met in recovery. A sober support system is essential to recovery, and cost-sharing makes housing more affordable for those seeking self-sufficiency. Further, if one tenant has qualified for the lease, a cosigner may not be necessary.[3] Given the prevalence of relapse in early recovery, however, if you are contractually liable to the landlord for the rent, you will want to understand the rules and boundaries for the house and how financial responsibilities will be handled if one or more of the housemates relapse.

Financial Considerations in the Presence of Disordered Gambling

The money chase is more complex when a qualifier has a gambling disorder. One could say that, for disordered gamblers, the substance of abuse is money. Just as individuals with eating disorders need to develop a healthy relationship with food, problem gamblers need to find ways to handle money appropriately. When their qualifier is actively gambling, family members need to take steps to protect their assets, finances, and credit. Experts suggest that family members identify and secure assets and exercise control over family finances. It is also recommended that the nongambling party take steps to close accounts held jointly with his or her qualifier and reopen them in the nongambler's own name as sole owner. Additionally, it is suggested that family members deactivate credit cards held jointly with their qualifiers and obtain credit in their own name. When the gambler commits to recovery, however, the family is advised to develop a plan for management of family finances that includes a budget, control over income, management of debt, and a mechanism for payment of bills.[4] Ideally, working with an addiction counselor and/or financial adviser would be an aid to this process.

A Community of Support

Given the nature of the disease, information from objective third parties may be of great value to you in confirming the well-being of your loved one. For this reason, you may find it helpful to broaden your network by connecting with those in your loved one's community of sober support, exchanging phone numbers with them and staying in contact. In times of crisis, they may be able to provide you with valuable information about what is happening to your loved one. Further, in the case of shared sober living, you would be well served to introduce yourself to and remain in contact with housemates and, if applicable, their family members to form a shared communication and support network. There may come a time when you will need information from these sources about the well-being of your loved one or when you will be able to share what you know with someone else who is worried about his or her qualifier. If you form these alliances, please honor them and share relevant facts, rather than hiding them.

Those of us who have loved ones with addictive disease are a community, and it is essential that we support each other in the common struggle. One of the things that has most confounded me while dealing with the issue of addiction in the family is how many people withhold crucial information about another's risky behaviors and relapses. Time and time again it has been discovered that, after the fact, those close to a family in crisis failed to share what they knew about another's son, daughter, or spouse. This critical information would have informed the family's choices and may have made a difference in the course of their loved one's illness. Any time you have information that someone else's loved one is engaged in the dangerous use of alcohol or other drugs, please find a way to share that information. You should not assume parents know their teenagers are at risk from the use of alcohol or other drugs. Make the tough telephone calls even when the news is not good. The family of the user needs and deserves any information you may have.

Healthy Patterns of Communication

In recovery, families can work on improved patterns of communication in which members listen effectively, respect and support each other, and clearly express their needs and feelings in a nonjudgmental way. What we say and how we say it matters. As we transition from trying to manage and control what others do to providing emotional support for their efforts to solve their own problems, we strive to provide less advice and to listen more supportively.

The technique of active listening involves repeating back what another has said to demonstrate that you have heard and understood. You don't have to comment on what another person says, provide advice, or offer a solution to a problem. Rather, you want to show that you have heard what was said and understand the situation. For example, if your family member describes a conflict with a coworker, you may say something like "I hear that you are very frustrated by what is happening at work; that is a difficult situation." It is suggested that you refrain from offering suggestions unless asked to do so. Similarly, asking detailed questions about what is happening in his or her life may cause your qualifier added stress. Rather, you may wish to try using general, open-ended questions (such as "How was your day?") to invite him or her to share what he or she wishes and solicit input, if desired.

Dr. Brad Reedy, the cofounder and clinical director of Evoke Therapy Programs, provides training in communication skills for families. He emphasizes that the purpose of effective communication is not to change another's behavior but to be "fully present in the relationship."[5] You have a right to express your feelings and emotions in a way that makes it about you and not someone else. Dr. Reedy recommends the use of "I feel" statements to describe feelings and events from a "dispassionate third person point of view," rather than attributing your feelings to another's behavior.[6] There are many ways to formulate and use "I feel" statements. As a general rule, start your statement with the word *I* rather than *you*. Starting a sentence with the word *you* sets up an adversarial tone and can make the respondent defensive. For example, rather than saying, "You are always late," the speaker could say, "I feel worried and can't sleep if it is after curfew and I don't know if you are safe." In other words, express your feelings and concerns directly, from your point of view, but without blame.

Dr. Reedy has written that one of "the most effective parenting tools" he knows of is elimination of the use of imperatives ("command words," such as "you should" or "you must") because a desire for control underlies use of such directives. He also cautions parents to avoid judgmental words such as *good* or *bad* and extreme overgeneralizations or black-and-white, all-or-nothing statements. According to Dr. Reedy, the avoidance of these "language traps" can "promote intentional and deliberate communications, and foster family intimacy."[7] These concepts represent sound advice for anyone with a loved one in recovery, not just parents.

Rebuilding Trust

President Ronald Regan is said to have quoted a Russian proverb while negotiating arms control agreements with President Gorbachev of the Soviet Union in the 1980s. The proverb, when translated, means "Trust, but verify." Trust is a subjective feeling that is based on past experience and cannot be forced. After a breach of trust, it may be possible to regain trust in someone if he or she demonstrates consistent reliability over a period of time. In other words, the perception of another's honesty and reliability may be restored by repeated demonstrations of trustworthiness. Words are not enough and our qualifiers need to show, not tell, us that we can trust them again. Dr. Reedy explains that individuals who do not own their past behaviors may become "indignant" when trust is withheld, while individuals who are "accountable" for their own actions may "tolerate" or accept the fact that they are not seen as trustworthy.[8] The rebuilding of trust in recovery is a process that requires time, patience, and cooperation by everyone involved.

RECOMMENDED RESOURCES

- Families Anonymous, "What Do I Say? A Helpful Guide for Difficult Phone Conversations" (Culver City, CA, 2008).

- National Alliance of Recovery Residences, http:// narronline.org/. (The website provides links to regional affiliates, and their websites identify recovery housing within their service areas.)

- National Endowment for Financial Education, "Personal Financial Strategies for the Loved Ones of Problem Gamblers," 2000: 23–29, https://store.samhsa.gov/ product/Personal-Financial-Strategies-for-the-Loved-Ones-of-Problem-Gamblers/BKD535.

- Brad M. Reedy, *The Journey of the Heroic Parent* (New York: Regan Arts, 2015, 2016).

CHAPTER 12 NOTES

1   Jean Chatzky, "Read This Before You Cosign a Loan," *AARP The Magazine*, October/November 2016: 28, https://www.aarp.org/money/credit-loans-debt/info-2016/before-cosigning-a-loan.html.

2   Ibid.

3   Ibid.

4   National Endowment for Financial Education, "Personal Financial Strategies for the Loved Ones of Problem Gamblers," 2000: 23–29, https://store.samhsa.gov/product/Personal-Financial-Strategies-for-the-Loved-Ones-of-Problem-Gamblers/BKD535.

5   Brad M. Reedy, *The Journey of the Heroic Parent* (New York: Regan Arts, 2016), 43.

6   Ibid., 47.

7   Ibid., 54.

8   Ibid., 186.

"Practicing These Principles in All of Our Affairs"

CONCLUSION: THE SEARCH FOR PEACE AND SERENITY

The Twelfth Step reminds us that "having had a spiritual awakening" we "practice these principles in all of our affairs." In many cases, those in recovery from addictive disease and their families emerge from the ordeal with strengthened bonds, greater self-awareness, and an enhanced view of life. In some cases, however, even after they have received quality treatment and positive support, our loved ones relapse into their old patterns of use. While at those times it may seem that we have come full circle, we have changed. We have knowledge of the disease and tools to confront it. When crises arise, we will have the means and the strength to respond appropriately. We can apply our understanding of the nature and progression of the disease to identify the best course of action for our loved ones and ourselves as determined by our own needs, resources, and core beliefs. It may come to the point that we are left with no cards to play and have no choice but to step back. Thus, in some circumstances our most informed choice may be a deliberate decision to refrain from any action and wait for a change in circumstances. Whatever happens, we can act deliberately to protect our own boundaries, our safety, and the safety of others. We have detached ourselves from enmeshment with our loved ones and are responsible for our own lives and our own happiness. We can continue to work our recovery program while remaining hopeful that our loved ones will someday find their way to their own. In essence, coping with another's addiction is about making reasoned decisions to do what we can, accepting what we are without power to change, and moving toward peace and serenity in our own lives.

Take what you will and leave the rest.

Families Anonymous

ACKNOWLEDGMENTS

I am indebted to my mentor, the late professor Lynn Boyle, LCSW, CADC, who conceived and developed the Advanced Accredited Alcohol and Other Drug Abuse Counselor Training Program for the Graduate School of Social Work at Loyola University Chicago and who encouraged me to bring my point of view to the field. I would also like to thank Patricia L. Bogie, MSW, LCSW, CADC, MISII, my supervisor at the Addiction Counseling and Education Services program at Catholic Charities of the Archdiocese of Chicago, who modeled the compassionate treatment of those suffering from addictive disease and whose positivity brought hope to those in the most desperate of circumstances.

My gratitude is further extended to the many individuals who encouraged me in the development of this project. I would particularly like to thank my friend Libby, whose professional edits to early drafts of my proposal were of enormous value to the presentation and refinement of the approach and concept. I am also indebted to my friend Alex B. Mahler, whose encouragement and editorial comments helped me move the project from conception to reality. My gratitude is also extended to a friend in long-term recovery whose insights were instrumental in my attempt to explain twelve-step recovery from addictive disease. Any remaining errors in my description of this experience are mine alone. I would also like to thank my friend Mary

Jan Rosenak, who challenged me and provided feedback on public policy issues; Beth Coleman, who introduced me to the practice of mindfulness and provided me with valuable resources on the subject; and my meditation teacher, Chuck Hutchcraft, LCSW, whose class is helping me to understand the benefits of the practice.

TABLE SUMMARIZING DRUGS OF ABUSE

The following table represents a snapshot of the various drugs of abuse, their street names, a description of what the drug looks like, methods of administration, effects on the body, imminent risks, and physical symptoms of use and withdrawal. Street names are included to assist readers in the identification of substances they have heard mentioned by their loved ones or their peers.

It is important to remember that many factors influence the effects of drugs on individual users, including the strength and purity of the substance, whether it has been combined with other psychoactive drugs or dangerous chemicals, the method of use, the user's prior experience and developed tolerance for the drug, the user's physical and emotional state at the time of use, and the environment in which the drug is used. No one will experience all of the potential symptoms or suffer from all the potential impairments to health listed for each drug. It should also be noted that many different drugs have similar effects. For this reason, individual symptoms cannot be used to identify the specific substance being used.

This general discussion is not intended as medical advice or as a substitute for professional assessment of a potential drug problem. Rather, it is offered as an aid to understanding the powerful impact of psychoactive substances on the body and mind of the user, the distinctive effects of the different classes of drugs, the generally opposite symptoms of intoxication and withdrawal from a given substance, and the range of potential health risks presented.

Commonly abused drugs are listed alphabetically, rather than by class of drug. Since reference to the class to which the drug belongs is crucial to an understanding of its effects, the class is listed directly below the name of the drug.

Drug Name, Classification, and Legal Status	Prescription, Brand, Chemical, or Street Names	Appearance	Method of Use
Alcohol Legal depressant	Booze, hooch	Liquid, ranging in color from clear to deep brown	Swallowed
Amphetamines Strong, synthetic prescription stimulants	Crosstops, black beauties (Biphetamine), beans, dexys (Dexedrine), and bennies (Benzedrine)	Often prescription medicines in tablet form	Consumed orally
Attention Medications Synthetic prescription stimulants	Methylphenidate (Ritalin and Concerta); Adderall and Dexedrine	Tablets, capsules, liquids	Swallowed or crushed and smoked, snorted, or injected

General Effects	Symptoms of Intoxication	Symptoms of Withdrawal	Short-Term and Long-Term Risks
Elevated mood; increased appetite, social confidence, and talkativeness; lessened inhibitions; and, at higher doses, observable depressive effects	Lowered blood pressure, slurred speech, loss of coordination, mental confusion, mood swings, memory loss, lack of control over emotions, and sleep or blackout	Increased pulse, heart rate, blood pressure, and insomnia; symptoms of acute alcohol withdrawal may be life-threatening and require medical management; and delirium tremens, the most serious complication of withdrawal, characterized by hallucinations, confusion, disorientation, frenzied motor activity, shakiness, and tremors	Accidents, injuries, violent behavior, loss of consciousness, coma, and death; and long-term risk of damage to all of the major organs of the body
Promotes euphoria, exhilaration, self-esteem, confidence, alertness, physical and mental performance; and suppresses appetite	Increases breathing rate, heart rate, temperature, and blood pressure, and may cause irregular heart rate and decreased appetite	Fatigue, sleepiness, sleep problems, depression, anxiety, and increased appetite	Irregular heartbeat, seizures, heart failure, heart problems, malnutrition, exhaustion, anger, violent behavior, paranoia, and psychosis
Promotes euphoria, exhilaration, self-esteem, confidence, alertness, and physical and mental performance; and suppresses appetite	Dilated pupils; sweating; nausea; increased blood pressure and heart rate; wakefulness; impaired judgment; and decreased appetite and thirst	Fatigue, depression, and sleep problems	Anxiety, irritability and restlessness, weight loss, paranoia, auditory and visual hallucinations, and aggression

Drug Name, Classification, and Legal Status	Prescription, Brand, Chemical, or Street Names	Appearance	Method of Use
Bath Salts (synthetic cathinones) Synthetic stimulants; some legal products, but not for human consumption	Bath salts, or by "brand names" such as Bloom, White Lightning, and Vanilla Sky	Usually a white, pink, or brown, crystal-like powder	Swallowed, sniffed, snorted, smoked, vaporized, or dissolved in liquid and injected
Barbiturates Prescription sedative-hypnotic depressants	Numerous prescription medications, including short-acting barbiturates such as Amobarbital (Amytal) and Secobarbital (Seconal); and a.k.a. barbs, barbies, red birds, reds & blues, yellow jackets, and yellows	Tablets; pills and capsules of many colors; and some are manufactured in liquid form	Swallowed, and the liquid is abused by injection

General Effects	Symptoms of Intoxication	Symptoms of Withdrawal	Short-Term and Long-Term Risks
Mimics the effect of natural cathinones or other stimulants such as cocaine; produces euphoria and alertness; and increases socialization and sex drive	Increases heart rate and blood pressure, and dilates pupils	Anxiety, depression, sleep problems, and tremors	Grinding of the teeth, anxiety, aggression, violent behavior, hallucinations, breakdown of muscle tissue, kidney damage or death from increase in body temperature, and may produce a state of excited delirium manifested in hyperstimulation, paranoia, hallucinations, and aggressive behavior
Alcohol-like effects; promotes euphoria; lowers inhibitions; disrupts memory; sedates; and incapacitates	Lowers blood pressure and respiration; slurred speech; confusion, dizziness; and poor concentration	Produces anxiety and agitation; increases heart rate; nausea and vomiting; sweating, stomach cramps, and tremors; and withdrawal, which can present serious risks, including convulsions and death, should be medically managed	Overdose presents a risk of coma and death; unmonitored withdrawal can result in potentially fatal seizures; associated with sexual assaults, aggressive behavior, and resulting injuries and accidents; high dose or chronic use can result in personality changes, mood disturbances, or depression; and IV users are subject to attendant risks

Drug Name, Classification, and Legal Status	Prescription, Brand, Chemical, or Street Names	Appearance	Method of Use
Benzodiazepines Prescription sedative-hypnotic depressants	Prescription medications including alprazolam (Xanax), lorazepam (Ativan), clonazepam (Klonopin), diazepam (Valium), and temazepam (Restoril); and a.k.a. benzos, trans, BDZs, and downers	Pills, tablets, or capsules	Swallowed or injected
Cocaine Plant-based stimulant; illegal but for rare medical uses	Blow, bump, C, candy, coca, coke, Charlie, crack, flake, rock, snow, soda cot, and toot	Fine, white, crystalline powder or hard, white or whitish lumps (rocks)	Snorted, smoked, or injected

General Effects	Symptoms of Intoxication	Symptoms of Withdrawal	Short-Term and Long-Term Risks
Alcohol-like effects; promotes euphoria, lowers inhibitions, disrupts memory, sedates, and incapacitates	Lowers blood pressure and respiration; slurs speech; causes confusion, dizziness, and poor concentration	Cravings, headaches, nausea, vomiting, muscle twitches, anxiety, high blood pressure, and sleep problems; and withdrawal, which presents risk of seizures, should be medically managed	Overdose presents a risk of coma and death; unmonitored withdrawal can result in potentially fatal seizures; associated with sexual assaults; IV users are subject to attendant risks
Produces feelings of euphoria, exhilaration, and well-being; increases mental alertness; and produces an immediate and intense but short-lived high when inhaled or injected	Raises blood pressure, body temperature, and heart rate; produces dilated pupils, sweating, nausea, and chest pain; suppresses appetite; and may manifest in anxiety or panic	Exhaustion, depression, unpleasant dreams, and feelings of sadness, isolation, and loneliness	Overdose is manifested by a very rapid heartbeat and hyperventilation, and may result in chest pain; while not usually fatal, deaths do occur from cardiac arrest, seizure, stroke, and respiratory failure; cocaine can provoke aggressive behavior; use may result in skin sores from formication; damage to the heart, cardiovascular system, brain, gastrointestinal tract, lungs, and nasal membranes; malnutrition, paranoia, and, in some cases, psychosis

Drug Name, Classification, and Legal Status	Prescription, Brand, Chemical, or Street Names	Appearance	Method of Use
Codeine Prescription opioid depressant	Includes promethazine-codeine cough syrups; a.k.a.Captain Cody, Cody, purple drank, sizzurp, and lean	Tablets, capsules, and liquids	Swallowed; often mixed with alcohol, soda, and hard candies, i.e., purple drank or sizzurp
Cough Syrups	See Codeine and DXM	See Codeine and DXM	See Codeine and DXM
DMT Illegal, synthetic hallucinogen	Businessman's special, Dimitri, and DMT	White, yellow, or brown powder	Most commonly smoked; can be snorted or injected
DXM (dextromethorphan) OTC opioid-like cough suppressant with hallucinogenic effects	DXM is contained in some cough medicines that are sold OTC such as Robitussin DM Dex, DXM, and a.k.a. orange crush and robo (as in robo tripping)	Cough syrups, tablets, and capsules	Orally ingested

General Effects	Symptoms of Intoxication	Symptoms of Withdrawal	Short-Term and Long-Term Risks
Euphoria and pain relief	Lowers blood pressure; reduces pulse and respiration; slurs speech; impairs coordination; constricts pupils; causes drowsiness; impairs judgment and memory	Raises blood pressure; increases pulse; dilates pupils; lowers mood; causes insomnia, diarrhea, muscle cramps, sweating, runny nose, stomach cramps, vomiting, fever, chills, and goose flesh	Respiratory arrest and potential death; more dangerous when combined with sedative effects of cough syrups (i.e., purple drank and sizzurp); nausea and constipation; long-term risks are not determined
See Codeine and DXM	See Codeine and DXM	See Codeine and DXM	See Codeine and DXM
Characterized by visual hallucinations and loss of connection with surroundings	Causes agitation, increased heart rate, high blood pressure, dilated pupils, rapid eye movements, dizziness, and lack of physical coordination	Not medically established	Coma and respiratory arrest have occurred at high doses; HPPD; and persistent psychosis
Causes euphoria at doses far above those recommended; dissociation from reality; and visual and auditory hallucinations	Increases heart rate and blood pressure; slurs speech; causes excitability, dizziness, nausea, vomiting, loss of coordination, confusion, and involuntary eye movements	Not medically established	Presents a risk of overdose, coma, and death, particularly when combined with alcohol, antidepressants, or other drugs; associated with accidental injuries or death due to dissociative effects; causes impaired perception of reality; and other medicines packaged with DXM can cause liver damage

Drug Name, Classification, and Legal Status	Prescription, Brand, Chemical, or Street Names	Appearance	Method of Use
Fentanyl Legal opioid pain reliever depressant; and illegally produced analogs	Illegal analog is acetyl fentanyl (desmethyl fentanyl); a.k.a. Apache, China girl, Chinatown, China white, dance fever, friend, goodfellas, great bear, he-man, jackpot, king ivory, murder 8, tango & cash, and TNT	For medical use, fentanyl is produced in liquids for intravenous use, oral lozenges (fentanyl lollipops), tablets, oral and nasal sprays, and transdermal patches. The illegal analog may be produced to look like pharmaceutical fentanyl; it is also sold as a powder or spiked onto blotted paper; it may be mixed into street heroin and sold as heroin	Swallowed, injected, snorted, or smoked; gel content of patches is injected; and patches are cut into pieces and placed in the mouth
Gamma Hydroxybutyrate (GHB) Legal sedative-hypnotic prescription depressant; and analogs (some legal, in household products not sold for human consumption)	Generic prescription drug Xyrem; analogs; a.k.a. easy lay, Georgia home boy, grievous bodily harm, and liquid ecstasy	Colorless liquid or a white powder that is undetectable in liquids	Often mixed with alcohol or water

General Effects	Symptoms of Intoxication	Symptoms of Withdrawal	Short-Term and Long-Term Risks
Like heroin; produces euphoria and relieves pain	Like heroin; depresses the CNS, resulting in lowered pulse, heart rate, blood pressure, and respiration rate; causes constriction of pupils, drowsiness (or coma), insensitivity to pain, confusion, impaired attention or memory, drooping eyelids, forward nodding of the head, slurred speech, and slowed coordination	Like heroin; causes bone, joint, and muscular pain; insomnia, depressed mood, anxiety, sweating, runny nose, nausea, vomiting, diarrhea, high blood pressure, rapid pulse, coughing, yawning, dilated pupils, teary eyes, hyperactive reflexes, muscle cramps, fever, chills, and/or goose flesh	Antagonists (drugs that block the effect of another drug), notably naloxone, can reverse an opioid overdose. **If you suspect a fentanyl overdose, immediately call 911.** Depression of the CNS, presents a high risk of overdose; is far stronger than heroin and has caused numerous deaths; presents a risk to emergency personnel and responders because even a few grains can be lethal
Promotes relaxation and euphoria; lowers inhibitions; and inhibits memory	Lowers heart rate and respiration; causes slurred speech and lack of coordination	Increases heart rate and blood pressure; produces anxiety, sweating, insomnia, tremors, and psychotic thoughts	Nausea, vomiting, depression, delusions, hallucinations, seizures, and risk of respiratory arrest or heart failure; associated with sexual assaults; and undetermined long-term effects

Drug Name, Classification, and Legal Status	Prescription, Brand, Chemical, or Street Names	Appearance	Method of Use
Heroin Illegal synthetic opioid depressant	Smack, H, horse, junk, brown sugar, skag, China white, and Mexican black tar	Powdered heroin is a white or brown powder; Mexican black tar heroin can be either a black, sticky substance or hard, coal-like lumps	Power is snorted, smoked, or dissolved in water and injected; black tar also dissolves in water and the liquid is usually injected into veins or muscles, or under the skin; a paste made from black tar can also be smoked
Hydrocodone Prescription pain reliever, opioid depressant	Prescription drugs: Hycodan, Norco, Tussend, and Vicodin; a.k.a. vike	Capsule, tablet, or liquid	Swallowed, snorted, or injected

General Effects	Symptoms of Intoxication	Symptoms of Withdrawal	Short-Term and Long-Term Risks
Euphoria, pain relief	Depresses the CNS, resulting in lowered pulse, heart rate, blood pressure, and respiration rate; constricts pupils; causes drowsiness or coma, insensitivity to pain, confusion, impaired attention, drooping eyelids, nodding of the head, slurred speech, and slowed coordination	Bone, joint, and muscular pain; insomnia, depressed mood; anxiety, sweating, runny nose, nausea, vomiting, diarrhea, high blood pressure, rapid pulse, coughing, yawning, dilated pupils, teary eyes, hyperactive reflexes, muscle cramps, fever, chills, and/or gooseflesh; after acute withdrawal (detoxification), the abstinent user may experience symptoms of post-acute and protracted withdrawal for three to eighteen months	Given depression of the CNS, presents a high risk of overdose and death; antagonists (drugs that block the effect of another drug), notably naloxone, can reverse an opioid overdose. **If you suspect a heroin overdose, immediately call 911.** IV users are exposed to attendant risks of HIV and hepatitis C; collapsed veins, skin abscesses, infections, and ulceration; infection of heart valves; heroin use also presents risks of severe constipation, stomach cramps, and diseases of the liver or kidney
Relieves physical, mental, and emotional pain; creates euphoria	Lowers blood pressure; reduces pulse and respiration; causes constricted pupils, drowsiness, and slurred speech; and impairs motor coordination, attention, judgment, and memory	High blood pressure, rapid pulse, dilated pupils, lowered mood, insomnia, diarrhea, muscle cramps, sweating, runny nose, stomach cramps, vomiting, fever, chills, and goose flesh	Respiratory arrest, death; risks attendant to IV use; and constipation

Drug Name, Classification, and Legal Status	Prescription, Brand, Chemical, or Street Names	Appearance	Method of Use
Hydromorphone Prescription pain reliever, opioid depressant	Dilaudid; a.k.a. D, dillies, dust, and juice	Liquid, suppository	Swallowed, injected, or used as suppository
Inhalants Legal products but not for human consumption and some prescription medications	Amyl nitrite, a prescription cardiac medication; the anesthetic nitrous oxide (laughing gas), and household products; a.k.a. gluey, huff, laughing gas, poppers, rush, snappers, and whippets	A wide variety of liquids that produce fumes, including gasoline, paint thinners, spray paint, certain glues, hairspray, nail polish remover, keyboard cleaners, and felt-tip markers	Popping and inhaling vials of medication; sniffing directly; spraying into nose or mouth; huffing (placing inhalant-soaked material over the nose and mouth or in the mouth); bagging (placing the inhalant or material soaked in the inhalant in a plastic bag and inhaling the fumes); soaking collars or sleeves in material and breathing from the clothing; capturing gas (e.g., from punctured cans) in a balloon and inhaling the gas from the balloon

General Effects	Symptoms of Intoxication	Symptoms of Withdrawal	Short-Term and Long-Term Risks
Relieves physical, mental, and emotional pain; creates euphoria	Lowers blood pressure; reduces pulse and respiration; constricts pupils; causes drowsiness, slurred speech; impairs motor coordination, attention, judgment, and memory	High blood pressure, rapid pulse, dilated pupils, lowered mood, insomnia, diarrhea, muscle cramps, sweating, runny nose, stomach cramps, vomiting, fever, chills, and goose flesh	Respiratory arrest; death; risks attendant to IV use; and constipation
Initially, inhalants provide stimulation, reduce inhibitions, and elevate mood	Dizziness, slurred speech, sleepiness, and lack of coordination; may be evidenced by odors or stains on clothing; and at higher doses, hallucinations and delusions	May include nausea, but symptoms are considered mild and are not used for diagnostic purposes	Death may occur from suffocation, cardiac arrest, seizures, choking, or coma; burns and injuries from explosions resulting from heating of products; inhalants also cause damage to the brain, heart, lungs, and liver; and impair memory and cognitive function

Drug Name, Classification, and Legal Status	Prescription, Brand, Chemical, or Street Names	Appearance	Method of Use
Ketamine Legal for medical and veterinary uses; dissociative anesthetic and hallucinogen	Cat valium, K, and special K	Clear liquid or white powder	Can be mixed with liquids and swallowed or injected; powder can be snorted or added to tobacco or marijuana and smoked
LSD (lysergic acid diethylamide) Illegal semisynthetic hallucinogen	Acid, blotter acid, dots, and window pane	Tablets or capsules; often added to decorated absorbent paper (marked to designate doses); and sometimes sold in liquid form	Swallowed; drug-soaked paper may be placed in the mouth where the drug is absorbed
Marijuana Hallucinogen that is illegal under federal law; legal in some states	Pot, dope, weed, ganja, herb, reefer, bud, and joint	Green, gray, or brown dried plant material containing shredded leaves, stems, and flowers that may look like tobacco; and concentrates may be sticky, black, or golden oils; golden or brown soft solids with the texture of wax, honey, or butter; or brittle solids	Smoked (joints, blunts, and pipes); mixed into food (edibles) or drink; or vaporized or dabbed

General Effects	Symptoms of Intoxication	Symptoms of Withdrawal	Short-Term and Long-Term Risks
Alters visual and audio perceptions; and causes the user to feel disconnected with or disassociated from reality and unable to control the situation	Dilated pupils, involuntary eye movements, stiff muscles, and difficulty moving	Withdrawal symptoms have not been scientifically established	In some cases, use can result in respiratory arrest and death; associated with sexual assault; depression, flashbacks, memory problems, stomach pain, ulcers, bladder pain, and kidney problems; and risks attendant to IV use
Heightens sensations and causes changes in sensory perceptions	May raise blood pressure and heart rate; increases temperature; and causes dizziness, dilated pupils, sweating, and impaired judgment	No generally recognized withdrawal symptoms, but may cause user to feel emotionally drained	Acute anxiety and panic reactions (bad trips); accidents or injuries; HPPD; and exacerbation of preexisting mental illness
Causes euphoria, relaxation, drowsiness, and heightened sensations, making ordinary things seem significant; lessens inhibitions; disrupts short-term memory; hinders judgment; disrupts focus and concentration; interferes with the perception of time, the ability to track moving objects, balance, coordination, motor skills, and reaction time; causes some	Causes bloodshot eyes, increased heart rate and appetite, dry mouth, and impaired visual tracking ability; and lessens coordination	Irritability, anger or aggression, nervousness or anxiety, restlessness, sleep disturbances, loss of appetite, weight loss, depressed mood, abdominal pain, shakiness, fever, chills, or headache; craving for the drug, aches, pains, or chills; slight tremors; sweating	Accidents; impaired attention, memory, and learning ability, presenting the attendant risk of academic failure; impairs ambition and life satisfaction; anxiety, paranoia; depression and suicide; cardiac and respiratory disease; and, with early onset, risk of long-term deficits in cognitive reasoning, attention, memory, learning ability, problem solving, and altered brain structure, volume, and IQ

(CONTINUED ON NEXT PAGE)

Drug Name, Classification, and Legal Status	Prescription, Brand, Chemical, or Street Names	Appearance	Method of Use
Marijuana (CONTINUED)			
MDMA (3,4-methylenedioxy-methamphetamine) Illegal synthetic drug with both stimulant and hallucinogenic effects	Adam, E, ecstasy, Molly, and X (Molly is often used to refer to the powdered or capsule form)	Usually in pill form; may appear as powder, capsules containing powder, or in liquid form; pills, which are manufactured in assorted colors, often contain an imprinted logo such as "E"	Generally swallowed, but powder can be snorted
Methadone Legal opioid depressant used for controlled medical management of opioid addiction	Dolophine; a.k.a. amidone, fizzies, methadose; street methadone	Liquid or tablets	Swallowed or injected

General Effects	Symptoms of Intoxication	Symptoms of Withdrawal	Short-Term and Long-Term Risks
users to experience fear, anxiety, panic, paranoia, and detachment; and, at higher doses, can cause delusions and hallucinations			
Causes muscle tightness and muscle spasms before the psychedelic effects are felt; increases energy; lowers inhibitions; induces feelings of happiness, clarity, self-awareness, and empathy; promotes human interaction, touching, and sexual activity; sensitizes user to visual stimuli and tactile sensation; and distorts perceptions and sense of time	Increases blood pressure and heart rate	Fatigue, lack of focus, depression, and anxiety	In rare cases, may cause organ failure and death because of significant increase in body temperature; highly unpredictable because it is often adulterated with other drugs such as ketamine, meth, or PCP; and long-term memory problems, sleep problems, anxiety, and depression
When used in controlled therapeutic doses, alleviates the symptoms of opioid withdrawal and craving without producing a high; but when abused, produces euphoric effects or enhances the effects of other opioids	Lowers blood pressure; reduces pulse and respiration; causes constricted pupils, drowsiness, and slurred speech; and impairs motor coordination, attention, judgment, and memory	High blood pressure, rapid pulse, dilated pupils, lowered mood, insomnia, diarrhea, muscle cramps, sweating, runny nose, stomach cramps, vomiting, fever, chills, and goose flesh	Respiratory arrest and death; IV users are exposed to attendant risks; and constipation

Drug Name, Classification, and Legal Status	Prescription, Brand, Chemical, or Street Names	Appearance	Method of Use
Methamphetamine (meth) Powerful synthetic amphetamine stimulant, illegal, but for rare medical uses	Chalk, chicken feed, crank, crystal, ice, glass, poor man's cocaine, shabu, shards, speed, stove top, Tina, trash, tweak, yaba, and yellow bam	Meth is a white powder or pill; crystal meth or crystal methamphetamine looks like shards of glass or crystals and is white or bluish white	Pills can be swallowed or crushed; powdered or crushed meth can be snorted or dissolved in water or alcohol and injected. Crystal meth can be smoked (analogous to smoking crack).
Meperidine Prescription pain reliever, opioid depressant	Demerol; a.k.a. demies	Tablet, liquid	Swallowed, snorted, or injected
Morphine Prescription pain reliever, opioid depressant	Dreamer, emsel, first line, hows, M.S., Mister blue, morf, morpho, and unkie	Liquid for injection, tablets, capsules, suppositories, and drinkable liquid	Injected, swallowed, smoked, or used as suppository

General Effects	Symptoms of Intoxication	Symptoms of Withdrawal	Short-Term and Long-Term Risks
Increases energy, self-esteem, confidence, alertness, and physical and mental performance; can produce feelings of euphoria, exhilaration, and well-being; and suppresses appetite	Increases breathing rate, heart rate, blood pressure, and temperature; and decreases appetite	Fatigue, sleepiness, sleep problems; sadness, loneliness, depression, and anxiety	At high doses, irregular heartbeat, seizures, and heart failure may occur; profound debilitating effects on the body, including damage to the brain, cognitive function, memory, the cardiovascular system, and teeth and gums; and formication resulting in skin sores from scratching
Relieves physical, mental, and emotional pain; and creates euphoria	Lowers blood pressure; reduces pulse and respiration; causes constricted pupils, drowsiness, and slurred speech; and impairs motor coordination, attention, judgment, and memory	High blood pressure, rapid pulse, dilated pupils, lowered mood, insomnia, diarrhea, muscle cramps, sweating, runny nose, stomach cramps, vomiting, fever, chills, and goose flesh	Respiratory arrest and death; IV users exposed to attendant risks; and constipation
Relieves physical, mental, and emotional pain; and creates euphoria	Lowers blood pressure, pulse, and respiration; causes constricted pupils, drowsiness, and slurred speech; and impairs motor coordination, attention, judgment, and memory	High blood pressure, rapid pulse, dilated pupils, lowered mood, insomnia, diarrhea, muscle cramps, sweating, runny nose, stomach cramps, vomiting, fever, chills, and goose flesh	Respiratory arrest and death; IV users exposed to attendant risks; and constipation

Drug Name, Classification, and Legal Status	Prescription, Brand, Chemical, or Street Names	Appearance	Method of Use
Oxycodone Prescription pain reliever, opioid depressant	Oxycontin and Percocet; hillbilly heroin, ocs, oxy, and o'cotton	Capsules, tablets, and liquids	Swallowed, chewed, crushed, and snorted; or crushed pills can be dissolved in liquid and injected
Oxymorphone Prescription pain reliever, opioid depressant	Opana, biscuits, Mrs. O, o-bomb, and octagons	Tablets	Swallowed, snorted, or injected
PCP Illegal dissociative anesthetic and hallucinogen	Angel dust, dust, hog, ozone, and peace pill; and fry and sherm (tobacco or marijuana cigarettes that have been dipped in liquefied PCP or embalming fluid)	White or colored powder with a dry, crystallized, or gummy consistency; tablets, capsules, and liquids	Smoked, snorted, dissolved in liquid, swallowed, injected; or added to marijuana or herbs (mint parsley or oregano) and smoked

General Effects	Symptoms of Intoxication	Symptoms of Withdrawal	Short-Term and Long-Term Risks
Relieves physical, mental, and emotional pain; and creates euphoria	Lowers blood pressure; reduces pulse and respiration; causes constricted pupils, drowsiness, and slurred speech; and impairs motor coordination, attention, judgment, and memory	High blood pressure, rapid pulse, dilated pupils, lowered mood, insomnia, diarrhea, muscle cramps, sweating, runny nose, stomach cramps, vomiting, fever, chills, and gooseflesh	Respiratory arrest and death; IV users exposed to attendant risks; and constipation
Relieves physical, mental, and emotional pain; and creates euphoria	Lowers blood pressure; reduces pulse and respiration; causes constricted pupils, drowsiness, and slurred speech; and impairs motor coordination, attention, judgment, and memory	High blood pressure, rapid pulse, dilated pupils, lowered mood, insomnia, diarrhea, muscle cramps, sweating, runny nose, stomach cramps, vomiting, fever, chills, and goose flesh	Respiratory arrest and death; IV users exposed to attendant risks; and constipation
Causes the user to dissociate from reality while feeling anger and the absence of pain	Initially increases blood pressure and pulse (manifests in flushing and sweating); at higher doses, lowers blood pressure, respiration, and heart rate, creating a risk of coma and death; may induce violence, anger, and suicidal actions; may cause nausea, vomiting, rapid eye movements, and blurred vision; may	Headache and sweating	At high doses, risk of coma and death; associated with injuries and violent altercations; memory loss, anxiety, weight loss, and depression; and IV users are exposed to attendant risks

(CONTINUED ON NEXT PAGE)

Drug Name, Classification, and Legal Status	Prescription, Brand, Chemical, or Street Names	Appearance	Method of Use
PCP (CONTINUED)			
Peyote (mescaline) Natural illegal hallucinogen	Button, peyo, and cactus	Fresh or dried crowns (buttons) of the peyote cactus	Crowns are chewed, boiled to make a tea, ground into a paste and stuffed into capsules, or added to another substance and smoked
Psychedelic Mushrooms (psilocybin and psilocin) Natural illegal hallucinogen	Shrooms or magic mushrooms	Mushrooms (fresh or dried) with long, slender stems and caps with dark gills on the underside	Stems and caps of the mushrooms are eaten fresh or dried
Rohypnol (flunitrazepam) Illegal benzodiazepine; sedative-hypnotic depressant	Forget-me pill, roach, roofies, roapies, and rufies	Olive-green tablet that when dissolved in liquid turns the liquid blue; generic formulations may not change the coloration of the liquid in which they are dissolved	Dissolved in liquid and swallowed

General Effects	Symptoms of Intoxication	Symptoms of Withdrawal	Short-Term and Long-Term Risks
	cause loss of balance and dizziness; and users may appear to walk in a zombie-like manner because they cannot feel the bottoms of their feet		
Causes colorful visual hallucinations and alters perception of time	Enlarged pupils, nausea, and vomiting; increased blood pressure, heart rate, and body temperature (resulting in sweating); muscle weakness; and lack of physical coordination	None known	HPPD and persistent psychosis
Causes hallucinations; alters visual, auditory, taste, and tactile perceptions; and undermines the user's ability to tell fantasy from reality	Nausea, vomiting, dilated pupils, and lack of physical coordination	None known	Accidental ingestion of poisonous mushrooms; memory loss; HPPD; and persistent psychosis
Lowers inhibitions, decreases anxiety, disrupts memory, sedates, and incapacitates	Lowered blood pressure, slowed respiration, slurred speech, confusion, dizziness, poor concentration, poor motor coordination, and muscle weakness	Headaches, anxiety, confusion, irritability, convulsions, and hallucinations	Depressant effects, especially when combined with alcohol; may cause respiratory arrest and death; amnesia; and associated with sexual assaults

Drug Name, Classification, and Legal Status	Prescription, Brand, Chemical, or Street Names	Appearance	Method of Use
Salvia (Salvia divinorum) Natural hallucinogen, illegal for human consumption	Sally-D and salvia	Fresh or dried leaves of a plant in the mint family	Chewed, smoked, or vaporized
Synthetic Cathinones	See Bath Salts	See Bath Salts	See Bath Salts
Synthetic Cannabinoids Hallucinogen, may be legal when sold for other than human consumption	Brand names such as Black Magic, Blaze, Cloud 9, Demon, Joker, K-2, Kush, Liquid Essence, Mojo, Ninja, Paradise, Sence, Serenity, Sacked, Spice, Spike, and Yucatan	Often sold in colorful foil packages; typically, powdered chemicals that are dissolved in acetate and sprayed on absorbent plant material; and may also be sold in liquid form	Used in the same way as marijuana: rolled in papers and smoked, smoked in a pipe or water pipe, vaporized, or brewed in a tea; and also sold in liquid form that can be vaporized

General Effects	Symptoms of Intoxication	Symptoms of Withdrawal	Short-Term and Long-Term Risks
Causes out-of-body sensations and a dreamlike state; hallucinations; visions of bright lights; overlapping objects; and physical sensations of motion or being pulled	Uncontrollable laughter, slurred speech, the inability to speak or move, loss of coordination, dizziness, mood swings, and sweating	Undetermined	Undetermined
See Bath Salts	See Bath Salts	See Bath Salts	See Bath Salts
Since the chemicals mimic the composition of marijuana, the general effects are the same, but synthetic cannabinoids are more potent	Like marijuana	Like marijuana	Has resulted in deaths from cardiac arrest; great risks presented due to unknown chemical composition and presence of additives, as well as unknown potency; and THC content produces risks like those of marijuana

GLOSSARY

A

Abstinence-based treatment. A theory of treatment based on the principle that recovery is best sustained by complete abstinence from the use of any mind-altering substances.

Abuse (of drugs). The abuse of drugs refers to a maladaptive use of a substance even though use of that substance can be medically appropriate or is socially accepted. For example, a person can use prescription drugs or abuse them by taking them other than as directed for the purpose of getting high. Similarly, it is socially acceptable to use alcohol, although excessive use may be referred to as the abuse of alcohol.

Acamprosate. A medication approved for use in the treatment of alcohol use disorders. It normalizes the reactions to alcohol in the brain's glutamate system to reduce cravings.

Acute withdrawal. Acute withdrawal is the period of withdrawal that occurs after cessation of the use of a substance and generally lasts for a period of days.

Active listening. Active listening is a process in which a listener confirms his or her understanding of something that is said by repeating the essence of the statement back to the speaker.

Addiction. The term *addiction* is generally used to refer to a severe substance use disorder or severe gambling disorder determined on the basis of the diagnostic criteria set forth in the *DSM-5*.

Adrenaline. Adrenaline is a natural neurochemical stimulant that provides a burst of energy in response to a crisis or perceived danger.

Agonists. Agonists are agents that bond with receptor neurons to facilitate the absorption of neurotransmitters.

Al-Anon. Al-Anon is a twelve-step recovery self-help group for individuals who have been impacted by the alcohol use of a family member or friend.

Alateen. Alateen is a twelve-step recovery self-help group for teenagers who have been impacted by the alcohol use of a family member or friend.

Alcohol dehydrogenase (ADH). ADH is an enzyme that partially breaks down alcohol in the stomach. Due to the fact that men have more ADH than women, more alcohol is broken down in the stomach of male users, and a greater percentage of alcohol passes through the stomach of female users.

Alcoholic hallucinosis. Alcoholic hallucinosis refers to the auditory or visual hallucinations that may be experienced by an alcohol-dependent person during withdrawal from alcohol.

Alcoholics Anonymous (AA). AA is a twelve-step recovery self-help group for individuals who wish to do something about their drinking problems.

Alcohol use disorder (AUD). An AUD is a substance use disorder based on the use of alcohol.

Amends. The making of amends is part of working a twelve-step program. A person makes amends to another in an effort to compensate the other for past harms or offense perpetrated upon them.

Amphetamine psychosis. Amphetamine psychosis is a condition associated with the chronic use of amphetamines that manifests in loss of contact with reality and hallucinations.

Amygdala. The amygdala is a part of the brain that processes emotions and memory and judges the emotional importance of stimuli.

Analog or analogue. An analog drug is a synthetically produced drug that is designed to copy the structure of another drug or mimic its effects.

Anandamide. Anandamide is a natural cannabinoid neurotransmitter in the brain that contributes to the regulation of sensory perception, emotion, memory, concentration, sense of novelty, appetite, anxiety, and motor coordination.

Antagonists. Antagonists are agents that block the acceptance of chemicals by receptor neurons.

Avoidant personality disorder. As described in the *DSM-5,* an avoidant personality disorder is a personality disorder that is manifested by a pervasive pattern of social inhibitions, feelings of inadequacy, and hypersensitivity to negative evaluation by others, that typically begins in early adulthood.

B

Bagging. Bagging is a method of using inhalants by placing an inhalant product, or material soaked in the product, into a plastic bag and inhaling the fumes from the bag.

Basic outpatient (BOP). BOP refers to outpatient treatment for addictive disorders. It is also known as outpatient level I.0, and generally involves individual and group-based treatment for one and a half to eight hours a week.

Betel nuts. Betel nuts are the seeds of the areca palm tree that are chewed for their stimulant effect. The practice is common in Asia.

Binge drinking. For men, binge drinking is the consumption of five or more alcoholic drinks on the same occasion. For women, it is the consumption of four or more drinks on the same occasion.

Blood alcohol concentration (BAC). BAC refers to the concentration of alcohol in the bloodstream.

Boundaries. Boundaries are self-defined personal limits that represent clearly defined ground rules for interaction with others.

Buprenorphine (Subutex). Buprenorphine is a synthetic opioid medication that has been approved for use in the treatment of opioid dependence. Buprenorphine is a partial agonist because, while it binds with opioid receptors, it is less strong than full agonists.

C

Cannabis arteritis. Cannabis arteritis is a serious peripheral vascular disease associated with the smoking of marijuana that may cause plaque and blockages in the blood vessels supplying the legs and feet.

Cannabis indica. Cannabis indica is one of the two main species of the marijuana plant. Most hash is derived from this species of the plant.

Cannabis sativa. Cannabis sativa is one of the two main primary species of the marijuana plant.

Cathinones. A naturally occurring stimulant drug found in the plant khat. Cathinones are related to the amphetamine family of drugs, which includes amphetamine and MDMA (ecstasy) and has similar effects.

Celebrate Recovery. Celebrate Recovery is an openly Christian support group for those in recovery from substance use or who are dealing with other problematic behaviors.

Central nervous system (CNS). The CNS consists of the brain and the spinal cord.

Chasing losses. Chasing losses refers to the gambling behavior of continuing to gamble after losing, in an effort to make up the loss.

Class of drug. Drugs fall within different classes or classifications. While terminology varies among sources, the generally recognized classes of drugs are stimulants, depressants, hallucinogens, and other substances (including steroids and inhalants).

Clinical assessment. A clinical assessment is an interview by a trained and licensed drug and alcohol counselor or specialist for the purpose of the investigation of an individual's use of substances to identify whether there are problematic patterns of use and to determine whether the individual satisfies the diagnostic criteria for an SUD as set forth in the *DSM-5*.

Closed meeting. Closed meetings are twelve-step fellowship meetings where attendance is limited to those who are members or potential members of the fellowship.

Club drugs. Clubs drugs are not a specific class or type of drugs. Rather, club drugs are those which, at a particular time, are favored as party drugs. Generally, they may be drugs that elevate mood and lower inhibitions.

Cocaine Anonymous (CA). CA is a twelve-step recovery self-help group for individuals who wish to do something about their use of cocaine and other drugs.

Codependent. A person is codependent if they are obsessed with controlling the behavior of another person to the extent that they fail to separate themselves from the person they are trying to control.

Cognitive behavioral therapy (CBT). CBT and related behavioral therapies such as cognitive therapy (CT) and dialectical behavior therapy (DBT) are often used in the treatment of SUDs. These behavioral therapies are based on the principle that learned behavior can be modified. The subjects are encouraged to examine the positive and negative consequences of prior behaviors, including drug use, and are taught coping skills and strategies to develop new responses to existing problems.

Combat Methamphetamine Epidemic Act of 2005. The Act controls and regulates the sale of cold medications and other products containing pseudoephedrine, which can be used to illicitly produce methamphetamine.

Comprehensive Addiction and Recovery Act of 2016 (CARA).
CARA contains numerous provisions to support the prevention
and treatment of SUDs, including expansion of access to overdose-
reversal medications.

**Comprehensive Drug Abuse Prevention and Control Act of 1970
(Controlled Substances Act).** The Controlled Substances Act
classifies drugs on schedules based on the potential for abuse and
dependence, weighed against their medical value, for legal purposes,
specifically, control of the manufacture, distribution, and sale of
potentially dangerous drugs and prosecution of drug offenses.

Contingency management. Contingency management is a model
of therapy that is based on a contractual agreement to take specific
actions, and offers tangible rewards to clients as incentives to achieve
the contractual goals.

Continuum of care. Treatment for addictive disorders includes
a variety of treatment options that vary in intensity along a
continuum. Clients are placed in an appropriate level of care based
on the severity of their condition and may progress from more
intense to less intense interventions along the continuum of care.

Controlled environment. A controlled environment is a setting
(such as a treatment center or jail) where access to drugs and alcohol
is precluded.

Controlled substance. Substances that are subject to federal
restrictions on their manufacture, distribution, and sale as defined in
the Controlled Substances Act.

Co-occurring disorders. A person has co-occurring disorders when
they have been diagnosed with more than one mental disorder at
the same time. For example, a client may have both an SUD and a
depressive disorder.

Craving. Craving is such a strong urge to use a drug that a person
can think of nothing else.

Cues. Cues are external or internal (emotional) stimuli that an individual associates with his or her prior use of substances or behaviors and that activate the individual's desire to return to that use or those behaviors.

Cultural competence. Cultural competence refers to the existence of an expertise regarding the language, beliefs, needs, and traditions of individuals in a cultural group or a specific population (such as women, trauma victims, veterans, the LGBTQ community, adolescents, or older adults).

D

Dabbing. Dabbing refers to the method of ingesting THC concentrates by placing a dab of concentrate on a hot surface and inhaling the vapors.

Defense mechanisms. Defense mechanisms (such as denial) are the means by which the subconscious protects individuals from painful realities and unwanted thoughts and feelings.

Delirium tremens (the DTs). The DTs represent the most serious complication of withdrawal from alcohol and are characterized by hallucinations, confusion, and disorientation accompanied by frenzied motor activity such as agitation, increased pulse, shakiness, and tremors. In its most severe forms, an alcohol-dependent person's withdrawal from alcohol is life-threatening and should be medically managed.

Delusion. Delusions are mistaken, illogical beliefs such as a person's conviction that they can fly.

Denial. Denial is a defense mechanism in which the mind unconsciously protects a person from recognition of things they do not want to accept and from harmful events and unwanted thoughts and feelings.

Depressants. Depressants are a class of drugs that generally slow down the functions of the CNS. Depressants can relax muscles, lessen anxiety, and induce sleep. They slow down heart rate, blood pressure, pulse, and breathing.

Designer drugs. Designer drugs have been manufactured to mimic the pharmacological effects of controlled substances.

Detoxification. Detoxification is a period of stabilization during which drugs leave the body. A person who is dependent on drugs will suffer symptoms of withdrawal in the absence of the drug. In some cases, these symptoms can be life-threatening. Detoxification in a medical facility is appropriate when withdrawal presents a potential health risk to the client.

Discharge plan. A discharge plan is a written plan prepared for clients prior to their discharge from treatment for addictive disease that addresses all major areas of the client's life and details the means by which the client will maintain abstinence and promote recovery.

Disease model. The disease model of addiction is the scientific theory that recognizes addiction as a chronic brain disease that has potential for recurrence and recovery.

Disordered gambling. Disordered gambling is another name for gambling behaviors of a person with a gambling disorder.

Disulfiram (Antabuse). Disulfiram is a drug approved for the treatment of alcohol use disorder that interferes with the body's elimination of acetaldehyde as part of the metabolism of alcohol, resulting in discomfort to the user and negatively reinforcing the use of alcohol.

Dopamine. Dopamine is a natural, feel-good chemical that is released by the brain to reward life-sustaining activities and thereby condition the repetition of the behavior.

Downregulation. Downregulation is a process by which the brain protects itself from overstimulation by drugs by slowing the production of or blocking the natural transmission of chemicals.

Drop. To drop is to provide a urine sample for testing.

Drug Enforcement Administration (DEA). The DEA is a federal law enforcement agency within the US Department of Justice that has the lead responsibility for enforcing the Controlled Substances Act and combating the smuggling and sale of illegal drugs in the United States.

Drug of choice. A drug of choice is the user's preferred substance.

Drugs of abuse. The Table Summarizing Drugs of Abuse lists the characteristics of common drugs of abuse.

DSM-5. *The Diagnostic and Statistical Manual of Mental Disorders (DSM-5),* published by the American Psychiatric Association, identifies criteria for the diagnosis of mental disorders, including addictive disorders (SUDs and gambling disorder).

E

Edibles. The term *edibles* refers to marijuana products made with THC-rich oils that are eaten, including candy, brownies, and cookies.

Enabling. Enabling is doing things for someone else that they can do for themselves and protecting them from the consequences of their choices.

Endorphins. Endorphins are naturally produced opioid neurotransmitters.

Enkephalins. Enkephalins are naturally produced opioid neurotransmitters.

Epinephrine. Epinephrine is a natural stimulant.

Evidence-based treatment (EBT). Treatment is evidence-based if its efficacy is supported by controlled trials that are independent, peer reviewed, and randomized.

Excited delirium. Excited delirium is a serious condition that may be brought about by the use of substances and is manifested by symptoms of hyperstimulation, paranoia, hallucinations, and aggressive behavior.

Externalizing disorder. An externalizing disorder is a medical disorder characterized by maladaptive behaviors directed toward the environment. ADD and ADHD are externalizing disorders.

Eye movement desensitization and reprocessing (EMDR). EMDR is an evidence-based therapy based on the use of eye movements, like those typical to REM sleep, to process traumatic memories, that is widely used by certified professionals in the treatment of trauma and PTSD.

F

Families Anonymous (FA). FA is a twelve-step recovery self-help group for individuals who have been impacted by the destructive behavior of someone near to them, whether caused by drugs, alcohol, or related behavioral problems.

Family fellowships. Family fellowships are twelve-step self-help groups for those affected by another's use of alcohol, other drugs, or gambling. These fellowships include Al-Anon, Alateen, FA, Nar-Anon, and Gam-Anon.

Family therapy. Family therapy involves the engagement of family members (spouses, parents, or children) in therapy sessions jointly with the client, allowing exploration of existing family dynamics and issues which may impact the client's long-term recovery.

Federal Analogue Act of 1986. The Act allows prosecution of individuals for the manufacture and sale of drugs chemically similar to those on Schedule I of the Controlled Substances Act.

Fetal alcohol syndrome (FAS). FAS is a serious disorder caused when an unborn baby is exposed to alcohol in utero. Symptoms of FAS include low birth weight, abnormal facial features, and long-term cognitive and behavioral problems.

Formication. The feeling of insects crawling across or underneath your skin. The name comes from the Latin word *formica*, which means ant.

Friends of Bill (FOB). A reference to Bill W., one of the founders of AA, which is used to subtly refer to the fellowship of AA.

G

Gam-Anon. Gam-Anon is a twelve-step self-help group for individuals who have been affected by the gambling problem of another.

Gamblers Anonymous (GA). GA is a twelve-step recovery self-help group for individuals who wish to do something about their gambling problems.

Gambling disorder. An addictive disease defined by the *DSM-5* that is related to persistent and recurrent problematic gambling behavior that causes significant impairment or distress.

Gamma-aminobutyric acid (GABA). GABA is a natural chemical neurotransmitter that controls impulses and generally slows down the brain.

Glutamate. Glutamate is a neurotransmitter in the brain that is essential to normal function of the brain and CNS. Its functions include the facilitation of communication, memory, and learning.

Group. The word *group* refers to group therapy.

H

Hallucination. A hallucination is a visual, auditory, or tactical experience that has no connection with external things, such as seeing an animal which is not present in the room.

Hallucinogen persisting perception disorder (HPPD). HPPD is a condition in which past users of hallucinogens experience flashbacks, causing them to reexperience the effects of the drug long after its use. The condition may also cause long-term visual disturbances, such as seeing light trails or halos around objects.

Hallucinogens. The drug class of hallucinogens (also known as psychedelics) is composed of a diverse variety of substances with different chemical structures that alter the user's perception of reality, thoughts, mood, and feelings.

Harm reduction. Harm reduction is a treatment theory based on the concept that if total abstinence cannot be achieved, it is beneficial for the client to reduce the risk of use.

Heavy drinking. Heavy drinking is generally accepted to mean binge drinking on five or more days within a thirty-day period.

Hemp. Hemp plants are part of the cannabis family, but they do not produce psychoactive effects, and their fiber is used to produce rope and other products.

Hippocampus. The hippocampus is a part of the brain that is important to the processing of information and memory.

Huffing. Huffing is the practice of placing a rag or other material that has been soaked in a toxic substance over the nose and mouth or in the mouth for the purpose of breathing fumes. The term *huffing* is also used more generically for all forms of inhalant abuse.

I

Illusions. An illusion occurs when a person views something real but perceives it to be something else. For example, a garden hose may be perceived to be a snake.

Inhalants. Inhalants include a variety of products ranging from prescription medicine and anesthetics to household chemicals, gasoline, and other petroleum-based products that produce fumes, which are inhaled to produce psychoactive effects.

Inpatient treatment. Inpatient treatment for substance abuse refers to residential treatment in a therapeutic sober environment for an initial period of between one and twenty-eight days.

Intensive outpatient (IOP). IOP or outpatient, Level II.1, is outpatient treatment for addictive disorders that occurs more frequently than BOP. IOP typically involves group and individual counseling for nine to fifteen hours a week.

K

Khat. Khat is a plant-based stimulant. Cathinone is derived from the leaves of the khat bush. The leaves are chewed or brewed in tea. Khat has long been used in East Africa and the Middle East.

L

LifeRing Secular Recovery. LifeRing Secular Recovery is a nonreligious support group based on theories of behavioral change and positive psychology.

M

Medical marijuana. Medical marijuana is the name given to products derived from marijuana plants and sold for medicinal purposes under state law. Medical marijuana is not an FDA-approved medicine.

Medication-assisted treatment (MAT). The use of medications in the treatment of SUDs, such as those that ease the symptoms of withdrawal and reduce cravings, in combination with behavioral therapies is called medication-assisted treatment.

Mental Health Parity and Addiction Equity Act of 2008 (MHPAEA). The MHPAEA is a federal law requiring that group health plans and providers afford benefits for mental health and SUDs that are on par with the benefits provided for medical and surgical services.

Met-enkephalin. A naturally occurring, endogenous opioid peptide that has opioid effects of a relatively short duration.

Methadone maintenance therapy (MMT). MMT originated as a harm reduction treatment methodology in which methadone was used to replace heroin. Methadone can also be used in conjunction with other therapies as part of MAT.

Mindfulness. Mindfulness is the practice of focusing attention on what is occurring at the present moment.

Mindfulness-based intervention therapy (MBIT). MBIT, as used in the treatment of addictive disorders, combines CBT with the practice of mindfulness.

Misuse of drugs. Misuse of drugs refers to use other than as directed or prescribed.

Monitoring the Future surveys (MTF). The Monitoring the Future surveys are annual surveys of secondary school students and young adults in the United States conducted by the National Institutes of Health that investigate the prevalence of drug use among the subject populations and identify trends in use.

Motivational enhancement therapy (MET). MET is a therapy model that is based on the use of motivational interviewing techniques.

Motivational interviewing. Motivational interviewing is a nonjudgmental, empathetic method of communicating with clients to assist them in defining their own goals for the future and in identifying obstacles to those goals to motivate and empower the client to effectuate change.

Mutual aid groups. Mutual aid groups are self-help peer-support groups. They may or may not be based on the Twelve Steps.

N

Naloxone (Narcan). Naloxone is an opioid antagonist, which means that it can block the effects of opioids. Naloxone is used in emergencies to reverse opioid overdoses.

Naltrexone. Naltrexone is an opioid antagonist that is used in the treatment of opioid dependence and alcohol use disorders.

Nar-Anon. Nar-Anon is a twelve-step recovery self-help group for individuals who have been impacted by the use of drugs by a family member or friend.

Narateen. Narateen is a twelve-step recovery self-help group for teenagers who have been impacted by the drug use of a family member or friend.

Narcotics. Narcotics is another word for opioids.

Narcotics Anonymous (NA). NA is a twelve-step recovery self-help group for individuals who wish to do something about their use of drugs, including alcohol.

Narrative exposure therapy (NET). In NET (also referred to as exposure therapy or narrative therapy), as used in the treatment of clients with a history of trauma, clients relate the story of traumatic events and explore traumatic memories and the feelings they create to help them process those experiences.

National Institute on Alcohol Abuse and Alcoholism (NIAAA). NIAA is part of the National Institute of Health. NIAA conducts and funds research on the impact of alcohol use on human health and well-being.

National Institute on Drug Abuse (NIDA). NIDA is an institute of the US government with a mission to advance science on the causes and consequences of drug use and addiction and to improve public health.

National Survey on Drug Use and Health (NSDUH). The US Department of Health and Human Services conducts an annual national survey of drug use based on in-person interviews of a representative, statistical sample of the national population aged twelve and older. The NSDUH is considered to provide reliable data quantifying the misuse of drugs and alcohol in the United States as well as the trends and changes in such drug use.

Neonatal abstinence syndrome (NAS). NAS occurs when a baby is born with a dependency on drugs due to the mother's use during pregnancy.

Neurons. Neurons are nerve cells.

Neurotransmitters. Neurotransmitters are chemical messengers that transfer messages between neurons.

Nodding off. The sedated state exhibited by the nodding forward of the head that is associated with heroin use.

Norepinephrine. Neurotransmitter that acts as a natural stimulant.

O

Open meeting. Open meetings are twelve-step fellowship meetings where attendance is not limited to those who are members or potential members of the fellowship. Interested observers are invited to attend.

Opiates. Opiates are naturally occurring depressant pain relievers that are derived from the sap of poppy plants containing morphine and codeine. Heroin, which is derived from morphine, is also considered an opiate.

Opioids. Opioids are synthetically produced depressant pain relievers such as oxycodone. The term *opioid* is commonly used to refer to refer to both opiates and opioids. As such, the term *opioid*, as used in this book, refers to both natural opiates and synthetic opioids.

Opioid treatment program (OTP). An opioid treatment program is a program that uses medicine in the treatment of opioid use disorders and that has been both certified by SAMHSA and registered by the DEA.

Over-the-counter (OTC). OTC products are those which are available for purchase without a prescription.

P

Partial hospitalization. Partial hospitalization is a day program for treatment of addictive disorders that consists of at least twenty hours a week, and where the client returns home at night.

Pathological gambler. The term *pathological gambler* is an outdated term used to refer to a person with a gambling problem. The *DSM-IV* identified the criteria for diagnosis of the impulse control disorder of pathological gambling. Currently, the *DSM-5* provides criteria for the diagnosis of gambling disorders, which are classified as a type of addictive disorder.

Peripheral nervous system (PNS). The human nervous system other than the CNS.

Pick-up. The term *pick-up* refers to a relapse, i.e., a user returns to or "picks up" use of a substance.

Polysubstance use. The term *polysubstance use* refers to the use of more than one substance.

Post-acute withdrawal syndrome (PAWS). PAWS are emotional and physical symptoms that begin after the symptoms of initial withdrawal subside (within seven to fourteen days after abstinence begins) and peak after about two or three months of abstinence. These withdrawal symptoms activate cravings and the desire to use drugs, presenting a significant challenge to recovery. PAWS may last from six to eighteen months or longer (as much as a decade in some cases).

Prefrontal cortex (PFC). The prefrontal cortex of the brain regulates decision making and the ability to control impulses.

Projection. Projection is a defense mechanism that occurs when one disavows their own unwanted feelings and attributes or projects them onto another person.

Psychedelic drugs. Psychedelic drugs are also known as hallucinogens.

Psychoactive drugs. Psychoactive drugs are drugs that interfere with the normal functioning of the CNS.

Posttraumatic Stress Disorder (PTSD). Stress responses to trauma can be identified as a continuum of symptoms which, in their most severe form, are manifested in PTSD.

Q

Qualifier. Your qualifier is the person in your life whose use of mind-altering substances or addictive behaviors has caused your life to become unmanageable.

R

Recovery. Recovery includes abstinence and remission from the symptoms of the disease and, as defined by SAMHSA, it is a "process of change through which individuals improve their health and wellness, live self-directed lives, and strive to reach their full potential" in all aspects of their life: health, home, purpose, and community.

Recovery coach. Recovery coaches monitor and assist individuals in planning for and maintaining abstinence.

Recovery fellowships: As defined herein, recovery fellowships are twelve-step self-help groups for individuals concerned with their own use of alcohol, other drugs, or gambling. They include AA, NA, CA, and GA.

Recovery management checkups (RMC). RMCs are periodic meetings between a former client and a representative of the treatment provider that provided care to allow staff to follow up on clients' continued abstinence and progress toward goals.

Recovery-oriented systems of care (ROSC). ROSC is a chronic care management model for the treatment of severe SUDs that includes the coordination of treatment and post-treatment support systems for the management of the disease.

Recovery plan. A recovery plan defines the specific actions that will be taken by an individual to support continued abstinence and personal growth. It sets forth both goals and the incremental steps to achieve those goals.

Recovery support services (RSS). RSS are community, faith-based, or governmental service programs that work with those seeking to recover from the use of substances by providing support for their basic needs such as health, housing, education, and job training and for managing preexisting legal issues. Twelve-step programs and other peer-support groups are RSS.

Relapse. A relapse is any use of a mind-altering substance after a period of abstinence.

Remission. Remission from addictive disease occurs when any problems associated with use are reduced to levels below the threshold for diagnosis of an addictive disease.

Resentment. A resentment is a feeling of permanent ill will that results when anger remains unresolved and is allowed to fester.

Resilience. Resilience is the attribute that helps some people to recover quickly from difficult situations and allows them to complete tasks and goals under difficult situations. Resilience can be innate, but actions that promote resilience can also be developed and practiced.

S

Scheduled substance. A scheduled substance or drug is one which is listed by the DEA on the schedules of controlled substances. Drugs may be identified on Schedules I through V, based on their potential abuse in the context of their medical value. Schedule I drugs are those deemed to present the greatest risk and have no perceived medical value.

Screening and brief intervention (SBI). SBI occurs when a medical provider asks a series of questions about a patient's use of drugs and alcohol as a means to identify problematic behaviors and provide brief counseling to the patient on any risks presented.

Screening, brief intervention, and referral to treatment (SBIRT). SBIRT occurs when a medical screening identifies a problem that requires more than a brief intervention and the healthcare provider refers the patient for further evaluation and treatment.

Secular Organizations for Sobriety. Secular Organizations for Sobriety is a recovery support group based on self-empowerment principles in a nonreligious context.

Sedative-hypnotics. Sedative-hypnotics fall within the drug class of depressants. These calming drugs include tranquilizers, sleep medications, antianxiety medications, and certain antidepressants.

Serotonin. Serotonin is a natural chemical neurotransmitter that controls mood.

Shakes. A person is said to have the "shakes" when he or she exhibits shaking of the hands or trembling as a symptom of withdrawal from alcohol.

Sinsemilla. Sinsemilla is a seedless, potent strain of marijuana that is cultivated by separation of the male and female plants before pollination. This process allows the harvest of high-potency, seedless buds from the female plants.

SMART recovery program. The SMART recovery program offers recovery support that emphasizes self-empowerment as a means for individuals to overcome addiction to substances and behaviors, including gambling.

Sober living. A sober house or sober-living facility refers to a variety of housing options, either managed as part of a treatment program or self-managed by residents, in which individuals in recovery live in a peer-supported sober environment.

Speedball. A speedball is the combination of a stimulant and a depressant. The term typically refers to heroin combined with cocaine or meth.

Sponsor. As used in twelve-step fellowships, a sponsor is a more experienced peer who works with a newer member on a person-to-person basis to assist the newer member in understanding the principles and how to work a program in the fellowship.

Stimulants. A class of drugs which generally increase energy, self-esteem, confidence, and physical and mental performance, and which may produce feelings of euphoria, exhilaration, and well-being.

Strengths-based. A strengths-based approach is one that draws on individual strengths and abilities.

Subcutaneous injection. A subcutaneous injection is one in which a needle is used to insert a substance just below the skin.

Suboxone. Suboxone is used in the treatment of opioid use disorders. It contains both buprenorphine and naloxone. The addition of naloxone acts as a deterrent since it is an antagonist and blocks opioids from binding with opioid receptors. This formulation is intended to minimize diversion of the drug for abuse.

Substance Abuse and Mental Health Services Administration (SAMHSA). SAMHSA is a branch of the US Department of Health and Human Services that seeks to reduce the impact of substance abuse and mental illness and advance the behavioral health of the nation.

Substance use disorder (SUD). As defined in the *DSM-5,* an SUD is an addictive disease based on a pathological pattern of behaviors associated with the use of a substance despite significant substance-related problems.

Sustained remission. A person is in sustained remission from addictive disease when the criteria for diagnosis of the disorder have not been met for a period of twelve months or more.

Synapses. Synapses are the spaces between neurons.

Synthetic drug. Synthetic drugs are man-made and are chemically manufactured to mimic the effects of naturally occurring drugs.

Synthetic Drug Abuse Prevention Act of 2012 (SDAPA). SDAPA classified additional substances, including two synthetic cathinones, as Schedule I controlled substances.

T

THC. Delta-9-tetrahydrocannabinol, commonly referred to as THC, is the chemical component in marijuana that is primarily associated with its psychoactive effects.

THC concentrates, extracts, and extractions. THC concentrates, extracts, and extractions are different names used to refer to concentrated forms of marijuana that are derived from the THC-rich resins of the marijuana plant.

Tissue dependence. Tissue dependence (or physical dependence) results from a biological process in which bodily tissues and organs become dependent on a substance to function following chronic use.

Tolerance. Tolerance refers to the fact that, with repeated consumption of a substance, the body needs more and more of the substance to achieve the same results.

Transdermal patches. Transdermal patches are adhesive patches containing prescription medication which are attached to the skin, allowing the medication to be absorbed through the skin.

Trauma-informed care (TIC). TIC is treatment that provides culturally competent services to clients with a history of trauma, acts to protect them from retraumatization within the treatment environment, emphasizes a strengths-based approach, and is based on recognition of the fact that a history of trauma may influence maladaptive behaviors such as substance abuse.

Treatment plan. A treatment plan is a written description of the services that will be provided during a course of treatment, including identification of the types of individual and group therapy that will be provided and any medications that will be used to support therapy, as well as the activities, skills training, and other services that will be provided as part of the care program.

Trichomes. Hairlike growths on marijuana buds and flowers that contain a THC-rich resin.

Triggers. Stimuli (people, places, things, sights, sounds, smells, and/or emotions) associated with drug use that precipitate cravings for drugs. Given the association with gun violence, the preferred reference is "cue" or "stimulus," which "activates" cravings.

Twelve-step facilitated treatment (TSF). TSF treatment teaches and incorporates the twelve-step philosophy as part of the treatment program.

V

Vape pen. Vape pens are devices used to heat products to release their psychoactive ingredients without combustion of the material. Thus, vape pens produce vapor, not smoke.

Vaping or vaporization. The ingestion of a drug through vaporization (inhalation of vapors released as a result of the heating of the product without combustion to contain the psychoactive elements of a drug without the production of smoke).

W

Withdrawal. When a person is dependent on a substance, the cessation of use of the substance will cause symptoms of withdrawal. Withdrawal symptoms are generally the opposite of the symptoms of intoxication from the same substance. In some cases, these symptoms can be life-threatening and require medical management.

Women for Sobriety, Inc. (WFS). WFS is a recovery program for women that encourages them to embrace an abstinent new life defined by positive life choices.

Working a program. Working a program refers to an individual's adherence to a plan to apply the principles of the Twelve Steps to their recovery and to their life.

BIBLIOGRAPHY

Al-Anon Family Groups. http://www.al-anon.org/. *How Al-Anon Works for Families and Friends of Alcoholics.* Virginia Beach, VA: Al-Anon Family Group Headquarters, Inc., 1995, 2008.

Alcoholics Anonymous. https://www.aa.org. *Alcoholics Anonymous.* 4th ed. New York: Alcoholics Anonymous World Services, Inc., 2001.

———. Twelve Steps and Twelve Traditions. New York: Alcoholics Anonymous World Services, Inc., 1953, 2006.

American Academy of Pediatrics. "American Academy of Pediatrics Reaffirms Opposition to Legalizing Marijuana for Recreational or Medical Use." Last modified January 26, 2015. https://www.aap.org/en-us/about-the-aap/aap-press-room/pages/American-Academy-of-Pediatrics-Reaffirms-Opposition-to-Legalizing-Marijuana-for-Recreational-or-Medical-Use.aspx.

The American Psychiatric Association (APA). *Diagnostic and Statistical Manual of Mental Disorders.* 5th ed. *(DSM-5).* Arlington, VA: APA, 2013.

Ammerman, Seth, Sheryl Ryan, William P. Adelman, the Committee on Substance Abuse, and the Committee on Adolescence. "The Impact of Marijuana Policies on Youth: Clinical, Research, and Legal Update." *Pediatrics* 135, no. 3 (2015): e771–85. doi: 10.15421/peds.2014-4147.

Arkes, Jeremy. "The Temporal Effects of Parental Divorce on Youth Substance Use." *Substance Use and Misuse* 48 (2013): 290–97. doi: 10.3109/10826084.2012.755703.

Batalla, Albert, Sagnik Bhattacharyya, Murat Yücel, Paolo Fusar-Poli, José Alexandre Crippa, Santiago Nogué, et al. "Structural and Functional Imaging Studies in Chronic Cannabis Users: A Systematic Review of Adolescent and Adult Findings." *PLOS ONE* 8, no. 2 (2013): e55821, 1–18. doi: 10.1371/journal.pone.0055821.

Beattie, Melody. *Codependent No More.* 2nd ed. (Center City, MN: Hazelden, 1986, 1992).

Brodzinsky, David M., Marshall D. Schecter, and Robin Marantz. *Being Adopted: The Lifelong Search for Self.* New York: Anchor Books, 1993.

Brown, Suzanne, Elizabeth M. Tracy, MinKyoung Jun, Hyunyon Park, and Meeyoung O. Min. "Personal Network Recovery Enablers and Relapse Risks for Women with Substance Dependence." *Qualitative Health Research* 25, no. 3 (2015): 371–85. doi: 10.1177/1049732314551055.

Center for Behavioral Health Statistics and Quality (CBHSQ). "Key Substance Use and Mental Health Indicators in the United States: Results from the 2016 National Survey on Drug Use and Health" (2016 NSDUH). Rockville, MD, 2017. https://store.samhsa.gov/shin/content/SMA17-5044/SMA17-5044.pdf.

Center for Substance Abuse Research. *National Drug Early Warning System (NDEWS).* University of Maryland. https://ndews.umd.edu/.

Chatzky, Jean. "Read This Before You Cosign a Loan." *AARP The Magazine,* October/November 2016: 28. https://www.aarp.org/money/credit-loans-debt/info-2016/before-cosigning-a-loan.html.

Chen, Chuan-Yu, Carla L. Storr, and James C. Anthony. "Early-Onset Drug Use and Risk for Drug Dependence." *Addictive Behaviors* 34, no. 3 (2009): 319–22. doi: 10.1016/j.addbeh.2008.10.021.

Clark, Luke, Bruno Averbeck, Doris Payer, Guillaume Sescousse, Catharine A. Winstanley, and Gui Xue. "Pathological Choice: The Neuroscience of Gambling and Gambling Addiction." *Journal of Neuroscience* 33, no. 45 (November 2013): 17617–23. doi: 10.1523/JNEUROSCI.3231-13.2013.

Cochran, Bryan N., K. Michelle Peavy, and Jennifer S. Robohm. "Do Specialized Services Exist for LGBT Individuals Seeking Treatment for Substance Misuse? A Study of Available Treatment Programs." *Substance Use & Misuse* 42 (2007): 161–76. doi: 10.1080/10826080601094207.

Coker, Kendell L., Elina Stefanovics, and Robert Rosenheck. "Correlates of Improvement in Substance Abuse Among Dually Diagnosed Veterans with Post-Traumatic Stress Disorder in Specialized Intensive VA Treatment." *Psychological Trauma: Theory, Research, Practice, and Policy* (2015): 1–8. doi: 10.1037/tra0000061.

Cosden, Merith, Jessica L. Larsen, Megan T. Donahue, and Karen Nylund-Gibson. "Trauma Symptoms for Men and Women in Substance Abuse Treatment: A Latent Transition Analysis." *Journal of Substance Abuse Treatment* 50 (2015): 18–25. doi.org/10.1016/j.jsat.2014.09.004.

Di Forti, Marta, Hannah Sallis, Fabio Allegri, Antonella Trotta, Laura Ferraro, Simon A. Stilo, et al. "Daily Use, Especially of High-Potency Cannabis, Drives the Earlier Onset of Psychosis in Cannabis Users." *Schizophrenia Bulletin* 40, no. 6 (2014): 1509–17. doi: 10.1093/schbul/sbt181.

Drug Enforcement Division. *Drugs of Abuse: A DEA Resource Guide.* Drug Enforcement Division, US Department of Justice, 2017. https://www.dea.gov/pr/multimedia-library/publications/drug_of_abuse.pdf#page=51.

Dunne, Eugene M., Jonathan J. Rose, and William W. Latimer. "ADHD as a Risk Factor for Early Onset and Heightened Adult Problem Severity of Illicit Substance Use: An Accelerated Gateway Model." *Addictive Behaviors* 39, no. 12 (2013): 1755–58. doi: 10.1016/j.addbeh.2014.07.009.

Families Anonymous, Inc. *Today a Better Way*. Des Plaines, IL: Families Anonymous, Inc., 1991, 2011, 2017.

Families Anonymous Recovery Fellowship. http://www.familiesanonymous.org/.

Farley, Melissa, Jacqueline M. Golding, George Young, Marie Mulligan, and Jerome Minkoff. "Trauma History and Relapse Probability among Patients Seeking Substance Abuse Treatment." *Journal of Substance Abuse Treatment* 27, no. 2 (2004): 161–67. doi: 10.1016/j.jsat.2004.06.006.

Ferguson, Gary. *Shouting at the Sky: Troubled Teens and the Promise of the Wild*. New York: St. Martin's Press, 1999.

Figueredo, Maraj, and Lynn Morris. "Cocaine and the Heart." *Clinical Cardiology* 33, no. 5 (2010): 264–69. doi: 10.1002/clc.20746.

Fleming, Michael F., Stacey L. Balousek, Paul M. Grossberg, Marlon P. Mundt, David Brown, Jennifer R. Wiegel, et al. "Brief Physician Advice for Heavy Drinking College Students: A Randomized Controlled Trial in College Health Clinics." *Journal of Studies on Alcohol and Drugs* (January 2010): 23–31. doi: 10.15288/jsad.2010.71.23.

Funk, Rodney R., Melissa McDermeit, Susan H. Godley, and Loree Adams. "Maltreatment Issues by Level of Adolescent Substance Abuse Treatment: The Extent of the Problem at Intake and Relationship to Early Outcomes." *Child Maltreatment* 8, no. 1 (2003): 36–45. doi: 10.1177/1077559502239607.

Furr, Susan R., W. Derrick Johnson, and Carol Sloan Goodall. "Grief and Recovery: The Prevalence of Grief and Loss in Substance Abuse Treatment." *Journal of Addictions & Offender Counseling* 36, no. 1 (2015): 43–56. doi: 10.1002/j.2161-1874.2015.00034.x.

Gabe, Janice E. "Marijuana Use in Teens and Young Adults." Online seminar, ATTP, 2016. http://aatpofillinois.com/.

———. "The Young Avoidant Adult: Peter Pan Is Alive and Well and Living in his Parents' Basement." Online seminar, ATTP, 2016. http://aatpofillinois.com/.

Gam-Anon International Service Office, Inc., and Gam-Anon Family Groups. http://www.gam-anon.org/.

Goldstein, R. Z., and Nora D. Volkow. "Dysfunction of the Prefrontal Cortex in Addiction: Neuroimaging Findings and Clinical Implications." *Nature Reviews: Neuroscience* 12, no. 11 (2011): 652–69. doi.org/10.1038/nrn3119.

Green, Kelly E., and Brian A. Feinstein. "Substance Use in Lesbian, Gay, and Bisexual Populations: An Update on Empirical Research and Implications for Treatment." *Psychology of Addictive Behaviors* 26, no. 2 (June 2012): 265–78. doi: 10.1037/a0025424.

Hall, Wayne, and Louisa Degenhardt. "The Adverse Health Effects of Chronic Cannabis Use." *Drug Testing and Analysis* 6 (2014): 39–45. doi: 10.1002/dta.1506.

———. "Adverse Health Effects of Non-medical Cannabis Use." *The Lancet* 374, no. 9698 (2009): 1386–91. doi: 10.1016/S0140-6736(09)61037-0.

Horvath, A. Tom, and Julie Yeterian. "SMART Recovery: Self-Empowering, Science-Based Addiction Recovery Support." *Journal of Groups in Addiction & Recovery* 7 (2012): 102–17. doi: 1:10.1080/1556035X.2012.705651.

Inaba, Darryl S., and William E. Cohen. *Uppers, Downers, All-Arounders: Physical and Mental Effects of Psychoactive Drugs.* 8th ed. Medford, OR: CNS Productions, Inc., 2014.

———. *Uppers, Downers, All Arounders: Physical and Mental Effects of Psychoactive Drugs.* 6th ed. Medford, OR: CNS Publications, 2007.

Johnston, Lloyd D., Richard A. Miech, Patrick M. O'Malley, Jerald G. Bachman, John E. Schulenberg, and Megan E. Patrick. *Monitoring the Future, National Survey Results on Drug Use,* 1975–2017: 2017 Overview, Key Findings on Adolescent Drug Abuse. Ann Arbor: The University of Michigan Institute for Social Research, 2018. http://monitoringthefuture.org//pubs/monographs/mtf-overview2017.pdf.

Kelly, John F., and William L. White. "Broadening the Base of Addiction Mutual-Help Organizations." *Journal of Groups in Addiction & Recovery* 7 (2012): 82–101. doi: 10.1080/1556035X.2012.705646.

Kessler, Ronald C., Irving Hwang, Richard LaBrie, Maria Petukhova, Nancy A. Sampson, Ken Winters, et al. "The Prevalence and Correlates of *DSM-IV* Pathological Gambling in the National Comorbidity Survey Replication." *Psychological Medicine* 38, no. 9 (September 2008): 1351–60. doi: 10.1017/S0033291708002900.

Kinney, Jean. *Loosening the Grip: A Handbook of Alcohol Information.* 10th ed. New York: McGraw-Hill Education, 2014.

Kornfield, Jack. "Meditations." https://jackkornfield.com/meditations/.

Lee, Benneth R. "Adolescents and Criminal Behavior: Rethinking the Problems and Answers." Seminar, Haymarket Center, Chicago, November 7, 2015.

Lion's Roar Staff. "Ask the Teachers: How Can I Accept the Suffering of Others?" *Lion's Roar: Buddhist Wisdom for Our Time.* July 21, 2017. https://www.lionsroar.com/ask-the-teachers-35/.

Lopez-Quintero, Catalina, Jose Pérez de los Cobos, Deborah S. Hasin, Mayumi Okuda, Shuai Wang, Bridget F. Grant, et al. "Probability and Predictors of Transition from First Use to Dependence on Nicotine, Alcohol, Cannabis, and Cocaine: Results of the National Epidemiologic Survey on Alcohol and Related Conditions (NESARC)." *Drug and Alcohol Dependence* 115, no. 1–2 (2011): 120–30. doi: 0.1016/j.drugalcdep.2010.11.004.

Maraj, Suraj, Vincent M. Figueredo, and D. Lynn Morris. "Cocaine and the Heart." *Clinical Cardiology* 33, no. 5 (2010): 264–69. doi: 10.1002/clc.20746.

Mayo Clinic, Mayo Medical Laboratories. "Test ID: THCU, Carboxy-Tetrahydrocannabinol (THC) Confirmation, Urine." https://www.mayomedicallaboratories.com/test-catalog/Clinical+and+Interpretive/8898.

McLellan, A. Thomas, David C. Lewis, Charles P. O'Brien, and Herbert H. Kleber. "Drug Dependence, a Chronic Medical Illness: Implications for Treatment, Insurance and Outcomes." JAMA 284, no. 13 (2000): 1689–95.

Meier, Madeline H., Avshalom Caspi, Antony Ambler, HonaLee Harrington, Renate Hours, and Richard S. Keefe. "Persistent Cannabis Users Show Neuropsychological Decline from Childhood to Midlife." *Proceedings of the National Academy of Sciences of the United States of America (PNAS)* 109, no. 40 (2012): E2657–64. doi: 10.1073/pnas.1206820109.

Metta Institute. "Metta Meditation." http://www.mettainstitute.org/mettameditation.html.

Meyers, William Cope. *Now What? An Insider's Guide to Addiction and Recovery.* Center City, MN: Hazelden, 2012.

Miech, Richard A., Lloyd D. Johnston, Patrick M. O'Malley, Jerald G. Bachman, John E. Schulenberg, and Megan E. Patrick. *Monitoring the Future: National Survey Results on Drug Use, 1975–2016: Vol. I, Secondary School Students (2016 MTF, Vol. I).* Ann Arbor: The University of Michigan Institute for Social Research, 2017. http://www.monitoringthefuture.org/pubs/monographs/mtf-vol1_2016.pdf.

Miech, Richard A., John E. Schulenberg, Lloyd D. Johnston, Jerald G. Bachman, and Patrick M. O'Malley. "National Adolescent Drug Trends in 2017: Findings Released." National press release, Ann Arbor, MI: December 14, 2017. http://monitoringthefuture.org/press.html. Tables at http://monitoringthefuture.org/data/17data.html#2017data-drugs.

Monte, Andrew A. "The Implications of the Marijuana Legalization in Colorado." *JAMA* 313, no. 3 (2015): 241–42. doi: 10.1001/jama.2014.17057.

Moore, Todd M., Amanda Seavey, Kathrin Ritter, James K. McNulty, Kristina C. Gordon, and Gregory L. Stuart. "Ecological Momentary Assessment of the Effects of Craving and Affect on Risk for Relapse During Substance Abuse Treatment." *Psychology of Addictive Behaviors* 18, no. 2 (2014): 619–29. doi: 10.1037/a0034127.

Nar-Anon Family Groups. http://www.nar-anon.org/.

Narcotics Anonymous. http://www.na.org.

National Center for Responsible Gaming (NCRG). "Prevalence of Gambling Disorders." http://www.ncrg.org/discovery-project/prevalence-gambling-disorders.

———. "Volume Six: Gambling and the Brain: Why Neuroscience Research Is Vital to Gambling Research." 2011. http://ncrg.org/sites/default/files/uploads/docs/monographs/ncrgmonograph6final.pdf.

National Council on Problem Gambling (NCPG). https://www.ncpgambling.org.

National Endowment for Financial Education. "Personal Financial Strategies for the Loved Ones of Problem Gamblers." 2000. https://store.samhsa.gov/product/Personal-Financial-Strategies-for-the-Loved-Ones-of-Problem-Gamblers/BKD535.

National Institute on Alcohol Abuse and Alcoholism (NIAAA). https://niaaa.nih.gov/.

National Institute on Drug Abuse (NIDA). https://www.drugabuse.gov/. "Treatment and Recovery." *Drugs, Brains, and Behavior: The Science of Addiction.* (2014). https://www.drugabuse.gov/publications/drugs-brains-behavior-science-addiction/treatment-recovery.

———. *Principles of Drug Addiction Treatment: A Research-Based Guide.* 3rd ed. (2012). https://www.drugabuse.gov/publications/principles-drug-addiction-treatment-research-based-guide-third-edition/frequently-asked-questions/what-drug-addiction-treatment.

———. *Principles of Adolescent Substance Use Disorder Treatment: A Research-Based Guide* (2014). https://www.drugabuse.gov/publications/principles-adolescent-substance-use-disorder-treatment-research-based-guide/principles-adolescent-substance-use-disorder-treatment.

———. Research Report on Cocaine. (2016). https://www.drugabuse.gov/publications/research-reports/cocaine/what-are-long-term-effects-cocaine-use.

———. *Research Report on Comorbidity: Addiction and Other Mental Illnesses.* (2010). www.drugabuse.gov/publications/research-reports/comorbidity-addiction-other-mental-illnesses/how-can-comorbidity-be-diagnosed.

———. *Research Report on Hallucinogens and Dissociative Drugs.* (2015). https://www.drugabuse.gov/publications/research-reports/hallucinogens-dissociative-drugs/director.

————. *Research Report on Heroin*. (2014). https://www.drugabuse.
gov/publications/research-reports/cocainettps://www.
drugabuse.gov/publications/research-reports/heroin/what-
heroin.

————. Research Report on Medications to Treat Opioid Addiction.
(2017). https://www.drugabuse.gov/publications/research-
reports/medications-to-treat-opioid-addiction/how-do-
medications-to-treat-opioid-addiction-work.

Olsson, Kurt L., R. Lyle Cooper, William R. Nugent, and Rory
C. Reid. "Addressing Negative Affect in Substance
Abuse Relapse Prevention." *Journal of Human Behavior
in the Social Environment* 26, no. 1 (2016): 214. doi:
10.1080/10911359.2015.1058138.

Petry, Nancy M., Frederick S. Stinson, and Bridget F. Grant.
"Comorbidity of *DSM-IV* Pathological Gambling and
Other Psychiatric Disorders: Results from the National
Epidemiologic Survey on Alcohol and Related Conditions."
Journal of Clinical Psychiatry 66, no. 5 (2005): 564–74.

Potenza, M. N. "Neurobiology of Gambling Behaviors." *Current
Opinion in Neurobiology* 23, no. 4: 660–67. doi: 10.1016/j.
conb.2013.03.004.

Rahula, Walpola Sri. *What the Buddha Taught*. 2nd ed. New York:
Grove Press, 1974.

Ramo, Danielle E., Mark A. Prince, Scott C. Roesch, and Sandra
A. Brown. "Variation in Substance Use Relapse Episodes
among Adolescents: A Longitudinal Investigation."
Journal of Substance Abuse Treatment 43 (2012): 44–52. doi:
10.1016/j.jsat.2011.10.003.

Rash, Carla J., Jeremiah Weinstock, and Ryan Van Patten.
"A Review of Gambling Disorder and Substance Use
Disorders." *Substance Abuse and Rehabilitation* 7 (2016): 3–13.
http://doi.org/10.2147/SAR.S83460.

Reedy, Brad M. *The Journey of the Heroic Parent.* New York: Regan Arts, 2016.

Rudd, Rose A., Seth Puja, David Felicita, and Lawrence Scholl. "Increases in Drug and Opioid-Involved Overdose Deaths—United States, 2010–2015." *Morbidity and Mortality Weekly Report* 65, nos. 50 & 51 (December 30, 2016): 1445–52. https://www.cdc.gov/mmwr/volumes/65/wr/mm655051e1.htm.

Salzberg, Sharon. *Real Happiness: The Power of Meditation, a 28-Day Program.* New York: Workman Publishing, 2011.

Sanders, Mark. "Gender Responsive Services: A Focus on the Unique Counseling Needs of Women and Men." Seminar, Haymarket Center, Chicago, IL, September 30, 2017.

Schulenberg, John E., Lloyd D. Johnston, Patrick M. O'Malley, Jerald G. Bachman, Richard A. Miech, and Megan E. Patrick. *Monitoring the Future, National Survey Results on Drug Use, 1975–2016: Vol. II, College Students and Adults Aged 19–55 (2016 MTF, Vol. II).* Ann Arbor: The University of Michigan Institute for Social Research, 2017. http://www.monitoringthefuture.org/pubs/monographs/mtf-vol2_2016.pdf.

SMART Recovery: Self-Management and Recovery Training. http://www.smartrecovery.org.

Spronk, Desiree B., Janelle H. P. van Wel, Johannes G. Ramaekers, and Robbert J. Verkes. "Characterizing the Cognitive Effects of Cocaine: A Comprehensive Review." *Neuroscience and Behavioral Reviews* 37 (2013): 1838–59. doi: 10.1016/j.neubiorev.2013.07.003.

Substance Abuse and Mental Health Administration (SAMHSA). https://www.samhsa.gov/. *Substance Abuse Treatment: Addressing the Specific Needs of Women, Treatment Improvement Protocol 51 (TIP 51).* Rockville, MD: SAMHSA, 2009.

————. *Trauma-Informed Care in Behavioral Health Services, Treatment Improvement Protocol 57 (TIP 57)*. Rockville, MD: SAMHSA, 2014.

————. *A Treatment Informed Protocol, Treatment of Adolescents with Substance Abuse Disorders, Treatment Improvement Protocol 32 (TIP 32)*. Rockville, MD: SAMHSA, 1999.

————. *Substance Abuse among Older Adults, Treatment Improvement Protocol 26 (TIP 26)*. Rockville, MD: SAMHSA, 1998.

Tashkin, Donald P. "Effects of Marijuana Smoking on the Lung." *Annals of the American Thoracic Society* 10, no. 3 (2013): 239–47. doi: 10.1513/AnnalsATS.201212-127FR.

Thomas, Grace, Robert A. Kloner, and Shereif Rezkalla. "Adverse Cardiovascular, Cerebrovascular, and Peripheral Vascular Effects of Marijuana Inhalation: What Cardiologists Need to Know." *American Journal of Cardiology* 113, no. 1 (2014): 187–90. doi: 10.1016/j.amjcard.2013.09.042.

US Department of Health and Human Services (HHS), Office of the Surgeon General. "Facing Addiction in America: The Surgeon General's Report on Alcohol, Drugs, and Health." Washington, DC, 2016. https://addiction.surgeongeneral.gov/.

Volkow, Nora D. "Drug Addiction: Free Will, Brain Disease, or Both?" Speech to the Town Hall Los Angeles, Los Angeles, CA, April 27, 2006, Vital Speeches of the Day, VSOD.com.

Volkow, Nora D., George F. Koob, and A. Thomas McLennan. "Neurobiologic Advances from the Brain Disease Model of Addiction." *New England Journal of Medicine* 374 (2016): 363–71. doi: 10.1056/NEJMra1511480.

Volkow, Nora D., and Marisela Morales. "The Brain on Drugs: From Reward to Addiction." *Cell* 162 (August 13, 2015): 712–25. doi: 10.1016/j.cell.2015.07.046.

Volkow, Nora D., and Ruben D. Baler. "Addiction Science: Uncovering Neurobiological Complexity." *Neuropharmacology* 76 (2013). doi: 10.1016/j. neuropharm.2013.05.007.

Volkow, Nora D., Ruben D. Baler, Wilson M. Compton, and Susan R. B. Weiss. "Adverse Health Effects of Marijuana Use." *The New England Journal of Medicine* 370 (2014): 2221–27. doi: 10.1056/NEJMra1402309.

Vuittonet, Cynthia L., Michael Halse, Lorenzo Leggio, Samuel B. Fricchione, Michael Brickley, Carolina L. Haass-Koffler, et al. "Pharmacotherapy for Alcoholic Patients with Alcoholic Liver Disease." *American Journal of Health-System Pharmacy* 71 (2014): 1265–75. doi: 10.2146/ajhp140028.

Williams, Pamela K. "Creating a 'Trauma Informed' Treatment Setting." Seminar, Haymarket Center, Chicago, IL, September 30, 2017.

Witkiewitz, Katie, Sarah Bowen, Haley Douglas, and Sharon H. Hsu. "Mindfulness-Based Relapse Prevention for Substance Craving." *Addictive Behaviors* 38 (2013): 1563–71. doi: 10.1016/j.addbeh.2012.04.001.

Women for Sobriety. http://womenforsobriety.org/beta2/.

Yalom, Irvin D., and Molyn Leszcz. *The Theory and Practice of Group Psychotherapy.* 5th ed. New York: Basic Books, 1995.